Variations

Also by Judy R. Rogers and Glenn C. Rogers

PATTERNS AND THEMES: A Basic English Reader, Second Edition

This extremely popular text contains forty-four short selections chosen for their appropriateness to developmental writing courses. The accompanying discussions and questions reinforce the connection between reading and writing and help students gain insights into the thinking and writing of professional writers. Organized into ten themes, the selections range from short stories and popular journalism to poems and student-written works.

Variations

A Rhetoric and Reader
for College Writing

ᐯᐯᐯᐯᐯᐯᐯᐯᐯᐯᐯᐯᐯᐯᐯᐯᐯᐯᐯᐯᐯᐯᐯᐯᐯᐯ

JUDY R. ROGERS
GLENN C. ROGERS
Morehead State University

WADSWORTH PUBLISHING COMPANY
A Division of Wadsworth, Inc.
Belmont, California

English Editor: Angela Gantner
Editorial Assistant: Julie Johnson
Production Editor: Donna Linden
Managing Designer: Kaelin Chappell
Print Buyer: Barbara Britton
Permissions Editor: Jeanne Bosschart
Text Designer: Adriane Bosworth
Copy Editor: Thomas L. Briggs
Technical Illustrator: TypeLink, Inc., San Diego, California
Compositor: TypeLink, Inc., San Diego, California
Cover Designer: Kaelin Chappell
Signing Representative: Mark Francisco
Cover Illustration: © 1990 The Estate and Foundation of Andy Warhol/ARS
N.Y. Photos courtesy Leo Castelli Gallery and the Estate and Foundation of
Andy Warhol

Credits and Acknowledgments appear on pages 285–287.

Printed in the United States of America   49

1 2 3 4 5 6 7 8 9 10—95 94 93 92 91

Library of Congress Cataloging-in-Publication Data
Rogers, Judy R.
    Variations : a rhetoric and reader for college writing / Judy R.
Rogers, Glenn C. Rogers.
        p.   cm.
    Includes index.
    ISBN 0-534-14658-9
    1. English language—Rhetoric.   2. English language—
Grammar—1950–   3. College readers.   I. Rogers, Glenn C.
II. Title.
PE1408.R645   1990
808′.0427—dc20   90-12929

For our parents, again

Sit memorasse satis, repetitaque munera grato
Percensere animo, fidaeque reponere menti.
    —Milton

Contents

Chapter 8   Building Better Sentences   105

Chapter 9   Writing Standard English Correctly   130

Reviewing Standard Written English   *137*

PART TWO   THE READER   163

Some Advice on Reading   165

Success   171

Drugs   191

Television   211

The Natural Environment   237

The Human Environment   257

Index   289

Rhetorical Table of Contents

 *Preface*

IDEAS BEHIND THIS TEXTBOOK

The last decade has seen seemingly countless variations in the teaching of composition as instructors have joined innovative concepts and methods with established techniques to create new teaching designs. Modern theories of the writing process are now widely applied. Reading selections—long welcomed in the composition classroom, then for a time treated like poor relatives—seem to be well accepted again. Critical thinking has received a fresh, strong emphasis. And these interrelated skills of writing, reading, and thinking are combined in infinite variety as our profession looks for new ways to improve teaching and learning.

The changes in teaching composition have come more slowly in basic writing than elsewhere. Yet, interestingly, ten years have passed since E. D. Hirsch, in an NCTE publication on basic writing, stated: "It is inherently obvious that we cannot write better than we can read." It has also been ten years since a Rockefeller Foundation Commission declared that critical thinking should be considered a basic skill.

Recently, however, basic writing teachers have shown increased interest in linking writing, reading, and critical thinking. This synthesis implies a teaching theory and method we have long believed in. Thus it is a foundation of this textbook in which we offer our variations: integrated skills especially adapted to the needs of basic writers.

THE RHETORIC SECTION

Part One, "The Rhetoric," combines instruction, short examples, thinking and writing activities, and suggested writing assignments. Chapters 1–3 cover (among other topics) the steps in the writing process, following the progress of a basic writer as she works on a descriptive essay.

Chapters 4–6 demonstrate a few of the various ways to organize essays. The methods of development emphasized are primarily those that rely on and sometimes mirror common thinking activities: observing and accurately describing, supporting a general statement with relevant examples, comparing and contrasting, analyzing the parts of a process, and supporting an opinion with evidence.

Chapters 7 and 8 deal in detail with the composition of paragraphs and sentences. Finally, Chapter 9 looks at some of the variations in standard and nonstandard English, offers advice on appropriateness, and closes with a mini-handbook of grammar, punctuation, and usage.

THE READER SECTION

Five groups of reading selections follow the "Rhetoric" section and comprise Part Two. These essays and excerpts from longer works are loosely arranged around broad topics: success, drugs, television, the natural environment, and the human environment. The writers' many ideas on these subjects make up another set of variations.

The readings present points of view that will stimulate thinking, generate discussion (or sometimes a bit of controversy), and lead to writing. Some selections, either wholly or in part, also demonstrate the techniques of successful writing, although serving as models is not their primary function.

CONNECTIONS

Variations contains numerous cross-references linking writing and reading, as well as numerous questions about both. It is our hope that students in basic or transitional writing courses will find this material helpful and interesting and that they will practice combining writing, reading, and critical thinking—those essential skills for college and beyond. We think with pleasure of those days in our own and others' classrooms when students encounter ideas, think and talk about them, then pick up their pens and begin work on their own variations.

ACKNOWLEDGMENTS

We wish to thank a number of people who have helped in the preparation of this book. Foremost among them are the reviewers who read part or all of the manuscript and shared their responses with us: Rebecca Argall, Memphis State University; Barbara Baxter, State Technical Institute; David D. Dahnke, North Harris County College; Jean M. English, Tallahassee Community College; Joseph Geckle, Westmoreland County Community

College; Claudia Greenwood, Kent State University; Chris Henson, California State University, Fresno; Robert G. Noreen, California State University, Northridge; Randall Popken, Tarleton State University; Nancy M. Posselt, Midlands Technical College; and Mark Reynolds, Jefferson Davis Jr. College. We are especially grateful to Susan Carkin, Utah State University, whose sensitive reading and thoughtful comments were of great value.

Our thanks also go to those with whom we have worked closely in the editorial and production departments at Wadsworth Publishing Company, especially Angie Gantner and Donna Linden. And it is a pleasure to acknowledge the contribution of Thomas Briggs, our accomplished and creative copy editor.

Finally, we want to say thanks to two of our co-workers at Morehead State University, Wanda Littleton and Vandy Trent, who give special meaning to the term "support staff."

J.R.R.

G.C.R.

In addition to those mentioned already, I wish to express my appreciation to the Morehead State University Sabbatical Leave Committee for recommending, and the administration for granting, a one-semester leave during the fall term, 1989. This provided much-needed time for reflection and revision. I also want to say thanks to my colleagues, especially Vickie Wier and Tom Stroik, who in our casual conversations often helped unawares.

G.C.R.

Variations

PART ONE

The Rhetoric

CHAPTER 1

〰〰〰〰 Writing in College and Beyond

If you want to be successful in this course, you must accept two facts: (1) you need to write well, and (2) you can learn to write well. If you already believe this, you have made a good start. If you do not yet believe it, then this first chapter will attempt to convince you. The major points in this chapter are that writing is important, that there is a writing process that can be learned and practiced, and that good writing is closely linked to clear thinking. If you begin right now to develop and sharpen your writing and thinking skills—along with the related skill of effective reading—you will have taken a necessary step toward success in college and beyond.

Why is writing important? For many years in this country, as in others, there was an easy answer: the ability to read and write divided the educated from the uneducated, the literate from the illiterate. Reading and writing opened the door to social and economic progress. Some people might still give this answer, but it is incomplete.

MODERN LITERACY

Since you are already college students, we are obviously talking about a stage of development beyond basic literacy. It remains true, however, that at a higher level these same skills—reading intelligently and writing well—can aid social, economic, and even professional progress. This is one important and very practical reason for learning to write well.

There are other reasons, of course, one of which should concern you right now. A number of your college courses will require written work. Many instructors include term papers and essay tests in their courses. You may have to prepare lab reports or written reports on assigned reading. Students in technical, vocational, and professional programs are often surprised to learn that they too must write. Those studying welding, construction, mining, and robotics find themselves writing technical reports. Others in nursing, health sciences, or veterinary technology keep records and write up case studies. In fact, because writing is an essential skill for any educated person, many colleges and universities now require students to pass a writing skills test before graduating.

Writing is also a key element in the learning process. A major part of any college education is organizing and transmitting information, and writing is an important way of doing this. No one will question that writing transmits information, but the previous sentence also mentioned organizing—a function of writing that too few people are aware of. Writing down what you know and what you are thinking is a good way to help you understand, categorize, and remember material from your classes. It is one of the many ways in which writing skills and thinking skills overlap. This is not something we just *hope* may happen; research proves it *does* happen. Even if there were no others, this would be one good reason for improving writing skills.

Thus, mastering writing skills, along with the related ones of intelligent reading and logical thinking, will help you not only now and during the rest of your formal education, but also far beyond your college years. There is a further point. These skills, like any others, require practice—now and in the future. If you can play a musical instrument, work with woods and metals, play a sport, ride a bicycle, type, sew, operate heavy equipment, or work with handicrafts, then you already know that it takes time to become competent and that if you do not continue to practice, you become rusty. This is equally true of the intellectual skills you are developing in college.

Activity 1.1

Write down several reasons for writing well. You may look back at the first few pages of this chapter, and you may want to add some reasons of your own. Read over your list several times; then put it away and write the reasons again without looking at your original list. As we said, writing information down helps you to remember it.

THE WRITING PROCESS

Although few writers work in exactly the same way, most people who have studied the subject agree that the writing process has three major steps, each of which draws on various kinds of critical thinking skills. The first step is usually called prewriting or planning—the stage of preparation. The second step is writing or drafting; here, the writer's thoughts are put into sentences and paragraphs. This, however, is not the stage that gives the writer a finished product. The third step is usually called rewriting or revision and involves improving and polishing. Every writer should understand these parts of the process and be able to move easily from one to another.

Planning

The prewriting or planning stage is absolutely necessary. One of the most common problems of inexperienced writers is poor planning. Let's suppose that Beth, a typical beginning college writer, is given a typical basic writing assignment: describe someone in her family. She thinks for a moment and decides to describe her grandmother. Then she gets paper, picks up a pen, and starts to write:

> My grandmother is named Mary Elizabeth. People who know her well usually call her Mary Lizbeth. She lives in New Orleans now with my mother. When she was young, she moved with her parents from Ireland to America. They settled in Chicago. She grew up there and married my grandfather. They had several children. My grandmother is very kind. She is a tall woman with gray hair, although it used to be reddish brown. She has brown eyes. My grandfather was a construction worker and he died in an accident when my mother and her brothers and sisters were young. My grandmother worked very hard and was able to send any of the children to college who wanted to go. I am very proud of her for this.

Let's not go any further. Beth has a major problem with this paper. She cannot see any clear direction and is not sure how to continue, so she just stops.

Where did Beth go wrong? She did not go through the steps of the process. She thought for a brief moment: "Description of a person. Who can I write about? Maybe my grandmother. Yeah." That was the end of her planning. She picked up her pen and started to write. Not certain in what direction she was going or even why she was going at all, she wrote whatever came to her mind and soon stopped—lost.

What should she have done? Once she decided to describe her grandmother, she should have continued her planning by asking herself several questions:

1. What do I want to write?

2. For whom am I writing it?

3. How am I going to write it?

These are questions that you as a writer must ask each time you begin a writing assignment. Then—and this is most important—you must answer them clearly before you actually begin drafting the paper. Answering these questions should make clear exactly what your task is and how you might accomplish it.

The first question asks you to determine not just what your subject is, but what you want to say about it. Suppose Beth asks herself this question and her answer is: "I want to write about my grandmother." Her problems have already begun. The question is not "What do I want to write *about*?" Beth does want to write about her grandmother, but *what* is she going to write about her? That is a very different question. Beth's answer for now may be: "I want to write a paper in which I describe my grandmother, especially telling what she has done for her family and why I am proud of her." Beth now has some sense of direction.

The second question simply asks: *Who is your audience?* Who is going to read what you write? The simplest answer, one that can cause you trouble, is: "I'm writing for my English teacher." Unless you are writing a letter, you usually do not write for an audience of one. And unless you are keeping a diary or a journal, you are not writing entirely for yourself either. If a writing assignment contains no specific instructions about audience, assume your readers will be at least your own classmates.

What do you know about these people? Who are they and what do they know? What do they have in common with you? Are there differences between you and them that may influence what you write? How are they likely to respond to the subject you are going to write about? As you try to answer these and similar questions about audience, you are using at least two common thinking skills: analysis and evaluation. You are examining or studying your readers and making judgments about them that will affect your writing.

What difference does audience make? Suppose you were asked to write a description of your first few days in college for three audiences: several very close friends, members of your family, and a teacher from several years ago who helped you and is still interested in your education. Would you describe your experience in the same way? No. You would try to make your descriptions suitable for each audience. You do not ordinarily speak in exactly the same way to friends, family, and teachers. You do not write to them in exactly the same way either. The decision you make about audience can affect everything from the overall organization to the details you include and even the words you use.

Beth needs an answer for this second question. If she knows that she is writing for an audience that includes at least a group of classmates and her instructor, this will help her make some decisions. In fact, if she had remembered that she was writing for anyone at all, it might have prevented some of her rambling. She probably feels comfortable jumping from one fact about her grandmother to another, but her readers are not comfortable trying to follow her.

Once you know what you are going to write and for whom, you have another question to address: *How am I going to do it?* In answering this question, you are making decisions about how you will organize your thoughts and present them to your readers. You now need a plan or a blueprint.

Let's return to Beth. She is especially interested in explaining what her grandmother did for the family and why she is proud of her grandmother. She is going to tell this to a group of people from various backgrounds who have about the same level of education she does. She has a topic and has decided who her audience will be. What will be her plan for doing this?

It is unlikely that any of Beth's readers will know her grandmother. Some, from backgrounds quite unlike her own, may know little or nothing about immigrant ancestors. Thus, Beth's task is to *show* (not just tell) what her grandmother's situation was and how she did whatever was necessary to provide for her family. She can accomplish this by including details, specific bits of information about her grandmother, that demonstrate what kind of woman she is. And because her readers are asked to be interested in a group of strangers, Beth must be sure they know who these family members are, how their lives were linked to her grandmother's, and why these people are interesting. Her point of view is clear: she will focus on her grandmother and her family. This is *how* she is going to accomplish her writing task.

Once Beth or you or any writer has answered these questions, the rest of the task becomes easier. We have spent several paragraphs looking at this initial step in planning, but actually it may not take long. As the writer, you are simply asked to be clear in your thinking about the task ahead, to know what you plan to do *before* you start doing it.

Activity 1.2

Select someone you know well, either a family member or a close friend, whom you would like to describe. Ask and answer the three early-planning questions:

1. *What do I want to write?* You do not want to say simply whom you are writing about. You want a statement that indicates your purpose for writing.

2. *For whom am I writing it?* Will you be sharing this paper with classmates, or is it meant for some other group?

3. *How am I going to write it?* What will your focus be? Will you concentrate on physical description or the details of this individual's life or personality?

Write down brief answers to these questions. Remember that the decisions you make here will influence everything else you do in the writing process.

Once you have a plan for writing, even if it is only a rough sketch, you need materials to work with. One of the simplest and most effective techniques for gathering writing material is **brainstorming**, which will be discussed more fully in the next chapter. During focused brainstorming the writer lets his or her mind roam freely so long as the thoughts are directed toward a single subject. The major thinking skill involved is association: one thing reminds the writer of another. The key to productive brainstorming is to focus on the topic and keep the mind thinking without trying to control what it is thinking. In Beth's case she can think actively about her grandmother and write down whatever comes to her mind.

The writer who is brainstorming does not worry about getting down complete sentences or about punctuation, spelling, and other features of "correct" writing. Fragments, even words and phrases, may be enough. The whole point is to keep the mind focused on the subject, not on spelling and sentence structure, and to write down as many thoughts as possible. At this point Beth should be concentrating on her grandmother, not on her writing.

Once the brainstorming is finished, or seems to be, it is time to organize. Again, there is a simple, effective technique. You can read through the brainstorming notes, looking for similar bits of information and clustering them together. This involves one of the most basic thinking skills—categorizing. Clustering will be discussed in detail in Chapter 2.

You are now moving from the planning to the writing stage. This is the time to refocus, to be sure of your sense of direction before moving on. Review the three questions and your answers to them. Are you sure what you want to write, for whom you are writing it, and how you plan to accomplish your writing goal? If so, you are ready to produce a draft.

Activity 1.3

Return to the planning that you did for Activity 1.2. Keeping in mind the person you will describe and the kinds of details needed for a description, do a few minutes of brainstorming. Write down your thoughts without worrying about sentence structure, punctuation, or spelling. Just try to keep yourself thinking and writing.

When you seem to have run out of thoughts on your subject, read over your brainstorming notes, looking for pieces of information that seem to fit together (for example, details about the color of hair, skin, and eyes or about other physical features; details about habits or about likes and dislikes; details about interests and activities). If some categories seem small, you may later add to them or decide not to use them. If some pieces of information do not seem to fit anywhere, put them in a "miscellaneous" category. This is not the time to toss anything out.

Now decide how you will organize your material. What kind of details will you put first, second, third, and so on? Look again at your answers to the three planning questions to see how the material from your brainstorming fits in with what you want to write.

Drafting

This is the hardest part of the process to describe because no two writers work in exactly the same way. In this book you will find much advice about planning and later about revision, but when you first begin to turn the words and phrases, the bits and pieces from your prewriting, into sentences and paragraphs, you are largely on your own. The best advice is probably this: get something down, whether you are satisfied with it or not. You will have plenty of time to rework your ideas and revise what you have written, but first you must have something on paper to work with.

This is the point at which many writers, especially those with limited experience, get stuck. The most frequent cause is concern with "getting it right," which usually means producing a draft that is ready to be read and graded. It is still much too early to worry about that. In brainstorming the task was to think and to list your thoughts on paper. Now the task is to develop those thoughts, to state them clearly and link them together in a pattern that your readers can follow.

The word *draft*, in the sense of a written document, has been part of the English language for nearly five hundred years, and it has always indicated something incomplete, something that is to be reworked and finished later. If you are going to complete a writing assignment successfully, convince yourself right now that the first draft is not the only draft. It is "first," which means that something else will follow. Of course, you want this first draft to be a good one; but you will write other versions, so don't spend time and energy now trying to make everything perfect. A "perfect" first draft for a writer is something like a hole-in-one for a golfer: both are rare occurrences that happen only to very talented—or lucky—people.

Writing Assignment

Using the material that you organized in Activity 1.3, write a draft of your paper describing a friend or family member. As with brainstorming, do not worry now about being "correct." There will be time for that later. The job now is to think your way through what you want to say and to get those thoughts down on paper.

Revision

This term sometimes causes confusion because it can refer to different procedures at different points in the writing process. Some student writers speak of revision when they might more accurately use the term *editing*; they are actually talking about correcting grammar, spelling, and mechanics. This is an important part of writing, one we will look at in detail in Chapter 9, but it is not really revision. Others use the term to refer to the rewriting they do when an instructor has graded and returned a paper. That is one kind of revision, but it comes much later in the process.

In this chapter the word *revision* refers to the third part of the process that finally leads to a satisfactory version of your work. You may revise several times before you are "finished" with a piece of writing.

As a writer you must be willing to try more than one way of completing your task. Once a draft is finished and your thoughts are down on paper, you can begin reworking and experimenting. Often, writers change words, rewrite sentences, and move whole paragraphs from one place to another. You may rewrite a short passage, reject the rewrite and try a third version, and finally return to the one you started with.

The main point is to try different ways of saying what you want to say until you are satisfied with the result. Your writing instructor may ask to see your work while it is in progress to make suggestions for revision. Often classmates will help by reading a draft and commenting on it. Learn to be comfortable with letting others look at your unfinished work and offer suggestions. Remember that you are creating a piece of writing that communicates your ideas clearly to your readers, not a piece of art that must be perfect before it is suddenly revealed to a dazzled audience.

Writing Assignment

Working in groups of two or three, share your drafts with others in the class. Let the readers in the group know the answers to your planning questions: tell them what you are writing, who your audience is, and how you intend to get your main ideas across.

As audience, members of the group should read or listen to each paper carefully, decide how well the writer achieved his or her purpose, and suggest how the writer might change the paper to better accomplish that purpose.

As a writer you must decide which of your readers' suggestions you will follow and which you will ignore. Decide also what changes you might want to make in addition to those suggested. Now write another draft of your description paper, using your and your readers' ideas for improvement.

Cycling Through the Process

Because the steps in the process are discussed in one-two-three order, it is easy for writers to think they will go through the process in that simple way, completing each step before beginning the next. In fact, the process does not work like that. It does not move in a straight line; instead, it moves in cycles or perhaps spirals.

Writing is often messy work. It does not go forward in an orderly way because it depends on thinking, and thinking is not always orderly. Before completing a task, a writer may move back and forth among the parts of the process many times.

Let's look at an example. Dave, a student in the evening college, is preparing to write a paper describing his daily routine. The first few lines of his brainstorming go like this:

> Alarm goes off at 6:00 A.M. Worst sound of the day—worse than sounds of traffic at rush hour or the cursing of my boss. Get up, shower, dress. Get myself together for another day at the warehouse. I work as a shipping supervisor from 8:00 to 4:00, take classes at night. Quick breakfast—usually strong coffee and a few glazed doughnuts. Bad idea. Sugar and caffeine get my body off to a bad start. Sometimes I'm tense and hyped up even before I get to work. Get in car and start the 45-min. commute to the city. Traffic gets real bad about ten miles out. Some mornings worse than others—bunch of real human garbage on the highway.

Dave finishes his brainstorming and then reads through it to see what material he has to work with. He especially likes the comparison he made in the second line: the sound of his alarm is worse than that of rush-hour traffic or his boss's cursing. He decides to move a few of the words unchanged into his first draft, and at the top of his brainstorming page he writes a couple of trial sentences using them:

> My first sensation is the worst sound of the day, my alarm. It is louder than the horns of traffic at rush hour and more irritating than the cursing of my boss.

He has moved for a moment from planning to drafting. As he returns to the task of sorting through the brainstorming, he is back in planning. These shifts can occur at almost any point in the process.

Most writing teachers caution against moving into revision during the drafting stage. This is sound advice, especially for inexperienced writers who may lose track of what they are doing if they interrupt their drafting very often. So most writers prefer to write straight through the drafting stage before revising.

Sometimes, however, our brains make revisions whether our hands want to or not. Some writers naturally think of minor revisions as they are drafting. When this happens it is probably best to make the revision right then, so long as it really is a small one.

Let's move Dave into the drafting phase. He decides the two trial sentences on his brainstorming page would make a good introduction:

> My first sensation is the worst sound of the day, my alarm. It is louder than the horns of traffic at rush hour and more irritating than the cursing of my boss.

If Dave is a revise-as-you-go writer, he may immediately make a change:

> It is louder than the horns of ~~traffic at rush hour~~ rush-hour traffic and more irritating than the cursing of my boss.

It is a small change, but for a moment Dave has moved from drafting to revising.

Again, a word of caution. It is always wise to complete drafting before trying large-scale revision like rewriting paragraphs or reorganizing sections of your paper. But if an idea for a small revision comes to you as you are drafting, make the change quickly and move on. This is the way we cycle through the writing process.

Let's return for a moment to the major points stated at the beginning of the chapter. First, writing is important. Developing good writing skills can help you learn, help you express yourself, and give you confidence during your college career and for years after. Second, there is a process that will produce more effective writing, and you will benefit from learning and practicing that process. Finally, good writing is related to sound thinking. To be literate in the late twentieth century, you must write well, read well, and think well.

CHAPTER 2

▚▚▚▚▚▚▚▚▚
▚▚▚▚▚▚▚▚▚ # Getting Ideas
▚▚▚▚▚▚▚▚▚

In this chapter we will look more closely at those writing activities that come before drafting, especially thinking, planning, and making lists or notes that help you explore ideas. You can get ideas about the writing topics you are assigned in several ways. You can look carefully at people and places around you. Even an ordinary room can be a good subject when it is described interestingly from your particular point of view. You can also search your memory for recollections of people and experiences. You can gather information from what you read. Finally, you can examine attitudes and ideas that come to mind as you make daily entries in a journal. Although this chapter is mostly about getting ideas, it also shows how you can begin to arrange and shape those ideas. And it again emphasizes that clear writing is related to clear thinking.

Many students think that the only way to begin a writing assignment is to sit at a desk, get a pen and clean pad or turn on a word processor, and start putting words on paper. They believe this process should continue without interruption until they have put the final period on the final page. But after completing Chapter 1, you know that you must prepare to write. (Remember the unfortunate Beth.) Thinking time comes before drafting time. Actually, you may begin the writing process while taking your morning shower, driving to campus, or sitting in the cafeteria.

Let us say that your instructor gives you a general subject or even a specific topic for writing. As you learned while working through Chapter 1, you must still decide what information you should include, what attitude you will take toward your subject, and what kind of readers you are writing for. These decisions are made during the planning or prewriting stage. As you now can see, a paper begun without basic planning is almost certain to be disorganized, underdeveloped, and difficult to write.

OBSERVATIONS AND INFERENCES

One of the easiest ways to collect information is to look around you. Careful observation can give you the kind of specific details you often need in writing. If your task is to write a physical description of a person, a place, or an object, you will need many precise details to show what that person, place, or object looks like and to find the words to share your information with others. In addition, you can use your written **observations**, which are statements about what you know, to make **inferences**, which are statements about what you think but do not know for sure.

Distinguishing Between Observations and Inferences

Let us look at an example. Suppose that at about 10:00 A.M. you see another student hurrying across the campus in the rain. She is quite wet. Her arms are full of books and notebooks, which are also wet. She manages to turn her left wrist enough to see her watch; then she frowns and begins to walk even faster. These are things you have observed and can describe factually. Now let us try making some inferences, statements based on what you have actually seen:

1. The girl does not have an umbrella with her.

2. Someone has stolen her umbrella.

3. She enjoys walking in the rain.

4. She is careless about her books and papers.

5. She is late for a class or an appointment.

Which of these inferences do you think can safely be drawn from the observations. Number 1? This seems safe. Of course, she may have an umbrella that she is not using, but it seems unlikely she would let herself and her possessions get wet if she could prevent it. Number 2? No, there is nothing to suggest that she owned an umbrella that was stolen. Be especially careful about a line of reasoning that goes: "I remember when someone stole my umbrella and I got caught in the rain like that. I'll bet the same thing happened to her." At the moment there is no evidence to suggest that her situation compares with yours. Number 3? No, this is not a good inference. She may well enjoy walking in the rain, but probably not in the middle of a class day and while she has her arms full of books and papers. The frown also suggests that this is not a pleasurable experience. Number 4? No, you cannot infer anything about her usual care of her books and notebooks. Without raising an umbrella, there is little she can do to keep them dry. Number 5? This is probably a safe inference. She looked at her watch, her face showed concern or dissatisfaction, and she began to move more quickly.

Inferences 1 and 5 are *valid*. This means the statements are based on enough facts that we can be fairly sure of them. To say they are valid does not mean they are absolutely true; it means there is a high probability they are true. In contrast, inferences 2, 3, and 4 are *invalid*. This means there is not enough information to base them on. To say they are invalid does not mean the statements are absolutely false; it means there are too few facts to support the inferences.

Activity 2.1   Listed here are the contents of a grocery cart that you observe while standing in the checkout line at a market. The shopper is buying for only one family. This is the only trip anyone in the shopper's family will make to the supermarket this week. Working in small groups, examine the list, look at the twenty inferences drawn from observation of the cart, and decide which are valid and which are invalid. Be prepared to defend your decisions based on available facts. Remember, you are looking for high probability, not absolute proof. If the group cannot agree on the validity of an inference, explain both points of view.

CONTENTS OF THE CART

six frozen dinners	two cans of pork and beans
two bags of potato chips	one carton of frozen chili
six two-litre bottles of Coke	one carton of potato salad
four two-litre bottles of Diet Coke	two packages of frozen macaroni and cheese
one six-pack of beer	one quart of ice cream
three boxes of cookies	five cans of chow mein
two loaves of bread	one bottle of aspirin (100 tablets)
one large jar of peanut butter	three pairs of white pantyhose
six candy bars	a box of sugarless candy
three frozen pies	one copy of *TV Guide*

INFERENCES

1. The shopper is not on a diet.

2. There is a diabetic in the shopper's family.

3. The shopper has a freezer at home.

4. There are no infants in the shopper's family.

5. The shopper's family does not have a balanced diet.

6. The shopper's family enjoys the convenience of modern foods.

7. The mother of the family hates to cook.

8. The shopper is eighteen or over.

9. The shopper works in a hospital or physician's office.

10. The shopper's kitchen has plenty of storage space.

11. The shopper likes sweets.

12. Someone in the family suffers from arthritis.

13. The shopper is female.

14. The shopper is going to spend more than $25.

15. Someone in the family eats Chinese food.

16. The shopper will stop at few, if any, other stores before returning home.

17. There are no smokers in the family.

18. The family has a TV set.

19. The shopper does not buy wisely.

20. The shopper is not on any sort of public welfare program.

Activity 2.2

Read the following mini-mystery story and, based on the facts of the case, decide whether the inferences that follow the story are valid or invalid. Be prepared to explain your answers. If your instructor wishes, you may work in groups.

1   Inspector Pludeau was called to the home of oil millionaire Lionel Parks to investigate a death. Parks's body was sprawled on a low sofa, the head resting on several cushions. A lamp at the end of the sofa was turned on. Parks's glasses were lying on his chest, and his shoes were under a table in front of the sofa. There was a small gunshot wound in his right

temple. A pistol, recently fired, lay near the sofa. Examination revealed a number of smudged fingerprints. Only those of Parks were identifiable.

2   On the table under which Parks's shoes were found, there were two nearly empty wine glasses and an ashtray containing a single cigarette butt. The cigarette was unfiltered; it had traces of bright red lipstick. Papers were scattered about the room. Among them was the most recent financial report from Multiglut, the huge oil company in which Parks and a partner owned controlling interest. In the margins of three pages of the report, someone had penciled question marks. Several desk drawers were pulled out. The books on the book shelves were shoved out of place; some were tossed on the floor. The French doors to the patio were ajar.

INFERENCES

1. Parks had been joined by a woman earlier in the evening.

2. The female was probably a brunette rather than a blond.

3. Parks committed suicide.

Assuming that Parks committed suicide, then:

4. He killed himself because he had embezzled large sums from the firm, and his business partner had discovered the loss.

5. His business partner was the woman who was with him earlier.

6. Parks was murdered.

Assuming that Parks was murdered, then:

7. He was killed as he napped on the sofa.

8. He was awake and saw his killer. It was someone he knew.

9. The killer shot Parks with his own gun.

10. The woman who had been with Parks can probably be eliminated as a suspect because women prefer poison, not a gun, as a murder weapon.

11. The murder took place during a robbery.

12. The robber did not know where to find Parks's money and valuables.

13. The murderer left through the French doors.

14. Death, whether by suicide or murder, occurred after dark.

Using Observations and Inferences in Writing

Making close observations and drawing inferences can be an entertaining pastime, as we have just seen. But for writers these activities are more than a game. They can encourage logical thinking and provide the kind of specific details that make writing concrete and interesting. For example, if you were to write a full description of the scene of the crime in Activity 2.2, you would certainly want to mention the wine glasses and the cigarette. Even if you could not draw inferences from these details (and you probably can), they would make your description more specific and interesting. And what of Lionel Parks's glasses lying on his chest? That fact not only suggests something about the way he died; it also gives your readers a clearer picture of the body. No doubt if you were assisting Inspector Pludeau, you would want to note what books had been pulled off the shelves and what papers had been scattered around the room. You would also need to be much more detailed about the wound in Parks's temple. The point is, the more closely you observe and the more carefully you make inferences, the more exact and thoughtful your writing will be.

Activity 2.3   Photographs are good subjects for observation because they can be studied at length. Take a close look at the photograph on page 19. Among the observable facts are these:

1. There are two people, one male and one female.

2. The male is dressed in running shorts and a Nike T-shirt.

3. The female is supporting the male, who is bent forward slightly and is reaching with his right hand toward his right lower leg.

4. The figures are standing on grass; there is pavement slightly in front of them.

Can you add other facts to this list?

Now let us make some inferences:

1. The male in the photograph is a runner.

2. He is suffering from exhaustion or from some sort of injury.

3. The female, who could be a runner or a bystander, is helping him.

Are these inferences valid or invalid? Can you add other inferences to this list?

*Writing
Assignment*

Suppose that you are a sports reporter who has witnessed the scene in the photograph. Write a paragraph describing the scene for your readers. Combine the facts and inferences, including any that you added to the lists. Use as many specific details as you can.

*Writing
Assignment*

On page 21 are two more photographs. Make a list of facts for each of them. Then make a list of valid inferences. Note that when you study these photographs, you can make observations about places as well as people. After you have drawn as many valid inferences as possible, write two paragraphs, one based on each photograph, describing these scenes for readers who have not observed them. As before, combine facts and inferences and concentrate on using specific details.

Activity 2.4

Another good way of learning to observe carefully and to draw valid inferences is to practice while going through your daily schedule. Here is a list of details that a student named Celia made as she sat in the University Center and watched people come and go. She made her observations over a two-day period.

FIRST-DAY OBSERVATIONS

The Place

five large plants in window: two hanging, three in floor urns, very green, no dead leaves

gray chairs, blue carpet, cream-colored walls

aluminum ashtrays in floor stands

several mobiles: blue and metallic geometric shapes

The Student

black hair and olive skin

talks to everybody

bends forward to listen to what is being said to him

speaks English with foreign accent, probably Middle Eastern

dressed in jeans, old black sneakers, striped belt, green T-shirt with gold letters that say "Donna's Li'l Brother"

talks to some people for quite a while—talks to Asian student about ballgame—girl looks worried—talks a long time

Dan is here; I'll come back tomorrow

SECOND-DAY OBSERVATIONS

same location

surprised to see same young man—my good luck

two students wave from stairway

one young man comes out of post office and stops—talks seriously for five minutes—smiles and waves goodbye

smell of food drifts out of cafeteria—I'm hungry and tired of writing this list

place is noisy today—footsteps, doors slamming, people talking and laughing, music on PA system

my husband is here—time to go

Now that you have looked at Celia's list of observations, read the paper that grew from her list. Working alone or in small groups, examine the paper to see which details were included, which were left out, and what inferences the writer drew from her observations.

DONNA'S LI'L BROTHER

1   Classes were over for the day, and it was time to go home. My husband had arranged to meet me in the lobby of the student center, so I sat and waited for him there.

2   Looking around, I noticed the well-tended plants in the window area. These healthy plants were an indication that someone cared about this place and worked hard to make it look its best. The navy blue carpeting complemented the gray of the furnishings and the off-white color of the walls. The blue and gold mobile added a finishing touch to the interior decoration.

3   My attention was drawn to one particular student seated in the lobby. While most of the other people were studying or simply staring into space, wrapped up in their own thoughts, this young man was busy talking or listening to people. Noticing his dark hair, olive skin, and foreign accent, I decided he was from the Middle East. He was dressed in blue jeans, a tan and brown striped belt, well-worn black sneakers, and a bright green T-shirt with gold letters.

4   For some reason he seemed to attract people to him. During the time that I watched him, I noticed that a large number of the students who walked through the lobby stopped to talk with him. Some greeted him casually and passed on by. Others stood and held extended conversations with him. He

attracted students of both sexes and of all nationalities. Middle Eastern students would sit down and share letters and photos with him. An Asian student stopped to talk about a recent ballgame. A black student sat down and held a conversation with him. A young Caucasian girl who looked depressed poured out her troubles to him while he listened with sympathy.

5   The next day I returned to the same place to sit and wait for my husband. Again I noticed the same young man seated in the lobby. Students on their way to lunch would notice him and lean over the stair rail to greet him. Others on their way to or from the post office would see him and come over to talk. He seemed to have the ability to say the right thing, to be a good listener, and to be available when people needed him. Students who talked to him always came away looking happier.

6   Just before my husband arrived, this young man got up, gathered his books, and left the building. I noticed these words written in gold letters on the back of his green T-shirt: "Donna's Li'l Brother." I smiled to myself, thinking how appropriate this slogan was, for this young man appeared to be a "brother" to so many of his fellow students.

Writing Assignment

Choose some place where you can sit and take notes. Observe the place carefully and make a list of what you see, hear, smell, and so forth. You do not need to worry about putting your observations in any order or about the spelling, punctuation, and grammar. But you do need to pay attention to vocabulary, using the most precise and exact words possible to describe what is around you.

First, make a list of the physical features. Use all your senses. Include any noticeable sounds, odors, colors, and textures. Try to make the list as complete as possible, using adjectives that will help you recall exactly what the place is like and what your attitude toward it is. For example, you may note that the carpet is a dark, dirty brown, that you can hear the hum of fluorescent lights, or that you smell a dreadful cigar.

If you have an opportunity while you are making notes, observe a person as well. Be sure to write down the person's physical features, such as approximate height and weight, hair color and style, clothing, and so on. Try to notice any characteristics that would help you draw inferences about this person.

When you finish observing, review your notes. Group similar details into separate lists. For example, put everything about the physical appearance of the place into one list, put everything about sounds into another, and so on. If you have observed a person, put those details into a list as well. Now, using the facts in your lists, write a description of the place and/or person you have observed. Make valid inferences whenever you can. Assume you are writing for readers who are not familiar with the place or person you are describing.

Activity 2.5   Exchange papers with someone else in the class. Each partner should read the other's paper and identify all the inferences in it. Based on the evidence given in the paper, decide whether each inference is valid or invalid.

Drawing Inferences from Reading

You can draw inferences from what you read as well as from what you observe directly. In fact, being able to draw valid inferences from assigned reading material is an essential thinking skill for successful college students. The thinking process is much the same as it is when you work from observation. What you read is the known; what you infer is based on the known. The inferences you draw from reading are valid if the text offers enough support to make your statements probable.

Be very careful, however, about making invalid inferences. Students in literature classes are sometimes taught (or at least think they are taught) that one person's interpretation is just as good as another's. They may have been told something like this: "It's what *you* think about this work that matters. Every reader has the right to his or her interpretation." To be blunt, this approach is wrong even in reading literature. And it is not only wrong but also dangerous when reading factual material. Every good reader must make inferences about what he or she reads, but those inferences must be valid. They must be based on what is actually in the text, not on what someone thinks may be there.

Let's consider an example. The two paragraphs that follow are from Svea J. Gold's book, *When Children Invite Child Abuse*:

1   Many preschoolers are brilliant. A two-year-old can name all the butterflies in the butterfly book after being told their names during just a few sessions on Mom's lap. He can tell the names of all the presidents from their pictures if someone shows him the pictures a few times. He may even know a Cadillac from a Chevrolet, a Mazda from a Toyota. Did Dad teach him that? He just seems to have picked it up. By three or four, given a modern mother, a child knows that chickens lay eggs, but the facts of life are different for animals like dogs and cats. At four, he knows all the four-letter words which circulate among the older boys in the neighborhood,

and at five, even before he enters kindergarten, he is fascinated by all those scary dinosaurs and knows their Latin names.

2   And then something terrible happens: He enters school. The more brilliant a child is, the more devastating the event may be, because the more brilliant he is, the more likely his parents are to push him into school too soon!

There are several inferences we can make. Based on the evidence of the first paragraph, we can infer that the main indicators of a preschooler's "brilliance," at least as discussed here, are more often recognition and recall than understanding. (Notice, however, that even the three-year-old makes an inference about the different reproductive patterns of mammals and non-mammals.) We can also infer that the child accumulates this knowledge from a variety of sources—personal observation, Mom, Dad, older children.

The most important inference, however, we draw from the second paragraph. These are the very children, says Ms. Gold, who are most damaged by entering school too soon. What inference can you draw? Be cautious. When you read the first sentence of this paragraph, you may jump to the conclusion that this author, like many others, is criticizing the American educational system for dulling the minds of bright children. This is not at all what she says. She says that parents "push [such a child] into school too soon!" We can infer that children should be placed in school according to their level of development and maturity, not simply according to their chronological age.

Activity 2.6   Read the following paragraphs in the "Reader" section of this text. Decide what valid inferences can be drawn from the material you read.

page 174, paragraph 8	page 244, paragraph 26
page 200, paragraph 1	pages 259–260, paragraph 6
page 213, paragraphs 3–5	pages 280–281, paragraphs 1–2

BRAINSTORMING

Brainstorming, which we looked at briefly in Chapter 1, is a technique often used in conferences to stimulate thinking, develop ideas, and solve problems. As a part of prewriting, brainstorming can be done in small groups, but most writers prefer to work through this thinking time alone.

Brainstorming is a way of searching your memory for details that you already know, but that may not be in your conscious mind. It opens up the memory. It can also help you think through an issue you want to examine thoroughly. Often, brainstorming can be combined successfully with inference drawing. As you think about and write down what you know, you can also write down inferences based on the facts you have recorded.

The technique is simple. You start with a topic, sometimes just a word, and think of anything you can about that topic. As your mind moves from one idea to another, you write these ideas down. You do not need to worry about grammar, spelling, punctuation, or mechanics. The important thing is to keep your mind moving and your pencil recording. You should not spend much time evaluating the thoughts that occur to you—that can come later.

Here is the result of one student's fifteen-minute, in-class brainstorming on the subject "pain." He was instructed to write down all thoughts and to keep writing, even if his mind went blank. Gaps and pauses in his thinking do not show on paper, but notice that he tries to push himself when he is stalled. He writes down his ideas in whatever order they occur to him, and he spends very little time examining them.

PAIN

First bad pain I remember—fell out of a tree—age 7. Real bad pain when I had appendicitis (?)—4th grade I think. Pain. Pain. What about pain? This is harder than I thought. Kinds of pain? OK, mental pain. That hurts too. Lots of mental pain the year I almost flunked algebra. Lost my girlfriend that same year. Really hurt. Guess I've had a lot of accidents—sprained ankle in 8th grade, shoulder injury in h.s. football, bruised ribs too. Accident prone? Accident makes me think of the time I lied to Dad about the car wreck. Physical *and* mental pain. Cuts and bruises hurt alot. Hurt when I was grounded for a month! But my conscience hurt too. I took keys to his car without asking, picked up some of the guys, had a few beers. We skidded into a pickup on a slick road. Lied to Dad about what happened. He found out anyway. Nothing right now. Brain's not working. What am I supposed to do now? Jim lifts weights. He all the time says "No pain, no gain." Is that true? I guess so. Is it true for mental pain too? Does that make sense? I'm stopping to reread this. Pain. One time I locked myself out of the house. Tried to climb on the porch roof to get in an open upstairs window and cut my leg on the gutter. My hand hurts! That's pain. This whole thing is getting to be a pain! Nearly time to stop. Good. What now? They say going to the dentist hurts alot. I don't know. Haven't been much. When people really don't

want to do something they say "I'd rather have a root canal."
I'm not sure what that is, something a dentist does. Times up.

Activity 2.7   Choose a subject for a brainstorming session of at least ten minutes. Do not interrupt your thinking to correct or criticize your list; just let your thoughts flow. Even if your mind goes blank, write down something. Keep the brain working and the storm brewing. If you do not have a subject in mind, you may choose one of the following: voices, eyes, walls, work, enemies, food, family, success, frustration, waste. If your instructor wishes, you may brainstorm in pairs or small groups. Select one person to jot down notes.

FROM BRAINSTORMING TO DRAFTING

Brainstorming is by no means the only way to start the writing process, but it is one you will use frequently. Therefore, you need to be sure that you can move logically from brainstorming to drafting, and that involves organizing your material.

The danger of not organizing, of never really getting past the brainstorming stage, is simple to illustrate. Let's look once more at a sample of writing from Chapter 1, Beth's attempt to describe her grandmother:

> My grandmother is named Mary Elizabeth. People who know her well usually call her Mary Lizbeth. She lives in New Orleans now with my mother. When she was young, she moved with her parents from Ireland to America. They settled in Chicago. She grew up there and married my grandfather. They had several children. My grandmother is very kind. She is a tall woman with gray hair, although it used to be reddish brown. She has brown eyes. My grandfather was a construction worker and he died in an accident when my mother and her brothers and sisters were young. My grandmother worked very hard and was able to send any of the children to college who wanted to go. I am very proud of her for this.

Compare this to the brainstorming done before her next attempt:

> Description—grandmother. Name: Mary Elizabeth Mullen Cooper. Everyone who knows her well calls her Mary Lizbeth. Lives in New O. with mother. Moved with family from

Ireland to Chicago when she was young. She was happy to be in America. Grew up in C. and married grandfather. Several children—two boys, three girls. Kind woman. Always nice to grandchildren. Looks: tall, gray hair—used to be reddish brown. Brown eyes. Grandfather killed in construction accident when kids young. G. worked hard to support family. Kids who wanted to went to college. I'm real proud of G. for what she did. Hope I can be like her.

In her description Beth has used complete sentences and taken care to be factually correct, but otherwise what she has written closely resembles brainstorming. Look at the organization, or rather the lack of it, in the "finished" description. Beth begins with her grandmother's name, then mentions her current home. Then there is a jump to her grandmother's early years when she came from Ireland to Chicago. She grows up, marries, has children. Now Beth mentions a few details of physical description and suddenly shifts to her grandfather, who dies almost before we are aware he existed at all. Now comes her grandmother's hard work for her family and Beth's pride in her.

Beth has not written an essay or even a good paragraph. What she has is like brainstorming that has been corrected and tidied up. Used as prewriting material, it may still be valuable, but it cannot be considered a finished product. Now Beth is stuck, out of ideas and uncertain what to do next. Her final two sentences sound as if they might be a conclusion, so she just stops. She could have avoided much of this trouble if she had planned first.

Clustering

This technique, as we noted briefly in Chapter 1, asks you to perform one of the most common thinking skills—categorizing. **Clustering** simply involves putting similar pieces of information together in categories.

If a teacher of logic asked you to create a categorizing system, you would have to be quite strict. Your categories would have to include every piece of information, or you would have to agree that a piece that would not fit into any of the categories must be tossed out. In categorizing for writing, however, you can be more relaxed. When you are clustering and you find some pieces of brainstorming or other information that do not fit, save these odds and ends in a "miscellaneous" category. You might find a place for them later.

Activity 2.8   Working alone or in small groups, look through the brainstorming data on pages 27–28 and pick several headings for categories. Then try to put each piece of information under one of those headings. What is left over? Can the categories be slightly expanded, or should the leftovers be put in "miscellaneous"?

Obviously Beth does not have enough information to write a description of her grandmother; but until the information she does have is clustered, it is difficult to tell what else she may need. Once the clustering is completed, it will be easier to see which categories may be adequate and which need additional information. At this point she can move back to the earlier parts of the cycle.

Beth may find, for example, that she wants more physical description of her grandmother. If so, then she can brainstorm that particular category, writing down everything she can think of concerning her grandmother's physical appearance. Then comes more clustering. There must be a category of things her grandmother did for her children because this is a major point of the description. That category, however, is weak. So, more brainstorming and more clustering. This process can continue until Beth is satisfied that she has enough information to write from. Even when she moves into the drafting or revising phases, if she feels some point is not well enough developed, she can return to brainstorming and clustering. The writing process, as you see, really is cyclical.

Activity 2.9   Return to the brainstorming you did in Activity 2.7. Decide on categories, and cluster your data under these headings. If you were going to write a paper on the topic of your brainstorming, what categories would need to be expanded?

Organizing

Later chapters will discuss various ways in which you can organize paragraphs and whole essays. However, organization begins here, as you near the end of the preparation stage and move toward drafting. If you have been successful in brainstorming and clustering, you have already begun organizing. Once you decide in what order you want to use the category headings you developed during clustering, you even have a kind of rough outline. You may make many changes in your organization before you finish your writing assignment, but a simple plan is necessary now if you are to avoid the problem Beth had. Here is a basic piece of advice that many writers forget: you must know where you want to begin, where you want to go from there, and where you want to end.

Activity 2.10   Look again at the brainstorming categories and clustering in Activity 2.9. If you were preparing to write a paper, how would you organize these categories? Why would you choose this particular order?

FREEWRITING

Although brainstorming is one of the most common and successful ways of generating ideas, there are a number of others. Many writers, both professionals and amateurs, like to warm up with freewriting. This is a useful technique when you are looking at a blank sheet of paper and cannot think of anything to write on it. The idea of **freewriting** is simply to start putting down words and to keep going. If you focus your freewriting, keeping your thoughts on one topic, you can follow the suggestions for brainstorming. In fact, focused freewriting may be thought of as brainstorming for one.

Sometimes, however, the best way to get your thoughts and your pencil moving is unfocused freewriting. For ten or fifteen minutes you simply write down whatever thoughts occur to you, giving yourself no instructions except to keep writing. If you find you cannot think of anything at all, write "I can't think of anything" until a thought comes. You may find unfocused freewriting especially helpful when you are asked to choose a topic for writing and cannot think of one.

Activity 2.11

For ten minutes practice unfocused freewriting. It does not matter what idea you start with; just begin writing and keep going. Record ideas and sensations. When your thoughts seem to stop, write down what is going on around you. If your mind seems a complete blank, write "I can't think of anything" until something occurs to you. It is absolutely necessary to keep working if you are to limber up your mental and physical writing muscles.

If you have trouble with this exercise, you may want to ask your instructor or another student to help you. Although freewriting is usually an activity for one writer alone, it is possible to have a partner—sometimes called a "goad"—whose job is to keep you working. When you stop writing for more than a few seconds, the goad will say, quietly and pleasantly, "Keep writing."

WHEEL DIAGRAMMING

Wheel diagramming is useful when you have a topic that is too large to be handled in your essay. It is a way of breaking down and narrowing a topic. Think of a wagon wheel. The large topic is the hub; the smaller ideas or subtopics are spokes radiating from the hub. Sometimes these subtopics will produce more radiating spokes of their own.

Let's look at an example. A student enrolled in an earth science class has been assigned to write a paper on a major environmental problem; the specific topic is up to her. Here is an early version of her wheel diagram:

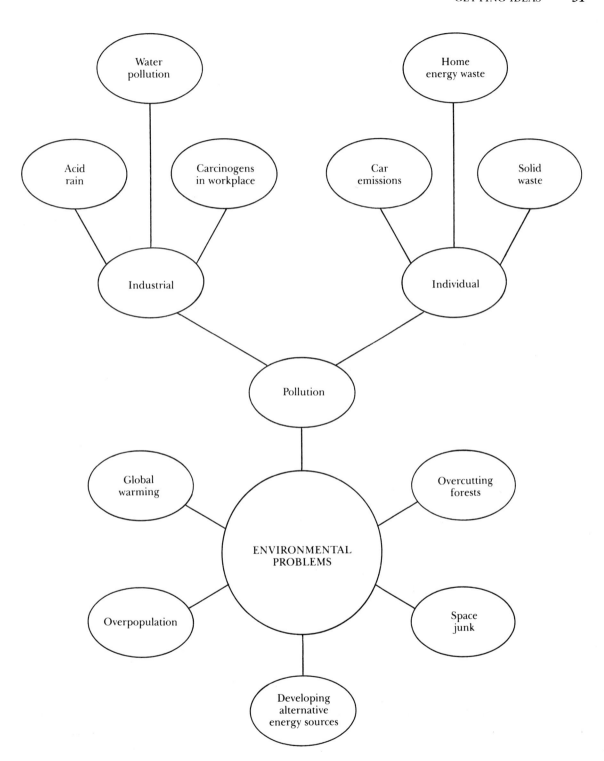

Activity 2.12   Make a wheel diagram for any topic you choose. If you have none in mind, you may use one of these: professional sports, careers in _____ (health, education, science, aviation, sales, management, radio/TV, stage and film, food services, the hotel/motel industry, and so forth), major social problems in America, summer jobs, problems of being a student/parent, challenges or difficulties facing handicapped students on your campus, different types of people you live or work with.

WRITING AND READING

Reading influences writing in several important ways. Sometimes the actual writing technique is affected. The more you read, the more words you can add to your own writing vocabulary. You can also learn by example about the structure of English sentences and paragraphs. Some student writers even begin to copy, consciously or unconsciously, sentence and paragraph patterns they see when reading. In this chapter, however, we will consider reading mainly as a source of material for writing, as another way of getting ideas.

Obviously, you can read for factual information to put into your writing. You have almost certainly done this in writing factual reports or research papers. But information gathered by reading can be worked into many writing assignments, not just those that call for research.

If you want to enrich your writing by adding "outside" information to your own thinking, you might follow two suggestions. Many writers keep what they call a commonplace book or writer's journal. You might try doing the same. There is nothing difficult about this, and you do not need any fancy materials. Simply keep a separate notebook or a part of your composition notebook for writing down quotations that impress you, facts that interest you, thoughts (your own or someone else's) that might be useful in writing, news items that catch your attention—anything, in short, that you might want to think more about or possibly use in your writing.

Another technique is to think about what you have recently read while you are in the prewriting stage of a writing assignment. Be especially alert for material read in other classes that might be useful in composition class. One example will show how this can work.

In her brainstorming Beth wrote that when her grandmother moved from Ireland, she was happy to be in America. Reading a book on Irish emigrants for her sociology class, she came across this sentence: "Female emigrants seemed especially prone to make realistic assessments of America's comparative advantages, less likely than husbands or sons to cling to old customs or romanticize the society left behind" (Kerby A. Miller, *Emigrants and Exiles: Ireland and the Irish Exodus to North America*). It is unlikely that she would copy such a sentence into a commonplace book or even remember the wording, but she might well remember the idea. Later, in describing her grandmother, she might write:

> Grandmother had to make many changes, some of them very hard. She missed her aunts, uncles, and cousins and her good friends in Cork. But like most of the women in her generation of Irish-Americans, she adjusted well to her new country.

It is not especially difficult to combine what you read with what you write. It depends on two good study habits: (1) paying close attention to what you read, and (2) merging information from different classes or subjects. When you combine information in this way, you are synthesizing, another of the thinking skills so important for your success in and out of college.

JOURNAL WRITING

Keeping a journal is one kind of personal writing. Each day, or several times a week, you make entries describing what is happening to you and how you are reacting. In addition to being a record of what you are doing and thinking at a particular time in your life, a journal is also an excellent source of ideas that can be developed as writing assignments.

You may already be keeping a journal. If you are not, try doing so for a few weeks. Make frequent entries, writing three or more times a week. Remember, when you keep a journal, you do not just record events. You also maintain a record of your ideas, reactions, and feelings.

Here is a sample journal entry that is merely an outline of a day's activities:

> *September 7*
>
> Not such a good start today. Tom woke early and turned off the alarm—again! I overslept and got to class 15 minutes late. Then there was a quiz in math, and I hadn't finished reading the chapter. At lunch I saw Laurie and asked her to go to the dance next week. She said yes. That improved my day. Mom called tonight. She wants me to come home this weekend. I guess I will—I can see everybody and get my laundry done!

The entry simply retells events. With some reflection and thought, however, the writer could use the activities that are recorded as the basis for a much better entry, one that has several possible theme topics in it:

September 7

1   Not such a good start today. Tom woke early and turned off the alarm—again!—making me late for my first class. This is the third time he has done this in two weeks. I don't know how to handle the situation. I've asked Tom not to shut off the alarm before I wake up, but he forgets. I wasn't so sure at first how I would get along with a roommate I'd never seen before, especially one from the northeast, but we're getting along great! We like a lot of the same things (like Italian food, Springsteen, and the N.Y. Giants), and I don't want any hassle. I'll mention the alarm again, but I'm not going to let a little thing like this cause trouble. I'll buy a second clock instead.

2   I saw Laurie at lunch. She's going to the dance with me next week. After I talked to her, my whole day seemed better. Guess that shows how I feel about Laurie! She's someone else I met only a few weeks ago, but it seems I've known her much longer. Who knows—this might turn into something special. I kind of hope so.

3   Mom called tonight. She wants me to come home for the weekend. She didn't say it, but it sounded like she and Dad and Andy really miss me. It's funny. I worried a lot before I left home that I would miss my parents and my brother, but I didn't think that *they* might miss *me*. I guess I was so busy thinking about myself that I didn't think how they would feel.

The first part of any writing assignment is the planning stage, a time for choosing ideas and collecting material. These ideas can come from your observation of the people and places around you, from your thoughts and memories, from your reading, even from your own journal writing.

These ideas are made richer by your analysis of your own responses to what you see, remember, read, or think. Thus, while you plan, you should decide how you feel about or react to the ideas you are collecting and what words you can use to communicate these ideas and responses to your readers. In all cases you need to know the difference between facts and the inferences you base on them. You also need to be sure that your inferences are valid, which means they are based on enough factual information to be probable.

CHAPTER 3

~~~~~~~~~~~ *Drafting*
~~~~~~~~~~~ *and Revising*

*In this chapter you will study in more detail two parts of the
writing process discussed in Chapter 1, drafting and revising. Drafting is actually getting your information down in
sentences and paragraphs so that you can work with it further. Revising is the refining and editing you do to prepare
a version of your writing that you will present to your
readers. These two activities may sometimes overlap; moreover, while drafting or revising, you may find you need to
return to planning, the first part of the writing process.*

We have seen the importance of thorough, careful preparation. But
after collecting and organizing the raw materials, a writer must move into
the drafting stage. Beginning writers sometimes use prewriting as a refuge
to hide in. They keep on planning and planning, putting off the task of
committing thoughts to paper. This may produce superior prewriting, yet
there comes a time when the writer must move on. Otherwise, he or she has
first-rate brick and well-made mortar, but no building.

Some writers who prepare well may still falter as they move into drafting. In Chapter 1 drafting was described as the stage where the writer's
thoughts are put into sentences and paragraphs. But writers who are not
comfortable writing sentences and paragraphs may hesitate to move into this
part of the process. The best advice is to go ahead, do the best you can, and
not worry unnecessarily about how well you write paragraphs and sentences.
You will work on improving these skills in Chapters 7 and 8.

REVIEWING THE PREWRITING

To see how at least one writer begins drafting, let's return to Beth's paper from Chapters 1 and 2. We will ignore the attempt on page 5 and call this draft her first. Here is her brainstorming:

> Description—grandmother. Name: Mary Elizabeth Mullen Cooper. Everyone who knows her well calls her Mary Lizbeth. Lives in New O. with mother. Moved with family from Ireland to Chicago when she was young. She was happy to be in America. Grew up in C. and married grandfather. Several children—two boys, three girls. Kind woman. Always nice to grandchildren. Looks: tall, gray hair—used to be reddish brown. Brown eyes. Grandfather killed in construction accident when kids young. G. worked hard to support family. Kids who wanted to went to college. I'm real proud of G. for what she did. Hope I can be like her.

In Activity 2.8 you considered how she might cluster her material. Here is one possibility:

Young Life	*Physical Description*
Moved from Ireland to Chicago	Tall
Was happy in America	Has gray hair that was once reddish brown
Grew up in Chicago	Has brown eyes

Later Life	*Miscellaneous*
Married grandfather	Now lives with Mom
Had children: 3 girls, 2 boys	She's kind
Grandfather killed	She's nice to grandchildren
G. supported family	I'm proud of her
Sent 3 kids to college	

For now, Beth decides to organize her paper by beginning with the physical description, then discussing her grandmother's early life, and finally describing her later life. Miscellaneous material will be worked in where it seems to fit.

THE DRAFTING PROCESS

Thesis Statement and Early Drafts

Beth will begin with a **thesis statement**, a sentence that states the main idea of her paper. The thesis may remain a permanent part of her paper, or it may be revised or even removed in the final version. She should begin with it now, however. It will help her keep the draft focused clearly on the central idea.

When Beth asked herself what she wanted to write, her answer was: "I want to write a paper in which I describe my grandmother, especially telling what she has done for her family and why I am proud of her." Her thesis statement can grow out of her answer. One possibility is:

> Whatever happened, my grandmother always took care of her family, and because of this I am proud of her.

With this statement, Beth has begun drafting.

BETH'S FIRST DRAFT

1   Whatever happened, my grandmother always took care of her family, and because of this I am proud of her.

2   My grandmother is a tall woman. She has gray hair but it was once a dark reddish brown. Her eyes are brown. I have seen some old photographs of her and she was beautiful when she was young. She is still very atractive. She has always been kind and generous to everyone. She is especially nice to her grandchildren. She now lives with Mom in New Orleans.

3   My grandmother was born in Ireland and her maiden name was Mary Elizabeth Mullen. People who know her well call her Mary Lizbeth, but she always uses both full names. When she was still a young girl, about 12 I think, she moved with her family to the United States to the city of Chicago. She missed some of her family and friends back in Cork, the town she came from in Ireland, but she was happy to be living in America.

4   Grandmother married Patrick Cooper who was a construction worker in Chicago. They had five children. Mary Elizabeth, the first, is my mother. The second child, Catherine Ann, died in infansy. The first boy was named Thomas Patrick after my grandfather. Then came Theresa Helen and then Francis Joseph. Mother says they were all named after my grandmother's favorite saints because grandmother was

very religious. Grandmother even once made a joke about the saints' names. She was good at sewing and made clothes for the family and sewed dresses for people in her home.

5   Grandmother was only 39 when Grandfather was killed in a construction accident. A high steel beam where he was welding collapsed. The children in age were from 6 to 17. Grandmother knew she had to support her family, so she got a job in a sewing factory. A friend watched the younger kids after school. Grandmother still sewed dresses at night.

6   She managed to get all four children through high school, and she told them if they wanted to go to college and would work she would help them. Mother wanted to take a secreterial course, so she did with Grandmother helping her. Uncle Pat went to college and so did Aunt Theresa. Uncle Joe went in the Army and liked it, so he stayed as an officer.

7   I'm real proud of my grandmother for what she did and I hope I will be like her.

As you can see, Beth is guided by her rough organization plan (the category headings and clustered items), but she adds or changes information as she writes. That is the way writing should go. A plan or outline should be your guide, not your dictator. As Beth writes, she thinks of things not included in her prewriting (for example, the early photograph and the joke about saints' names), and she feels free to include them.

The students in Beth's writing class will read and discuss their papers in small groups before beginning major revisions. However, Beth will make some changes even before her paper goes to the group.

Activity 3.1   Beth's major revisions will come after her group has read and commented on her paper. Before she gives it to them, she will do some "clean-up" work: eliminating unnecessary material from her sentences, making minor word changes, checking for obvious errors in spelling and punctuation, and so forth. Read through her paper and locate errors or problem areas that can be corrected easily before the group works with the paper. Check to see how your suggestions match up with the corrections Beth makes in her second draft.

BETH'S SECOND DRAFT
WITH MINOR REVISIONS

1   Whatever happened, my grandmother always took care of her family, and because of this I am proud of her.

2   My grandmother is a tall woman. She has gray hair, but it was once a dark auburn. Her eyes are brown. I have seen

some old photographs of her, and she was beautiful when she was young. She is still very attractive. She has always been kind and generous to everyone, especially her family. She now lives with Mom in New Orleans.

3   My grandmother was born in Ireland, and her maiden name was Mary Elizabeth Mullen. People who know her well call her Mary Lizbeth, but she always uses her full name. When she was still a young girl, about 12 I think, she moved with her family to Chicago. She missed some of her family and friends back in Cork, but she was happy to be living in America.

4   Grandmother married Patrick Cooper, who was a construction worker in Chicago. They had five children. Mary Elizabeth, the first, is my mother. The second child, Catherine Ann, died in infancy. The first boy was named Thomas Patrick after my grandfather. Then came Theresa Helen and Francis Joseph. Mother says they were all named after my grandmother's favorite saints because grandmother was very religious. Grandmother even once made a joke about the saints' names. She was good at sewing. She made clothes for the family and sewed dresses for people in her home.

5   Grandmother was only 39 when Grandfather was killed in a construction accident. A high steel beam where he was welding collapsed. The children were then from 6 to 17. Grandmother knew she had to support her family, so she got a job in a sewing factory. A friend watched the younger children after school. Grandmother still sewed dresses at night.

6   She managed to get all four children through high school, and she told them if they wanted to go to college and would work, she would help them. Mother wanted to take a secretarial course, so she did with Grandmother's help. Uncle Pat went to college, and so did Aunt Theresa. Uncle Joe went in the Army and liked it, so he stayed as an officer.

7   I'm real proud of my grandmother for what she did, and I hope I will be like her.

Revision

Some student writers think that the sort of thing Beth has done is all that revision amounts to; they would assume that she is finished. Such a view underlies many writing problems, so it is important to look more carefully at this part of the process. There are several kinds of revision intended to accomplish different ends. Let's make a comparison. Revising a paper can be like changing a room. You may take the furniture you have and rearrange it.

You may remove pictures or knickknacks that you are tired of or that no longer seem to fit in and replace them with new ones. If you want greater changes, you may put new upholstery on a chair or get a new bedspread. You might buy two or three new pieces of furniture to mix with the old, repaint the walls, and put up new curtains. You might even change the function of the room: what was once an extra bedroom can become a nursery.

Revision is like that. You can revise words, sentences, paragraphs, and groups of paragraphs. You can add, eliminate, and reorganize material within the paper. You can even change the function of a paper: what was once a simple description of an automobile accident can become an argument for tougher drunk-driving laws.

So far, Beth has made a few revisions and corrected some obvious errors. To return to our essay/room comparison, she has just dusted, tidied up, and perhaps added a couple of new throw pillows. To make major improvements in her paper, she needs to rethink and rewrite.

Her reading group will make several suggestions for revision. Just as important, they will ask questions. Readers' questions must be taken seriously. They are not always good suggestions or questions; sometimes they show that a reader simply is not paying attention. But often they point out places where something is not clear or where the writer makes the reader curious and then does not satisfy that curiosity. Look at the comments Beth receives on her second draft.

BETH'S SECOND DRAFT WITH PEER COMMENTS AND QUESTIONS

1   Whatever happened, my grandmother always took care of her family, and because of this I am proud of her.

2   My grandmother is a tall woman. She has gray hair, but it was once a dark auburn. Her eyes are brown. I have seen some old photographs of her, and she was beautiful when she was young. She is still very attractive. She has always been kind and generous to everyone, especially her family. She now lives with Mom in New Orleans.

This doesn't fit here.

3   My grandmother was born in Ireland, and her maiden name was Mary Elizabeth Mullen. People who know her well call her Mary Lizbeth, but she always uses her full name. When she was still a young girl, about 12 I think, she moved with her family to Chicago. She missed some of her family and friends back in Cork, but she was happy to be living in America.

Sounds awfully vague
You could describe her early years in U.S.A.

Maybe describe grandfather

4   Grandmother married Patrick Cooper, who was a construction worker in Chicago. They had five children. Mary Elizabeth, the first, is my mother. The second child, Catherine Ann, died in infancy. The first boy was named

What was it? Don't leave me wondering! These details don't seem to go with the rest of the ¶. Maybe in ¶ 5?

Thomas Patrick after my grandfather. Then came Theresa Helen and Francis Joseph. Mother says they were all named after my grandmother's favorite saints because grandmother was very religious. Grandmother even once made a joke about the saints' names. She was good at sewing. She made clothes for the family and sewed dresses for people in her home.

5   Grandmother was only 39 when Grandfather was killed in a construction accident. A high steel beam where he was welding collapsed. The children were from 6 to 17. Grandmother knew she had to support her family, so she got a job in a sewing factory. A friend watched the younger children after school. Grandmother still sewed dresses at night.

I'm not sure what you mean here — work at a job?

This is a really important point, and you should make more of it.

6   She managed to get all four children through high school, and she told them if they wanted to go to college and would work, she would help them. Mother wanted to take a secretarial course, so she did with Grandmother's help. Uncle Pat went to college, and so did Aunt Theresa. Uncle Joe went in the Army and liked it, so he stayed as an officer.

7   I'm real proud of my grandmother for what she did, and I hope I will be like her.

Activity 3.2   Assume that you are revising this paper. Which suggestions would you accept and which would you reject? Which questions are important to answer? Is further prewriting needed on any points? If so, which ones? Are there other changes you would make that have not been suggested here?

The Final Draft

After considering the questions and suggestions of those in her group, Beth will write one more draft. This one will be submitted for the instructor's comments and a grade. If she or her instructor wishes, there can be further revisions after that. The paper that Beth will submit is printed here. Following it are some questions about her final revisions.

BETH'S FINAL VERSION

1   My grandmother is a tall woman, almost 5 feet 8 inches, and she still holds herself very straight. Her hair is gray now, but it was once a dark auburn. Her eyes are dark brown. I have seen old photographs which show how beautiful she was when she was young, and even in her sixties she is very attractive.

2   Grandmother was born Mary Elizabeth Mullen. The name sounds very Irish, and it is. Most people who know her call her Mary Lizbeth, but she is very proud of her name, and she never shortens it when she says it.

3   She was born in Cork, but she moved to Chicago with her family when she was twelve. It was not easy for a young girl to make such a big change. Grandmother had to make many changes, some of them very hard. She missed her aunts, uncles, and cousins and her good friends in Cork. But like most of the women in her generation of Irish-Americans, she adjusted well to her new country. One of Grandmother's favorite sayings is "You can't see where you're going if you're looking behind you."

4   When Grandmother was 20, she married Patrick Cooper, an Irish-American construction worker. They had five children. My mom was the first, named Mary Elizabeth like Grandmother. The second child, Catherine Ann, died in infancy. The first boy was named Thomas Patrick after my grandfather. Theresa Helen and Francis Joseph followed.

5   All the children were named for saints. Grandmother is a very religious woman, but she isn't stuffy about it. In fact, she once joked that she and grandfather would have had a larger family except she had used up all her favorite saints. I think her faith probably helped her get through the hard times she had.

6   She was only 39 when Grandfather was killed. He was welding on a high steel beam that collapsed. Mom was 17 and not yet out of high school. Uncle Joe was only 6. So Grandmother knew she had to do something to support her family. She was a good seamstress. She had always made clothes for her family and sewed dresses for other people. Now she went to work in a sewing factory. At night Mom and Uncle Pat took care of the younger children while Grandmother still made dresses.

7   Grandmother insisted that all her children finish high school, and she told them she would help them go to college if they would work and help themselves too. Mom wanted to go to a two-year secretarial school. Uncle Pat went to college, and so did Aunt Theresa. He's a businessman now, and she is a teacher. Uncle Joe is the only one Grandmother didn't have to help. He joined the Army and liked it, so he became a career officer.

8   A few years ago Grandmother moved to New Orleans to live with Mom. She says leaving Chicago after so many years

was almost like leaving Cork when she was a girl. But she adjusted again. She goes to Mass every day, and she has made lots of new friends, especially in her church. She still sews. Her fingers are not as fast as they must have been when she sewed eight hours a day and at night too, but she likes to make things for her grandchildren. When I told her goodbye before I left for college, she was working on a christening dress for her first great-grandchild.

9   I'm proud of my grandmother. She had to make a lot of changes during her life, and she always handled them. When she had to make sacrifices for her family, she seemed happy to do it. I inherited my grandmother's name, and I hope I inherited her strong character too.

Activity 3.3   Answer the following questions about Beth's fully revised paper:

1. What changes have been made in the organization of the paper? What material has been moved from one place to another? Why do you think Beth moved this material?

2. What material has been added in this version? Do the additions improve the paper, or are they just padding?

3. Beth has dropped her original thesis statement. Is her main idea now clear from the paper? Should she still open with a thesis statement? Why or why not?

4. In paragraph 3 Beth added some information she had come across in her reading for a sociology class. (See pages 32–33.) From that same source she had learned that during the time she is writing about, there was a large Irish-American community in Chicago and that many of the male immigrants went into construction work. Should she have mentioned these facts? Why or why not?

5. What inferences are made in paragraphs 5, 8, and 9?

Drafting and revising complete the writing process. As you have seen, writers cycle in and out of the different steps. After the prewriting, you need to get a first draft on paper so there is actually a text to work with. Then comes revision, both minor and major. The revising and redrafting and perhaps even some additional planning continue until you are satisfied with the result.

A final, very practical, piece of advice. Few writers, whether professionals or students, are completely satisfied with what they write. In theory, the planning, drafting, revising, replanning, redrafting, and rerevising could go on forever. You want to produce the best writing you can, but at some point you must let go.

There comes a time when the most helpful step is to turn your writing over to readers, either your peers or your instructor. When you have gotten their response, you may need to do further work. However, even this process of communication, response, and further communication must have a practical limit. Eventually, you must say: "For right now, I have done as much with this piece of writing as I can reasonably do." Then you go on to the next assignment. That is the way writers grow.

When the planning or prewriting is finished (or at least seems to be), it is time for drafting, for actually getting ideas down in sentences and paragraphs. Then comes revising, which may involve rewriting, reorganizing, even rethinking, and certainly careful editing. Finally, your work is given to your readers, who may offer suggestions for even more revision. In theory, the writing process could cycle on forever; but in practice, you and your instructor must decide when a writing assignment is complete so that you can move to the next one.

CHAPTER 4

Writing Description and Narration

A piece of writing can be organized and developed in several ways, depending largely on your purpose. Two of the most common and useful types of writing are description and narration. In fact, if you have used the chapters of this book in order, you have practiced these types already. Even though you will often use other methods of development in your writing for college or business, you will frequently combine description or narration with these other methods.

Generally, methods of arranging ideas on paper are similar to methods of arranging ideas in our minds. That is, we tend to write in the same ways we think. We may think random thoughts and jot them down in any order during the planning stage, but later we work to arrange our ideas in a pattern that our readers can follow. That way, the readers can think along with the writer. As we begin to practice these patterns, it is important to point out that writers (and thinkers) often use several of them together. It is unusual to find just one method of development in a piece of writing.

DESCRIBING AND NARRATING

People have always felt the need to picture what they experienced or how they felt and to tell stories or explain how something happened—that is, to describe and to narrate. Usually, they have kept this information in a written record. Even before the development of alphabets and written languages, cave dwellers used pictures to show what something looked like or to tell how a hunt or battle took place. The desire to describe and narrate seems to be part of what makes us human.

Generally speaking, when you describe a subject, you picture it with little or no action—that is, you use **description**. When you begin to describe action, especially a series of events, you have moved into **narration**. Let's look at an example.

1   I saw her as soon as I left my house. She was sitting quietly on a bench, waiting for the 43rd Street bus. When I came nearer, I could see that she was thin and her hair was gray, but her skin was clear and almost unlined. Her navy suit and white bow-blouse were of good quality but slightly out-of-date. She also wore low-heeled navy shoes. I quickly stereotyped her as a typical middle-class senior citizen.

2   It was then that I noticed something strange about her ears. Hearing aids? No, she was wearing a Walkman. When I sat on the bench beside her, she smiled at me, and I could just hear the music she was listening to. It was rock! I began to reconsider my earlier description.

3   Just then the bus arrived. She rose from the bench slowly, apparently suffering slightly from arthritis. She crossed to the curb and climbed with some difficulty onto the bus. She pulled herself up the three steps, using the handrail, and only then did she open her large purse and begin to rummage for her fare. The driver snapped at her, "Hey, lady, you're supposed to have your money ready when you get on the bus. We ain't got all day. There's people behind you waitin', and they're in a hurry." In fact, I was the only one, and I was standing patiently with my fare already in my hand.

4   The driver's grumbling didn't disturb the old lady. She pulled out an old-fashioned leather change purse, opened the clasp, and carefully took out three quarters. She deposited these one at a time, watching them drop into the fare box. Then she snapped her change purse, replaced it carefully in her handbag, closed that, and started toward the seats.

5   The driver spoke again, this time more rudely than before. "Next time, granny, have your change ready or I won't let you on the bus. Now move out of the way and find a seat—quick." The old lady acted as if she had not heard the insults. She smiled and said, "Thank you, young man. Oh, by the way, you forgot to say 'Have a nice day'." Several passengers laughed loudly, and the driver looked angrier than ever as the woman made her way toward an empty seat.

If you organize your paper this way, you move quite smoothly and naturally from telling how someone looks to telling how she and others act during a short series of events. You move from description to narration.

WRITING DESCRIPTION

When you are writing description, you can ask the same questions you ask before beginning any other kind of writing:

1. What do I want to write?

2. For whom am I writing it?

3. How am I going to write it?

When you can answer these questions, you can be certain of your purpose.

People

Often, the purpose of description is a very simple one: to tell readers who do not know a particular person just what that person is like. The aim of the brainstorming, drafting, and revising is to produce a description that is clear and creates a picture for your readers. This means using accurate details that are suitable for the audience and are put together in logical order. And if you want to keep your readers' attention, it also means using material that is interesting. (Recall the process that Beth went through in describing her grandmother or that you went through in describing a relative.)

Fiction writers learn to use interesting, descriptive details about a character that help their readers form clear mental pictures. In the following example Ernest Hemingway describes a fictional character, a big-game hunter in Africa:

> He was about middle height with sandy hair, a stubby mustache, a very red face and extremely cold blue eyes with faint white wrinkles at the corners that grooved merrily when he smiled. He smiled at her now and she looked away from his face at the way his shoulders sloped in the loose tunic he wore with the four big cartridges held in loops where the left breast pocket should have been, at his big brown hands, his old slacks, his very dirty boots and back to his red face again. She noticed where the baked red of his face stopped in a white line that marked the circle left by his Stetson hat that hung now from one of the pegs of the tent pole. ("The Short Happy Life of Francis Macomber")

The writer's purpose here is to help readers "see" a person they have never seen before. And we do see him. Not only do we know what he looks like; we have some hints of his personality as well. Hemingway gives us this information quickly by using exact, interesting details.

Writers of nonfiction use these same techniques. In the following example Maxine Hong Kingston describes a Chinese relative. Notice that she concentrates first on her uncle's personality (shown in part by his conversation) and later on his general appearance.

> We had an uncle, a second or third cousin maybe, who went back to China to be a Communist. We called him Uncle Bun, which might have been his name, but could also be a pun, Uncle Stupid. He was a blood relative and not just a villager. He was very talkative. In fact, he hardly ever stopped talking, and we kids watched the spit foam at the corners of his mouth. He came to the laundry and sat, or if it were hot, he stood near the door to talk and talk. It was more like a lecture than a conversation. He repeated himself so often that some of what he said seeped into the ears. He talked about wheat germ. "You ought to eat wheat germ," he said, "because wheat germ is the most potent food in the world. Eat it and you'll stay young for a long time; you'll never get sick. You'll be beautiful and tall and strong, also intelligent." . . . Wheat germ would fatten up my father and also fatten up the skinny children. Unlike the rest of the men in the family, who were thin and had white hair, this uncle was round and bald with black hair above his ears and around the back of his head. He wore a pearl gray three-piece suit and a necktie with a gold tiepin, the gold chain of his pocket watch linking one vest pocket with the other, the last button of his vest open over his prosperous paunch. He opened his eyes wide to see everything through his round gold-framed eyeglasses. (*China Men*)

Writing Assignment

In one or two paragraphs, describe a person's physical appearance. You may choose someone you know and write from memory, or you may choose someone whom you can observe directly. Remember that you cannot include everything, so use details that are definite and interesting.

Places

In addition to describing people, writers often must describe places. Again, we must consider purpose: Why are we writing the description? Sometimes, writers simply want to tell what a place looks like; but often they want their readers to glimpse the personality of a place, just as they do with the personalities of people. Here is an example from fiction, again by Ernest Hemingway, describing a railroad stop in Spain:

> The hills across the valley of the Ebro were long and white. On this side there was no shade and no trees and the station was between two lines of rails in the sun. Close against the side of the station there was the warm shadow of the building and a curtain, made of strings of bamboo beads, hung across the open door into the bar, to keep out flies. The American and the girl with him sat at a table in the shade, outside the building. It was very hot and the express from Barcelona would come in forty minutes. It stopped at this junction for two minutes and went on to Madrid.   ("Hills Like White Elephants")

Activity 4.1

Later in "Hills Like White Elephants," Hemingway describes another part of this scene:

> The girl stood up and walked to the other end of the station. Across, on the other side, were fields of grain and trees along the banks of the Ebro. Far away, beyond the river, were mountains. The shadow of a cloud moved across the field of grain and she saw the river through the trees.

How is this part of the scene different from the part described earlier? Pick out the specific details that make the two descriptions different.

In his book *Blue Highways*, William Least Heat Moon describes many of the places he visited while driving the secondary highways and back roads of America. Here is part of his account of a town in Tennessee:

1   Nameless, Tennessee, was a town of maybe ninety people if you pushed it, a dozen houses along the road, a couple of barns, same number of churches, a general merchandise store selling Fire Chief gasoline, and a community center with a lighted volleyball court. Behind the center was an open-roof, rusting metal privy with PAINT ME on the door; in the hollow of a nearby oak lay a full pint of Jack Daniel's Black Label. From the houses, the odor of coal smoke.

2   Next to a red tobacco barn stood the general merchandise with a poster of Senator Albert Gore, Jr., smiling from the window. I knocked. The door opened partway. A tall, thin man said, "Closed up. For good," and started to shut the door.

Activity 4.2   Writers use many visual details, telling us what they see. But they may also want readers to share what they hear, smell, taste, or touch. Here is part of Heat Moon's description of the general merchandise store and the time he spent visiting there. (As you will see, Heat Moon mixes description with narration in these paragraphs.) Read this selection, along with the earlier paragraphs. Then, working in small groups, classify the details according to the sense they appeal to: sight, hearing, smell, and so on.

1   The old store, lighted only by three fifty-watt bulbs, smelled of coal and baking bread. In the middle of the rectangular room, where the oak floor sagged a little, stood an iron stove. To the right was a wooden table with an unfinished game of checkers and a stool made from an apple-tree stump. On shelves around the walls sat earthen jugs with corncob stoppers, a few canned goods, and some of the two thousand old clocks and clock-works Thurmond Watts owned. Only one was ticking; the others he just looked at. . . .

2   "Hilda, get him some buttermilk pie." He looked at me. "You like good music?" I said I did. He cranked up an old Edison phonograph, the kind with the big morning-glory blossom for a speaker, and put on a wax cylinder. "This will be 'My Mother's Prayer'," he said.

3   While I ate the buttermilk pie, Watts served as disc jockey of Nameless, Tennessee. "Here's 'Mountain Rose'." It was one of those moments that you know at the time will stay with you to the grave: the sweet pie, the gaunt man playing the old music, the coals in the stove glowing orange, the scent of kerosene and hot bread. "Here's 'Evening Rhapsody'." The music was so heavily romantic we both laughed.

Activity 4.3   Recall what you learned about observations and inferences in Chapter 2. Factual observations are statements about what you know; inferences, which are based on observations, are statements about what you think but do not know for sure. (If you wish to review this material, see pages 14–15.) Using the observations in William Least Heat Moon's description, make several inferences about Nameless, Tennessee. This activity will help you understand why Heat Moon chooses the particular details he does.

Writing Assignment   In a few paragraphs describe a place, either one you can recall or one you can observe directly. In your planning make a list of observations. Arrange these in order; then write the description. You can use your observations to make inferences about the place. (You may wish to look again at the writing process that led to the description of place in "Donna's Li'l Brother" on pages 20–23.)

Objects

Another common writing task is describing things. Such description is often a part of some larger assignment. For example, if you are writing about a carpentry project, you might include a short description of an adz. If you are explaining how to make a cheesecake, you might briefly describe a springform pan. If you are describing the architecture of a building, you might need to explain what a Romanesque arch looks like. As always, a writer is guided by purpose: the objective is to help readers see, hear, smell, or otherwise respond to what is being described.

Often, such descriptions are short, sometimes only a few sentences. Here is the way an expert on American antiques describes beakers for readers who may know little about the subject:

> *Beakers* are handleless cups. The typical early form is tall, slender, and tapering, with a flaring lip and a molded base. By the late 1700's it had become more squat and straight sided. This shape, often with a molding around base and top, persisted up to the mid-1800's in the South. . . . They are now often called julep cups.   (Alice Winchester, *How to Know American Antiques*)

Two other writers help inexperienced houseplant growers identify familiar plant problems:

> *Mealybug*, one of the most common houseplant diseases, is a white, furry-looking inanimate insect that gathers in white, furry-looking clusters on your plant. (Inanimate insect here means one that doesn't move—not one that's dead.) You can't miss it. It's white and furry-looking and a bit sticky, too.   (Lynn and Joel Rapp, *Mother Earth's Hassle-Free Indoor Plant Book*)

Activity 4.4

Reread the two descriptions just quoted. You will notice that they do not sound alike. (In fact, we would describe these descriptions as having different *tones*.) What methods do the writers use to make their work sound different? What does this suggest about their audiences? Which description do you think is more helpful?

Writing Assignment

Choose some ordinary object in your dormitory room, apartment, or home, and write a one-paragraph description of its appearance. For such an assignment planning will be brief. Begin by listing all the object's characteristics. Then select those that seem most important. Remember that in a brief description you may not be able to include every detail, so when you write your paragraphs, pick those details that will best help your readers see what you see.

Writing Assignment

Several volunteers should bring to class a common fruit or vegetable. (Your instructor may wish to assign specific objects or even supply them.) Good choices include apple, pear, orange, lemon, cucumber, bell pepper, or small squash.

During the planning stage small groups should observe and list as many details as possible about the object given them. What does this object look like, both outside and inside? How would you describe its size, shape, and color? How would you describe its smell, taste, and feel? When you bite it, what sort of sound does it make? Learn as much about the object as you can.

Now, working alone, rearrange the details in your list into categories. You can organize by sense (sight, smell, and so forth), by direction (outside to inside, top to bottom), or even by growth pattern (small to large, stem end to blossom end). In a few paragraphs describe this object (without naming it) so that your readers get a clear idea of what you are writing about.

You may wish to share papers with others in your group to see how different papers can be written from the same facts and observations. Read carefully to see if you or the other writers drew any inferences from these observations. If so, were they planned or not? Sometimes, we make inferences when we think we are writing nothing but factual description.

Situations

Sometimes, writers want to explain or tell about a set of circumstances in which they or others find themselves. Such a description may include people, places, objects, and anything else helpful in picturing these particular circumstances. This type of writing may involve brief bits of narration as well, since there may be some action taking place within the situation being described.

In the following example Donald Hall describes some of the conditions during the first winter after he and his wife Jane moved into his grandmother's house in New Hampshire:

> The next morning was cold, thirty below, cold enough to notice. January is the coldest month, in fact, although many would argue for February. Usually our cold is dry, and it does not penetrate so much as damp cold. December of 1975, our first full winter here, I tried starting the Plymouth one morning with normal confidence in the old six and without cold-weather precautions; I flooded it. When I looked at the thermometer I was astonished to find it minus seventeen

degrees, for my face and forehead had not warned me it was *cold*. . . . Later that winter we did not complain of mildness. In January of 1976, morning after morning was thirty below; one morning on the porch the thermometer read thirty-eight degrees under—a temperature we did not equal again until 1984. . . . Jane and I had never lived without central heat. Now we had a parlor Glenwood stove for heating, two kerosene burners in the kitchen, and on occasion an electric oven with the door open. This twelve-room house, in January of 1976, dwindled to a one-room house, with a kitchen sometimes habitable. Working at the dining room table, twenty feet from the living room's Glenwood, I felt chilly. At the time, we were too excited or triumphant to complain. We were camping out; we were earning our stripes. . . .   ("Winter")

In another example Joan Didion describes the beginning of the 1989 fire season in Los Angeles:

. . . There is nothing unusual about fires in Los Angeles, which is, after all, a desert city with only two distinct seasons: one beginning in January and lasting three or four months, during which storms come in from the northern Pacific and it rains—often an inch every two or three hours, and sometimes, in some places, an inch a minute—and one lasting eight or nine months, during which it burns, or gets ready to burn. What was unusual this year, after two years of drought and a third year of less than average rainfall, was that it was ready to burn while the June fogs still lay on the coastline. On the first of May, months earlier than ever before, the California Department of Forestry declared the start of the fire season and began hiring extra crews. By the last week in June, there had been more than two thousand brush and forest fires in California. Three hundred and twenty of them were burning that week alone.   ("Letter from Los Angeles")

Activity 4.5   In small groups or as a whole class, discuss answers to these questions:

1. Which of the descriptions you just read seems more personal? How does the author make it sound that way?

2. When we say that one example sounds more personal than the other, we are again talking about the *tone* the of writing. What purpose (beyond just describing) do you think each author has? How does the personal tone help the writer fulfill the purpose?

*Writing
Assignment*

In one to three paragraphs, describe a situation. You may be either directly involved in the situation or merely observing it. Some possible subjects are: a time of great heat or cold, the final moment of waiting just before something exciting or important happens, the feeling in a classroom during a major test or final examination, the feeling during a gathering of family or friends. You may also choose a subject not in this list.

When you have finished, exchange papers with a classmate. Read your partner's paper, and then, in your own words, explain what you think he or she intends to do in the description. Your partner will then do the same with your paper. How well did each of you communicate with your reader? How could you improve your description?

WRITING NARRATION

By now it should be clear what narration is and how it is related to description. A simple way of expressing the difference is to say that narration is a description of action. When you write about a series of events, large or small, you narrate. We have already seen how narration mixes with description so that the two types of writing often work together. In fact, in all the examples that follow, you will find many descriptive details within the narratives.

Let's begin with a narrative of events that cover a short period of time. In "Winter" Donald Hall recalls how his grandfather lived during the frozen months on his New Hampshire farm, getting up at 4:30 to begin his chores. This paragraph comes only a few lines after the one quoted earlier, showing description.

> My grandfather worked all day without any heat except for the bodies of his cows. When he sat at morning and evening between two great steaming black-and-white Holstein hulks, pulling the pale thin tonnage of blue milk from their cud-chewing bodies, he was warm. I can remember him, on my winter visits to the farm as a boy, scurrying into the house for a warm-up between his other daily chores, rubbing his hands together, opening the drafts of one of the woodstoves and looming over it for a moment. Early and late, he moved among cold sheds and unheated barns. In the cowbarn, he fed the cattle hay, grain, and ensilage, and provided his horse Riley with oats and hay and water. He let the Holsteins loose to wander stiff-legged to the old cement watering trough next to the milk room, from which he first removed a layer of ice. Their pink muzzles dipped one by one into the near-freezing water. And he fed the sheep in the sheepbarn

and sheepyard. From the sheep's trough, he dipped out water for the hens, who lived next door to the sheep, and carried feed for his hens from the grainshed beside the cowbarn.

The next example tells briefly of events that took place during a period of a few weeks. In an earlier paragraph from "Letter from Los Angeles," Joan Didion described Los Angeles at the beginning of an early fire season. Here, she narrates some of the events that followed a short time later:

> A week or so later, thirty-seven hundred acres burned in the hills west of the Antelope Valley. The flames reached sixty feet. The wind was gusting at forty miles an hour. There were two hundred and fifty firefighters on the ground, and they evacuated fifteen hundred residents, one of whom returned to find her house gone but managed to recover, according to the *Los Angeles Times*, "an undamaged American flag and a porcelain Nativity set handmade by her mother." A week after this Antelope Valley fire, fifteen hundred acres burned in the Puente Hills, above Whittier. The temperatures that day were in the high nineties, and the flames were as high as fifty feet. There were more than nine hundred and seventy firefighters on the line. Two hundred and fifty families were evacuated. They took with them what people always take out of fires— mainly snapshots, mementos small enough to put in the car. "We don't have a stitch of clothing, but at least we'll have these," a woman about to leave the Puente Hills told the *Times* as she packed the snapshots into her car trunk.

Activity 4.6

Some verbs show action, others (especially the various forms of the verb *to be*) simply show existence. Look carefully at the verbs in this paragraph and those in Didion's earlier paragraph. Which has more verbs indicating action? Why would you expect this to be so?

A third, longer example of narration comes from Maxine Hong Kingston. Earlier, we read her description of Uncle Bun. (Reread that passage on page 49.) In the following paragraphs Kingston tells how her uncle slips into paranoia, a mental illness that causes him to think the rich "white devils" are trying to kill him because he has discovered their plot against the American poor. Influenced by his version of Chinese Communism, her uncle believes that there should be no rich and poor; everyone should be valued equally. One way to accomplish this, and to solve a number of other world problems as well, would be for everyone to eat wheat germ.

1   Amazing! His two big ideas—wheat germ and Communism—connected!

2   His ideas had come together neater and neater as the months and years passed. "Not just China," he would say, "and not just America, but the world. We will organize the whole world. End world hunger. And we will have world peace." What scope. What neatness. World peace. How amazingly his ideas connected up.

3   Then one day, he announced in a whisper, "The milk demon is poisoning me. The grocer demon is poisoning me. They have a plot against me. They put poison in my milk and eggs."

4   My mother said, "It's impossible to inject poison into eggs. Look how perfect the shells are."

5   But he said, "Science. Science can do anything."

6   When he connected his two big ideas, he touched wrong wires to each other, shot off sparks, and shorted out. He had become a paranoiac. "They are trying to poison me," he said, running into the laundry, his red face bursting above the collar and tie. "I've discovered their plot. They think they can get away with it but because of the sharp senses I've developed on wheat germ, I can detect poisons. I smelled the poison, and did not eat or drink it. I've discontinued milk delivery, and I'm going to buy groceries at a different store." He looked canny. "Why do you suppose they're after me," he asked. "It must be because I've hit on the truth and discovered the plot against the poor. And so they want to get me." He entered rooms as if pursued, stepping in and out of doorways, checking behind him, peeping out of windows, and pressing his back to walls. He continually surveyed the street. "I've noticed a pattern," he said. "They put the poison into white food—eggs, bread, milk, vanilla ice cream, flour, sugar, white beans. They're thinking that the seeming purity of white food would fool me, and it would disguise the poison, but I know that they have developed an invisible dissolvable poison. I'm outsmarting them. I'll shop at a different store every day. I'll keep changing stores."

7   "He's gone crazy," my mother diagnosed. "He is getting crazier. When he comes to the house, and we're at the laundry, you kids don't let him in."

8   He became more and more agitated. "I saw the wholesale demon open a bottle of milk. Yes, I saw him lift the lid. He dropped in a pellet of poison. I could tell by the way he cupped his hand. Then he pressed the lid back on. Sleight of hand. Lately the tops of milk bottles have been looser. That's

evidence. And today's evidence is that I saw the wholesale demon tampering with the vacuum seal. He placed the bottle
in the exact spot where I had picked my last bottle. They're
out to get me because—" and he held his breath on "because"—"I am a Communist." "FBI," he whispered. "Secret
police. House Un-American Activities Committee. Coconut.
Inside the husk. They've even gotten inside the coconut with
their scientific know-how."

9   "His head is a coconut," said [my father].

Activity 4.7   When you write narration and description, you can give your readers information both directly and indirectly. In this example Kingston directly tells
her readers some things about Uncle Bun. Other things are revealed indirectly, mostly through what Uncle Bun says. We hear his ideas, and we draw
inferences from them. Working in small groups, read this passage again,
making a list of the information that you receive directly from the writer and
the information that you receive indirectly. Does most of your specific knowledge about Uncle Bun come to you directly or indirectly? Why do you think
the writer presents her ideas this way?

WRITING ABOUT PERSONAL EXPERIENCE: USING DESCRIPTION AND NARRATION TOGETHER

In Chapter 1, when we were talking about brainstorming, we briefly
watched Dave, a student attending evening college, as he began work on a
personal experience paper describing his daily routine. Let's return to him
and look at the total results of his brainstorming:

Alarm goes off at 6:00 A.M. Worst sound of the day—worse
than sounds of traffic at rush hour or the cursing of my boss.
Get up, shower, dress. Get myself together for another day at
the warehouse. I work as a shipping supervisor from 8:00 to
4:00, take classes at night. Quick breakfast—usually strong
coffee and a few glazed doughnuts. Bad idea. Sugar and caffeine get my body off to a bad start. Sometimes I'm tense
and hyped-up even before I get to work. Get in car and start
the 45-min. commute to the city. Traffic gets real bad about
ten miles out. Some mornings worse than others—bunch of
real human garbage on the highway. Sometimes in bad
mood by the time I get to work. Have to lose that attitude to

get job done. Other workers don't like it when somebody brings personal problems to work. I work from 8 to 12 noon with one 15 min. break. Then lunch. Forgot: should have said first I hate to get up any day—even when I'm not working. Just not a morning person. If I had my way, nobody would work before ten. After lunch (12 to 1) there's lots to do before quitting. Most shipping is in morning, but paper work takes all afternoon. Forms, reports, sometimes calls or letters to people that called or wrote about late shipments. Should I talk about the group I eat lunch with? No—who cares! More about paper work? Probably dull to read, but it takes a lot of my time. The shipping department records are mostly computerized now, but there's a lot of paper to keep track of anyway. Years ago my dad worked in this same department. Then all records were kept by hand. There weren't so many, though. It's interesting how different things are now from when dad worked here. A lot has changed since then—market, product line, job requirements, even the company name. This is off the track. My day again—I quit at 4, get something to eat, get to campus about 5:30 and start class at 6:00. Classes meet from 6 to 9. I take 3 classes, so I'm here Monday, Tuesday, and Thursday nights. Sometimes it's hard to keep my mind on the classes if I'm already tired. If a professor lectures the whole time, I just about can't take it. Home by 10, usually asleep by 11:30. In six and a half hours I start it all over again. Right now it doesn't seem like much of a life. When I get out of college, I can get a better job with the company. "Supervisor" sounds important, but it doesn't pay much. Right now it seems like a long haul. I don't want to keep these hours forever. If I had a family I don't think I could keep it up. This is off the subject again. My day's over.

Activity 4.8   Answer the following questions. Your instructor may ask you to share your answers with others.

1. Several possible essay topics are suggested by this prewriting. Dave is going to write about his daily routine, but he need not cover everything. What individual parts of his day could be pulled out of this prewriting and written about? (Remember that additional prewriting might be required, focused on the smaller subject.)

2. Judging by Dave's prewriting, what part of the day is toughest for him? Would he need further planning before writing a paper on that topic?

3. What items in the prewriting need to be moved to go with similar material? (This is part of clustering.)

4. One of the benefits of prewriting like Dave's is that it sometimes contains possible subjects for other writing assignments. What topics other than his daily routine might grow out of this prewriting? (Again, further planning would be needed before writing.)

When Dave finishes rereading his prewriting and rearranging some of the material, he decides that his best topic might be getting up—something he clearly dislikes. He will need more material, so he jots down a few more ideas. Other thoughts will come to him as he is writing. We can skip over the early drafts and see what he decides to submit to his peer readers. Here is Dave's edited draft. Notice how he combines description and narration to relate his personal experience.

SIX TO EIGHT—IT'S NOT SO GREAT!

1. My first sensation is the worst sound of the day, my alarm. It is louder than the horns of rush-hour traffic and more irritating than the cursing of my boss. That steady "Beep! Beep! Beep!" means it's 6:00 A.M. and time for me to get myself together for another day at work.

2. First, getting up. For someone who hates mornings, this isn't as easy as it sounds. I can push the covers back, but it takes a lot of determination to make me swing my legs over the edge of the bed and put my feet on the floor. Then on to the shower. Let's see. Hot is left, cold is right. I'd better remember, or I could be in for a shock.

3. The shower helps. At least I can now open my eyes enough to see myself in the mirror when I shave. After that I brush my teeth—very carefully. Putting shaving cream on your toothbrush is an old joke in movies, but I really did it once. Maybe I deserved soap in my mouth because of some of the things I've said about early morning.

4. Getting dressed is pretty automatic. The routine doesn't change: shorts, socks, shirt, pants, belt, shoes. Then I put on my watch and pick up my money and keys. If anything interrupts the routine, I may forget a step. If I'm lucky, I won't leave the house not wearing something essential.

5. Since I live alone, breakfast has to be quick and easy. I usually have several cups of strong, black coffee and two or three glazed doughnuts. Of course, the caffeine and sugar make a bad situation worse. Now I'm hyped up and edgy when I start my 45-minute commute to work.

6   The drive to the city is the worst part. About ten miles out the traffic gets really bad. I'm stuck in the middle of six lanes of cars, bumper to bumper, trying to move toward the right so I won't miss my exit. It's like running with a pack of wild dogs. But I'm one of the wild dogs myself. I hate the other drivers, but really they're no worse than I am.

7   It's 7:45. I'm in the parking lot now, circling like a vulture, looking for an empty space and hoping I can park and get to the shipping department by 8:00. There's a digital clock on my desk, and the eight-double zero flashes just as I sit down. I'm hassled and I'm grouchy, but I'm here!

Writing Assignment

Write a narrative that describes the activities you go through during some part of your day. You might choose getting up, going to a class, having lunch, studying for a test, writing a paper, working at your regular job, fixing a meal for your family, helping children with their homework, getting ready for bed, or any other activity you think would be interesting to write about. During your planning write down all the details you can think of that describe what you do, and arrange them in some order. (You may use time order, as Dave did, or choose some other type of organization.) Then write your narrative. In groups or pairs, exchange and comment on the papers, as you have done before.

When you describe something or someone, you give your readers information about the subject as it exists—what it looks like, how it acts, what it does or does not do, and so forth. When you narrate, you share with your readers a series of events; some action is involved. Both kinds of writing are useful in college and beyond, and they are often combined with other types of writing to fulfill a number of purposes. Watch for examples of description and narration as they appear in different combinations in the next two chapters.

CHAPTER 5

~~~~~~~~~~~~~~ *Writing Exposition*

*This chapter will help you learn to write essays that give information clearly to your readers. This type of writing, called **exposition** or **expository writing**, is intended to make ideas clear and understandable. You will often have opportunities to use exposition both in college course work and in your business or profession. There are several methods of organizing expository essays to develop and clarify their main ideas. You will examine and practice three common methods of organization in this chapter: illustration, comparison and contrast, and process analysis. As you might expect, these patterns of writing imitate patterns of thinking. Studying these types of organization will help you to use them when you write exposition and to recognize and understand them when you meet them in your reading.*

ILLUSTRATION

As you gain knowledge and experience, you use the information to form general ideas, or generalizations. Some of these general ideas are inferences, as you have already learned, based on the facts that you have encountered. Some ideas are opinions that reflect your beliefs and values. You probably have examined some of these ideas thoughtfully and carefully, for they are the basis of many of your most important decisions. Some are ideas that you pursue out of curiosity or as a matter of only slight interest. Some ideas are constantly changing as you gain new information and test their soundness.

A general idea that has grown from your knowledge, your experience, or your self-examination can become the main idea or thesis of an essay. The challenge you then face as a writer is to clarify this main idea so that the reader understands it as you do. One of the best ways to make the general idea clear is to show your readers **examples** or **illustrations** of it, perhaps drawing on the same pieces of knowledge or bits of experience that led you to the generalization. Thus, a pattern of thought can become a pattern for writing.

When you use this method of development, the generalization is the main idea of the essay, which is clearly stated in the first or one of the first paragraphs. The other paragraphs present details or specific examples that help the reader to better understand the main idea. These supporting details are called illustrations. The following brief essay is an example of organization by illustration:

THE SINGLE PARENT

1   The life of a single parent is both rewarding and frustrating. The man or woman who takes on the task of raising children alone should be prepared for both. Knowing that the hard times will surely be followed by better days may help the single parent be more courageous and persistent.

2   Recently, I talked to my friend Ellen who is busy working her way up the career ladder in a realty company and raising six-year-old Gerald alone since her divorce. Her voice over the telephone sounded the smile which I was sure shone on her face. Gerald had just brought home his first progress report from first grade. He had been rated "satisfactory" in every category with a very complimentary note from his teacher.

3   This good report was a significant victory for Ellen and Gerald. The divorce had left Gerald, then a bright pre-schooler, sulky and uncooperative. He could not sleep well at night, did not feel like playing during the day, and whined for Ellen each morning as she dropped him off at the child-care center. By giving Gerald extra attention—in fact every moment she was off from work—Ellen had convinced him that he was not to blame for Daddy leaving and that he was good, smart, and important. The good report card rated the success of her efforts as well as Gerald's.

4   Right now it would be difficult to convince Ray, a thirty-five-year old accountant who is singlehandedly raising a teen-age daughter, that there are any compensations for his problems with Jenny. He is convinced that his daughter is missing a significant part of the pleasure of being young by not having a mother to model at this important stage in her development. He cannot get Jenny to be the least interested in her clothes or general appearance. She balks at even showering

or bathing and flies into a rage when he objects to her tangled hair and dirty jeans. Of course, her social life suffers as
a result of her unusual lack of concern about herself. Ray
blames himself for Jenny's problems and is angry with her at
the same time. No one can convince him that many teenagers develop unconventional behavior, whether they have
one parent or two.

5   The single parent must shoulder many burdens that
would feel lighter if shared. A child who is sick in the night, a
tangled schedule, a problem in school are easier to deal with
when shared with a partner. On the other hand, the close-
ness of the bond between parent and child and the sweetness
of the successes when they come are compensations for those
who accept the responsibilities of being the only parent.

The writer of this essay wanted to explain one main idea—that being a
single parent is both rewarding and frustrating. This writer decided that a
detailed example or illustration of the rewards and another of the difficulties
would make the point clear. The essay could be developed further with other
examples of the triumphs and the problems, examples that could be presented more briefly if the writer chose. Not all the supporting illustrations
need to be paragraph length, as these are.

The writer could also move to the related idea that single parents often
seek help from family, neighbors, or single-parent support groups to solve
problems. With the further illustration of this new idea, the essay would
become longer and more complex.

When you choose to illustrate a main idea to clarify it for your reader,
you must have enough knowledge of the topic to recall or to create specific
examples. If this is not the case, you should include some outside reading in
the planning stage of your writing to gain the information you need to develop your paper.

Activity 5.1   Turn to page 212 of the "Reader" section of this text and examine the essay
entitled "Exposing Media Myths." Read the essay carefully to determine its
main idea. Then examine the essay to see what illustrations the author uses
to clarify and develop this main idea. Are there many illustrations mentioned briefly or a few developed in detail?

*Writing
Assignment*   Listed here are several generalizations that could be the main idea of an
essay. Notice that while these statements reflect the opinion of the writer,
they are not strongly argumentative, a type of generalization that will be
discussed in the next chapter.

1. Mystery novels challenge the reader to think logically and to observe carefully to solve the mystery from the clues given.

2. People's lack of concern about the environment causes harm and sometimes death in the animal world.

3. Dogs (or cats) of different breeds have different personalities and require different kinds of care.

4. The pro-democracy movement has caused remarkable change throughout Eastern Europe.

If these are not generalizations that you have information about, then write a thesis or main idea of your own that is similar to one of these.

When you have chosen a thesis statement, spend at least fifteen minutes in focused brainstorming for information related to the main idea. Try to call to mind examples and details—any bits of information that might help you write illustrations of the thesis. If the brainstorming proves that you do not have enough information on the topic, try to do some reading to add to what you already know.

After you have completed your list of information on the topic, review it thoughtfully to choose the clearest, most interesting details to use. As the writer, you may choose whether to include many brief examples or only a few that are developed more fully. The short essay you read earlier in this chapter uses only two examples. Consider also the best order in which to present the examples. (You may have to try more than one arrangement to decide which is most effective.)

If your instructor agrees, work in peer groups to review your first draft before you revise or rework it. Your classmates should tell you if you have used enough examples and have chosen good examples to make your thesis clear. Be sure also to ask them if they find the essay interesting and informative to read. Their answers will help you decide how to rework the essay before submitting it to your instructor.

COMPARISON AND CONTRAST

Another way to think about people, events, or items of any type is to think about how they are alike and how they are different. Focusing on similarities and differences helps you to identify details and specific information that can increase the amount and depth of knowledge you have about a topic. Comparing and contrasting can also lead you to draw inferences.

Sometimes, the details that are compared or contrasted are illustrations, just like the ones discussed in the first part of this chapter. When this is the case, you are comparing and contrasting the details of the illustrations to clarify or increase your understanding of the subject.

When you use this pattern of thinking to help organize material for an essay, then you are using a familiar writing pattern called **comparison and contrast**. The purpose of an essay that compares or contrasts two or more items is to clarify and give information about them. You assume that the reader can understand the items more easily by thinking of them together and by seeing how they are alike or different.

Presenting Information

The following paragraphs organize information about two types of elephants in a way that is both clear and easy to remember by using comparison and contrast as a way of presenting information.

1.   Elephants are the largest of all land animals. And they are among the strangest-looking animals in the world, with their long trunks, big ears and pointed tusks. There are two basic kinds of elephants—African elephants and Asiatic (or Indian) elephants. It is rather easy to tell one kind from another.

2.   Asiatic elephants have smaller ears than African elephants. They have a high forehead with two rather large "bumps" on it. The back of an Asiatic elephant bends up in the middle, and usually only the males have tusks. African elephants have very large ears. Their foreheads don't have big bumps on them. The back of an African elephant bends *down* in the middle, and both the males and females have tusks.

3.   African elephants are larger than Asiatic elephants, and the males of both kinds are larger than the females. The average Asiatic male is about 9 feet tall at the shoulder (2.74 meters) and weighs about 10,000 pounds (4,535 kilograms). African males average about 10 feet tall (3 meters) and weigh about 12,000 pounds (5,443 kilograms).   (John Bonnett Wexo, "Elephants")

Obviously, there must be some logical reason for comparing and contrasting within an essay. There would be little point to comparing and contrasting your part-time job at a fast food restaurant and your part-time job on campus if there is no main idea or thesis that you can clarify and develop. If there is no basis for comparison between the two, there will be no central idea for the essay to develop and illustrate. On the other hand, you may be able to show that both jobs take up a similar amount of time and pay a similar salary, but one contributes nothing toward your future career while the other gives you valuable experience. Then you can focus on the benefit of part-time work that helps you prepare for the job market.

In the elephant essay there is enough similarity between the two types of elephants with their "long trunks, big ears and pointed tusks" to use comparison and contrast to organize additional specific information about them. Notice that the writer arranges the information so that details are given in the same order for each type of elephant: ears, forehead, back, and general size. Placing the details in this consistent order is an additional help to the reader.

Drawing Inferences

The essay on elephants simply gives information, but using comparison and contrast can also allow the writer to draw inferences or conclusions based on the information presented. You may recall from Chapter 4 that a student named Dave, who is taking courses in the night college, was doing some focused brainstorming about his daily routine. Dave's brainstorming notes included some comments about how his job is different from his father's even though they work at the same company and his father once held the same job that Dave now has. Later, Dave decides to write an essay on this topic using comparison and contrast as the method of development. Of course, more brainstorming will be needed. As he starts to work on his prewriting again, Dave is not sure whether he will focus on how his life or how his job is different from his dad's.

TWO JOBS? ME AND DAD?

Dad went to work for Metropolitan Cleaning Supply Co. in (check year). He was 18, just out of high school. Worked in shipping dept. By age 24 he was a supervisor—one of only two. Still a small company then. Shipping was mostly in metro area, a few customers statewide. Company sold cleaning products mostly to businesses and schools. When he became supervisor, Dad was already married and had one kid (older sister Rita). He didn't make a lot, but his money went further than mine. I did like Dad—went to work right out of high school, same age, same company, same department. Now I'm 24 and also a supervisor but the title doesn't mean as much as it used to—I'm one of four supervisors just in the shipping department. It means I mostly handle paperwork instead of really loading and unloading stuff. Most records are computerized now, not like when Dad was here. What else? Market? Sales have changed. Years ago salesmen visited customers, wrote up orders and brought them in to the company. Now a lot of our business is in contract sales. Lots of customers telex their orders. But I still have to write a lot of letters or make phone calls about late or incomplete shipments, breakage, that kind of thing. What other differences? Family responsibilities. Dad really was a family man at my age, only source of income. Jeannie and I will probably get married next year, but we're not in any hurry to have kids. I want to get more college behind me and she wants to work a while longer before kids. Am I off the subject? I don't know for sure what the subject is yet. I have the same job title in the same company as Dad, but things have changed. (Main idea?) Even the name's different—it's now MCS, Inc. That's supposed to sound more modern or something. And it's a lot bigger than it used to be. We now sell the latest electronic cleaning equipment and handle lots of industrial strength cleaners and things of that sort. My department ships mostly heavy-duty cleaners and solvents, big drums full of the stuff, and the supervisors see that it gets loaded for the right locations and that the records are up to date. MCS isn't just a local company any more, we ship all over the Southeast. That's another difference from when Dad worked here. *Here* means this department. He still works for the company. He's been promoted several times and has a good job. I want a better job too—maybe staying with this company—but that means more education. That's why I'm taking night classes. I plan to get a degree in business, maybe in marketing. One of the top guys in the company (a "real" boss, not my boss in my department who's a jerk!) told Dad I could probably advance pretty far. But there's a company rule about having a college degree before you can reach certain levels, so here I am. Dad encourages me. He says if he had it to do over again, he probably would get some college. He says it would have made his moves up the ladder easier.

Activity 5.2

During his brainstorming session Dave draws several conclusions. One seems suitable to become the main idea of his comparison and contrast essay: "I have the same job title in the same company as Dad, but things have changed." Review the text of the brainstorming and make a list of the details showing how Dave and his dad are similar and a second list of details showing how they are different.

After you have completed your lists, decide how you might organize and develop a comparison and contrast essay. Compare your organization with Dave's. Here is his essay:

LIKE FATHER, LIKE SON, BUT . . .

1   In 1954 my dad went to work in the shipping department of the Metropolitan Cleaning Supply Company. He was 18 years old and had just graduated from high school. Six years later, at 24, he was a supervisor and a family man with a wife and year-old daughter. In 1980 I went to work in the same department of the same company. Six years later I am also a supervisor. It looks like my life is a copy of my dad's. But there are some major differences.

2   First, although I have Dad's old job title, I don't really have the same job. When he was in the shipping department, the title really meant something. There were only two supervisors in the small company, and they had a lot of responsibility. Most of the paperwork was done by hand, and there wasn't any computer backup system if something went wrong. Now I am one of four supervisors in just one department. We handle the paperwork, but most of it is computerized, so it's pretty routine. We also see that shipments are sent to the right place, but that doesn't exactly take a genius either. I don't think I feel the kind of personal responsibility for the company that Dad did.

3   In a way, the whole job used to be more personal. Dad knew most of the salesmen who took orders for the company, and he knew a lot of the customers—mostly small businessmen and buyers for schools. If a buyer needed a rush order or had a problem with a shipment, he would call and Dad would straighten it out right then. Today the company is larger and more modern. It even has a new, modern name: MCS, Inc. The "sales reps" are scattered all over the Southeast. We now have a lot of contract sales, and we get stacks of telex orders. When I write or telephone a customer, I usually am dealing with an unknown clerk in a purchasing department.

4   At 24 Dad didn't make a lot of money, and what he made had to stretch. He supported himself and Mom and my older sister. Still, he managed. He was even able to save a small amount. The company was still family-owned, and management provided pretty good benefits for that time. My salary is much bigger than Dad's was at my age, but it doesn't seem to go as far. If I had to support a family, I don't think I could make ends meet. Our jobs are alike in one way though—my benefits don't amount to much more than his did almost 30 years ago!

5   The difference in the company helps to explain the difference in our outlooks, though I guess changing times make

our views different too. At 24 Dad had been married three years and was a settled family man. I am engaged and plan to be married soon, but my fiancee and I intend to postpone our family for a few years. I want to get more college hours, maybe even go a few semesters as a full-time student, before taking on the added responsibility of kids. Jeannie wants at least a couple more years' work before taking a leave. We both want careers.

6   After 32 years and several promotions, Dad has a good job with the company. I think he's been very successful, though he's gone about as far as he can. But if I stay that long the way things are now, I'll just be the oldest guy in the shipping department. I can't go much further with my high school diploma. In fact, company policy requires a college degree for the kind of job I hope for. So if I want to be compared with my dad when I'm 50, I've got to keep working on my business degree. Maybe I'll change that old expression a little: like father, like son—but with a difference.

Activity 5.3   Turn to page 238 of the "Reader" section of this text, and examine the essay entitled "A Fable for Tomorrow." Read the essay carefully to determine its main idea. Then examine the essay to see what specific details are compared and contrasted to help the author clarify and develop the main idea. Make a list of these points of comparison and contrast.

Writing
Assignment   Choose one of the following pairs as the subject of a comparison and contrast essay:

two friends

two pets

two ways of studying for a test

two products

two theories of creation

two styles of classroom teaching

You may substitute a similar pair if you prefer. As you plan your essay, create a list of the similarities and differences that come to mind as you think of the two items. The planning stage for your essay should also include reviewing your list to add, regroup, or temporarily eliminate items.

To begin drafting your essay, write a brief introduction to state the main idea of the essay and to introduce the reader to the two subjects being compared and contrasted. Then develop a paragraph on each point you want to make. The last paragraph should restate the idea you want the reader to understand from reading the essay.

If there is an opportunity, share the first draft with a peer group before revising it.

PROCESS ANALYSIS

Communicating information about how to do something so clearly that the reader should be able to perform the process or explaining how something was done in step-by-step detail is a type of writing called **process analysis**. Process analysis requires that the writer think and plan especially carefully before drafting.

The purpose of a process analysis is to break a complicated process into parts or steps so that it can be understood more easily. Of course, it is essential that the parts of the process be placed in logical sequence. The writer must outline or list carefully to be sure of maintaining the correct order. Generally, it is necessary to give some information about each of the parts or steps so that the reader can fully understand the process. Remember, however, that you are still writing an essay and not just a set of instructions to be followed. Your essay needs to have an appropriate introduction, body, and conclusion.

Look at the following brief essay as an example of process analysis:

YOUR ENTRY FOR THE CHILI COOK-OFF

1   A recent TV new program covered the international chili cook-off held for several days in Colorado. Men and women came from a number of different states to prepare their favorite chili recipes for the judges. Their ingredients ranged from steak to beer. Obviously, a part of the fun of preparing chili is inventing your own personal recipe with your own secret ingredients. You do, however, need a good basic chili recipe to begin with. Then you can allow your imagination to take over.

2   The basic recipe that I recommend has the advantage of being inexpensive to prepare and easy to change to suit individual taste. Start by crumbling one pound of lean ground beef in a heavy skillet that has been sprayed with Pam. (Extra cooking oil really is not needed.) Add one small, coarsely chopped onion. Add garlic also, if you like. Brown this mixture over medium heat. When the browning is finished, drain away any liquid that has cooked from the meat.

3   Now that you have prepared the basic meat mixture, you are ready to add the liquid. You will need at least one large can of tomatoes (28 ounces). For a stronger tomato flavor, add one 6-ounce can of tomato paste. If you want your chili to have the consistency of a thick soup, add one cup of tomato juice or water.

4   Just before you are ready to serve your creation, add one medium-sized can of red kidney beans (18 ounces) and heat through. Here is an optional step. If you want your chili to go further or to be your main dish, try adding one to two cups of cooked macaroni or spaghetti. Adding the cooked pasta may require that you increase the water or tomato juice also. You can decide how thick you want the chili to be. If you add macaroni or spaghetti, you should have about six servings.

5   This recipe is fun to use because it allows even beginners to experiment and make their own decisions. As you become a more experienced chili chef, you can be even more adventurous. You can substitute cubed round steak for the ground beef and change the seasonings to suit your own taste. Just remember, you are preparing an inexpensive dish, suitable for family or company, that is rarely dull. Someday you may be ready to enter the international chili cook-off yourself.

The process described here is really a recipe, a very simple set of instructions. This recipe becomes an essay when it is given an introduction, when the ingredients and the steps for combining them are clarified with comments and explanation, and when the instructions are concluded with further remarks on the topic.

Activity 5.4

Turn to page 179 of the "Reader" section of this text and examine the essay entitled "Dress for Success." Read the essay carefully to determine its main idea. Then examine the essay to identify the steps of the process being described. Try making a list of these steps. Does the author present the steps clearly enough that you feel you understand the process thoroughly? What does the writer do to make the process a part of an essay and avoid presenting it as a set of instructions?

Writing Assignment

Choose a topic about which you have sufficient knowledge to write a process analysis essay in which you give your reader information about how to do something. You may need to do some focused brainstorming to come up with an appropriate topic. You are hoping to find a process that you understand so thoroughly that you can explain it perfectly clearly to your reader. You could start your brainstorming by thinking of skills you have—rappelling, cross-country skiing, cake decorating, baby-sitting, tie-dyeing, showing horses, and so on.

When you have selected the process you want to analyze, make a list of the steps necessary to complete the process. Check the list carefully to make sure that no step has been omitted; check again to see that each step is in the appropriate order.

Now you are ready to draft the first version of your essay. If possible, share this draft with a peer group to find out if your explanation of each step is entirely clear. Ask your group members if they could perform the process following the steps as you have described them. Also ask them if your paper is interesting to read.

Sometimes, process analysis explains not how to do something, but how something happens. Phyllis Lafarge describes a complex process in her book *The Strangelove Legacy*. She explains how young children develop a fear of nuclear war from what they learn from the world around them. This "context" or environment in which they first hear of nuclear destruction determines what kind of attitudes they will form.

1   A nursery school child came up behind his teacher with a construction made of Lego blocks, poked her in the back, and said, "This is an atom bomb and I'm going to kill you."

2   The same teacher told the following anecdote. She had created a Valentine calendar for the month of February featuring many hearts pierced by arrows, and had hung it on her bulletin board. Above the Valentine calendar was a large photo of an airplane, part of a quite separate display about transportation. One day she noticed a boy gazing at the bulletin board in a reverie while the other children ate their snacks. At last he said, "Those are the missiles the plane is dropping aren't they?" He meant the arrows that pierced the hearts.

3   In relating these anecdotes his teacher took them as proof that the child knew about nuclear weapons and nuclear war. But what did she mean by "knew"? What does a young child understand of war? What can a young child understand about the conflicts and rivalries that lead to war? . . . Is the impact of nuclear fear on young people different from what it is on adults? And is the impact different on younger children from what it is on older children?

4   At four or five children do not have the same conception of war as adults—or even children of eleven or twelve. Their

thinking is very concrete, and they have a very modest supply of information at their disposal about the "big world" beyond their family. Nevertheless, their imagination is already being furnished with the vocabulary and images of their culture's aggressive and destructive forces. They can easily draw on this vocabulary or these images to express feelings of aggression or hostility. . . .

5   Learning about war and the instruments of war is colored, like everything else, by the context of learning. Is the child's learning the result of direct experience or does it come from books or television? Learning about war in Beirut is different from learning about war in Scarsdale. Context includes the more subtle experience of picking up the tone with which adults or older peers convey information. To illustrate the latter with a personal example, my first memory of the "big world" beyond home, neighborhood, or community was a radio broadcast of a speech by Adolf Hitler. I was five, living safely and peacefully in Connecticut, but I was alarmed. In retrospect, I realize that the anxiety of the adults in my family as they listened, and the very exceptional fact that the radio was on at all in the middle of a perfectly ordinary afternoon, contributed to my feelings as much as Hitler's ranting voice speaking in a language I could not understand through the static of the short-wave reception.

6   As the child absorbs the vocabulary and images of power, destruction, and vulnerability, he learns who talks about them, who does not, and how they talk. He may learn that the men in his family talk one way and the women another, or that nuclear weapons, for instance, are just about never mentioned by anyone in his family yet are referred to on the nightly television news. As a preschooler he will feel less bound to abide by the rules implicit in the behavior he observes than he will a little later, when he is six or seven, but they are still part of the context of what he learns.

Activity 5.5

Working in peer groups or as a class discussion, decide which paragraphs from the previous selection are developed by process analysis. When these paragraphs have been agreed upon, list the steps or the parts of the process that lead children to the development of particular attitudes toward nuclear war.

A close look at this selection will show that Lafarge uses more than one type of exposition to clarify the information she presents. Point out several examples of development by illustration. Can you identify any other pattern of exposition used in the selection? Try to explain in each case why the author chose to use this way of organizing her ideas.

Expository writing is used to develop and clarify the main ideas of essays that are intended to give information to your reader. The patterns of organization used for such essays often follow closely the ways people think. Expository writing developed by illustration uses examples and other types of specific details to illustrate and make clear the main idea of the essay. Comparison and contrast focuses on the ways in which two topics are alike and different. Looking at similarities and differences often will help you draw inferences about the topics. Process analysis explains in clear detail how to do something or how something happens. There are other methods of developing expository writing, but these three are common and useful types.

Writing exposition requires careful planning. Sometimes, additional reading is needed to supply enough information for drafting. More than one draft is nearly always necessary to produce an essay that clearly and fully develops the main idea.

As you look at other examples of these patterns of writing, you will find that professional writers often use more than one pattern in an essay. For example, a comparison and contrast essay may rely on illustration to present similarities and differences clearly. A process analysis essay may have a few paragraphs of comparison and contrast to help explain clearly how to accomplish a particular procedure. In fact, it is far more common to see combinations of these patterns than to see only one used alone.

CHAPTER 6

~~~~~~~~~~~~~~~~~~~~~ *Writing Persuasion*

This chapter will emphasize a type of writing that you may already have practiced briefly: persuasion. Persuasive writing uses many of the same techniques you have employed in description and exposition, but here the emphasis and the purpose are different. The chapter does not deal with formal argument; instead, it stresses effective ways to state, support, and convince others to agree with an opinion.

Many composition teachers agree that much writing is persuasive, whether or not we give it that label. They believe that almost any time we write for readers, we intend for those readers to agree with what we say. Thus, consciously or not, we mean to persuade them.

If you think of some of the samples of writing included in earlier chapters, you can see **persuasion** at work. When Beth describes her grandmother and tells us why she hopes she will be like her, she persuades us that her grandmother is an unusually fine person who would make a good role model. When Maxine Hong Kingston describes her Uncle Bun, she persuades us that he was always quite odd and became at last quite mad. Or when Dave explains how circumstances have changed since his dad held the job that Dave now holds, he persuades us (as he has already persuaded himself) that he must continue his education in order to get ahead.

There are some highly specialized techniques of writing argument, and sometimes entire courses are devoted to this subject. What you will be working with in this chapter, however, is **informal persuasion**: writing in such a way that you convince others to agree with certain ideas. You may use several types of writing you have studied earlier. Let's say you want to persuade your readers that the federal government should increase aid to independent farmers. You picture the typical family farm, and you explain how young people who want to continue the farm life nevertheless must often move and choose other careers because they cannot make a living farming.

76

You tell how a young couple struggled to keep the land that had been in the family for three generations but at last gave up and sold out to an agricultural corporation. You are now using description and narration to persuade.

To take another example, let's suppose you argue that the food at Tony's Pizzeria is both better and cheaper than the food at Casa Italiana. You can use comparison and contrast to persuade. Or, if you argue that teenage drivers who do not drink have fewer accidents and therefore should have lower insurance rates, you are trying to persuade by pointing out cause and effect. The main difference between persuasive writing and exposition is that when you write persuasively, your number one purpose is to convince rather than just to explain.

CHOOSING A TOPIC AND
STATING A PERSUASIVE THESIS

As you consider topics for persuasive writing, it is usually best to avoid arguing opinions for which you cannot offer evidence acceptable to those you are trying to persuade. Arguing that there are life forms in other galaxies may be entertaining; but as long as there is no available evidence either way, the argument seems to have no practical value.

Be aware, too, that when you argue theological or moral issues by offering religious texts as evidence to readers who do not accept the truth of those texts, you are probably wasting your time and words. No matter how strongly you believe in your position, try to examine it carefully before you set out to persuade someone else. Too many writers, especially inexperienced ones, end up reasoning this way: this opinion is true because I believe it is true.

Even when you have found a truly debatable issue, you must be careful how you put it into words. To begin with, avoid statements like this:

> I think there should be more parking spaces on campus for freshmen and sophomores.

This is not truly a debatable statement; it is just an announcement of what you think. Rephrase it this way:

> The university should provide more parking spaces on campus for freshmen and sophomores.

Or suppose that you begin with this statement of opinion:

> Universities should work to eliminate substance abuse among students.

It's hard to imagine that anyone would argue against such a statement. Specifically how, in your opinion, should universities go about this task? Here are two possible statements:

> Universities should ban alcoholic beverages from all food service facilities, dormitories, and sorority and fraternity houses.

> Universities should begin compulsory drug testing for all student athletes.

Now, you may be sure, you have a couple of debatable opinions.

Another early task is to make certain that your opinion is clearly stated. What a terrible waste of time it is for people to argue over an issue when they are not really talking about the same thing, and yet how often this happens. Look again at the second statement: *Universities should begin compulsory drug testing for all student athletes.* What does *all student athletes* mean? Does the term include those who play intramural sports? Does it cover anyone who joins a pickup game on an outdoor basketball court or who plays a game of tennis with a roommate? Of course not. What the writer surely means is students who compete in intercollegiate sports. Very well, the writer should say so. This should be an unbreakable rule of persuasive writing: try to say exactly what you mean.

SUPPORTING A PERSUASIVE THESIS WITH EMOTIONAL APPEAL

There are two powerful tools of persuasion: emotion and reason. Emotional statements appeal to your readers' feelings. Specific evidence appeals to their reason or intellect. Used correctly, both kinds of support are effective, but you must be cautious in using emotional appeal. Some readers, of course, may be easily persuaded by a writer who only plays on their feelings; they enjoy an emotional wallow. This may be especially true when a writer appeals not only to readers' emotions, but to their prejudices as well. Most readers, however, will reject an argument based on emotional appeal alone. They will want some solid evidence as well, for they know that an argument that depends on emotion alone is false. Often, the best arguments will make limited use of emotionalism and offer plenty of sound evidence as well.

Activity 6.1

The passage that follows is from Phyllis Schlafly's popular book, *The Power of the Positive Woman.* Schlafly is an experienced persuasive writer who depends on both facts and feelings to make a point. Working alone or in small groups, list the facts Schlafly uses to support her thesis. Then pick out words or phrases that make an emotional appeal. Note that even factual statements can have an emotional overtone based on the words a writer chooses. Do you think this is an effective piece of persuasive writing? Why or why not? Do you think the argument is sound? Why or why not?

1   The energies and dedication of the Positive Woman are needed as never before to fend off the attacks on the moral, the social, and the economic integrity of the family.

2   Take, for example, the tremendous drive to set up child-care centers—taxpayer-financed, government-managed, "universally" available for "all socioeconomic groups" regardless of means. This adds up to an attempt to make it public policy to remove babies from the family unit and place them in an institutional environment.

3   Several groups see it as in their self-interest to promote a policy to replace mother care with government care. The women's liberationists are persistent pushers for this objective, based on their dogma that children are a burden from which women must be liberated.

4   Certain branches of the teachers' lobby also share this goal because they see it as the solution to the growing problem of empty classrooms and teacher unemployment caused by the severe decline in the American birth rate. Obviously, if our society can be induced to accept and finance the notion that every child should be put in school or a school substitute at age two or three instead of at age five or six, this would eliminate teacher unemployment.

5   The third force working resourcefully and effectively to move babies out of the home into government kiddy-care centers and mothers out of the home into the job market is the consortium of vested interests that always works toward more government (especially federal) spending and control. It is obvious that the American people are now paying all the taxes they are willing to pay; they vote against higher taxes every chance they get.

SUPPORTING A PERSUASIVE THESIS WITH EVIDENCE

There are several kinds of evidence that persuasive writers can use. In this chapter we will look at three: illustrations or examples, statistics, and the statements of authorities.

Illustrations

In Chapter 5 you saw how illustrations or examples can support a generalization or inference. These illustrations or specific examples can also support a persuasive thesis. In order to be effective as evidence, the illustrations should be interesting and fitting. Perhaps the trickiest job for writers using examples as evidence is sensing when they have used enough but not too many. This comes only with practice.

In a recent study of sexism in English, Alleen Pace Nilson writes that language can slyly influence our attitudes toward each other. She argues that our language suggests "that women are expected to play a passive or weak role while men play an active or strong role." As evidence she offers these examples:

> The grammar used in talking or writing about weddings as well as other sexual relationships shows the expectation of men playing the active role. Men *wed* women while women *become* brides of men. A man *possesses* a woman; he *deflowers* her; he *performs*; he *scores*; he *takes away* her virginity. Although a woman can *seduce* a man, she cannot offer him her virginity. When talking about virginity, the only way to make the woman the actor in the sentence is to say that "She lost her virginity," but people lose things by accident rather than by purposeful actions, and so she's only the grammatical, not the real-life, actor.

Activity 6.2

Here is another paragraph from Nilson's article. She is now developing a somewhat different thesis: ". . . many positive connotations are associated with the concept of masculine, while there are either trivial or negative connotations connected with the corresponding feminine concept." Do you find her examples persuasive? Based on your own experience, can you agree with these examples or perhaps add to them? Can you think of others that would work against her thesis?

> Early in life, children are conditioned to the superiority of the masculine role. As child psychologists point out, little girls have much more freedom to experiment with sex roles than do little boys. If a little girl acts like a *tomboy*, most parents have mixed feelings, being at least partially proud. But if their little boy acts like a *sissy* (derived from *sister*), they call a psychologist. It's perfectly acceptable for a little girl to sleep in the crib that was purchased for her brother, to wear his hand-me-down jeans and shirts, and to ride the bicycle that he has outgrown. But few parents would put a boy baby in a

white and gold crib decorated with frills and lace, and virtually no parents would have their little boy wear his sister's hand-me-down dresses, nor would they have their son ride a girl's pink bicycle with a flower-bedecked basket. The proper names given to girls and boys show this same attitude. Girls can have "boy" names—*Chris, Craig, Jo, Kelly, Shawn, Teri, Toni,* and *Sam*—but it doesn't work the other way. A couple of generations ago, *Beverley, Frances, Hazel, Marion,* and *Shirley* were common boys' names. As parents gave these names to more and more girls, they fell into disuse for males, and some older men who have these names prefer to go by their initials or by such abbreviated forms as *Haze* or *Shirl.*

Statistics

Collecting statistics seems almost to have become a craze; we want to count or quantify everything. But perhaps because of this, some people have become suspicious of statistics. Statistical evidence can surely be useful and effective, but before you use it, you should be reasonably certain that it is sound. Beware of statements such as this:

> Seven out of ten doctors who use sleeping tablets use Extra-Strength Knockout.

In the first place you have no way of knowing how this statistic was arrived at. And, even if the statement happens to be true, how many doctors use sleeping tablets anyway?

The following passage shows how statistics can be used effectively. Melinda Beck, writing about the effects of an increasingly older population, uses statistics to show what medical problems may face many American families in the twenty-first century. Notice that she keeps these figures from being dry and boring by personalizing them with just a touch of emotional appeal.

> Sadly, longer life expectancy—up 28 years since 1900—will only prolong the problems of aging for many families, while dramatically increasing health-care costs. Medical advances are extending life faster than they are slowing the onset of chronic disabling conditions such as arthritis, stroke and senile dementia. Today, some 6 million Americans 65 or over require help in dressing, eating, bathing and going to the bathroom. That number will swell to 13.8 million by 2030, according to an Urban Institute study. Unless a cure is found, Alzheimer's disease alone could debilitate 7 million

people by 2040, up from 2.5 million today. In the advanced stages, "the care required is total," says Susan Nowicki of the Alzheimer's Association. "And the family becomes the second victim."

Activity 6.3

Here is another paragraph from Beck's article. As you examine it and look again at the previous example, decide (1) what details Beck uses to give life and meaning to her statistics and (2) how she leads us to believe that these statistics are trustworthy.

Even if government does provide more funding, the nation will face a critical shortage of nursing homes. Researchers estimate that 220 new nursing-home beds must be added *every day* between now and the year 2000 just to meet the demands of the next decade—long before the baby boomers arrive in their wheelchairs. "We're looking at an 85-and-older population that's quadrupling within 40 years and no place to put them," says Paul Willging of the American Health Care Association, a nursing-home trade group. As it is, the average cost of a nursing-home stay is $23,000 annually—some run as high as $60,000—and costs will soar higher if supply doesn't catch up with demand. Yet with 65 percent of nursing-home residents supported by Medicaid, Willging says, "you can see why government doesn't want to build 75,000 beds a year, because it will have to support whoever is sleeping in 50,000 of them."

Authorities

Another common type of support is the use of authorities. You have already seen in the paragraphs on health care for the elderly how a writer can strengthen an argument by quoting or referring to experts in the field. Remember, however, that your readers will want to know that these people really are experts and that their expertise is in the area you are talking about.

Often, it may be necessary to identify the person briefly. Note how Beck explains who Susan Nowicki and Paul Willging are. Another person quoted elsewhere in her article is John Rother of the American Association of Retired Persons. Once she gives the credentials, readers are willing to grant that these people should have solid information and worthwhile opinions on the topic.

Be certain, too, that the authority you mention has expertise in the field you are discussing. No matter how famous your experts may be or how well known in one field, you need to show that they are knowledgeable on *your* topic. Thus, you should be cautious about using well-known people to support your argument just because they are well known.

This is a common technique among advertisers (who perhaps use persuasion more than any other group). A familiar actress who for years played the mother of six on a popular TV show now talks about the importance of using a certain brand of cooking oil to keep our families healthy. A former president of the United States personally recommends a particular magazine. And at least three actors who played doctors in long-running TV series now advertise over-the-counter medicines. If these people were talking (in one case) about governing or (in all cases) about acting, then they would clearly be authorities. But as long as they are talking about cooking oil, reading material, and pain killers, theirs is not expert opinion. Celebrities can, of course, become experts on a subject (for example, wildlife preservation, children's charities, or even politics). But before you use them to support an argument, make sure you choose them for what they know, not just for who they are.

Be careful, too, about recognized experts who make public statements about subjects not related to their fields of expertise. For example, a famous chemist may get involved in a controversy over preventing the common cold; a well-known pediatrician may take a stand against war; the mayor of a large city may make moral judgments about the criminal justice system. It is unfair to say their opinions are not sound; they may be. But just because they are wise in one area does not automatically mean they are wise in all.

In an article on extended adolescence—the refusal of many young Americans in their twenties and even thirties to accept the responsibilities of maturity—Kenneth Woodward mentions several authorities to support his point. Notice how he identifies them in order to establish their expertise.

1   Another striking feature of extended adolescence is the . . . rise in cohabitation [living together]—in effect, the commitment not to be committed. Today half of all men and women in their 30s cohabited before marriage, many of them on the assumption that it is better to look—deeply—before they leap. But studies now demonstrate that couples who cohabit before marriage are more likely to divorce than those who do not. "It's a relationship that attracts those, mainly men, who are looking for an easy out," observes sociologist Glen Elder of the University of North Carolina, "and it is uncertain what, if anything, it contributes to marriage." . . .

2   Like love, work, too, has become an opportunity for immediate gratification, rather than for long-term growth and commitment. In the '70s, [John S.] Coleman and other American sociologists warned that the young were becoming expert consumers before they were learning how to produce. . . . By the '80s, three out of four high-school seniors

were working an average of 18 hours a week and often taking home more than $200 a month. But their jobs—often in fast-food chains—were rarely challenging and earnings were immediately spent on cars, clothing, stereos and other artifacts of the adolescent good life. Indeed, researchers at the University of Michigan find that less than 11 percent of high-school seniors save all or most of their earnings for college or other long-range purposes.

3   In short, teenage employment has only intensified the adolescent drive for immediate gratification. Instead of learning how to delay desires, students are indulging in what University of Michigan researcher Jerald Bachman calls "premature affluence."

STATING AND SUPPORTING
PERSONAL OPINIONS

The examples of persuasive writing that you have looked at so far in this chapter might be considered public argument: they concern broad topics or large groups of people. Thus, it is not too difficult for the writers to supply illustrations, gather statistics, or find authorities. This is the kind of persuasive writing you may encounter often in a university when you are asked to prepare a research paper or to write an essay examination.

But often you may wish to persuade readers of the value of your opinion on a subject of local or perhaps personal interest. Statistics and experts may be nearly impossible to find, and good illustrations may be your best (or only) evidence. In such a case an important part of your support is your own image. You must present yourself to your readers as a reasonable, trustworthy writer who has some personal knowledge of the subject.

The best ways to do this are to (1) use a reasonable, nonthreatening tone, (2) offer evidence of your personal experience and knowledge, and (3) whenever possible, anticipate objections to your point of view and be prepared to deal with them. You may also use emotional appeal in this sort of persuasion, but as always, use it with care.

Writing for a university newspaper, student Cary Conley offers and supports a personal opinion on the problem of insufficient campus parking. In the paragraphs quoted here, note how Conley works to establish an effective image of himself as one who has knowledge of the problem and has considered possible solutions carefully.

1   I feel that the two groups in the worst situation right now are the married students and the commuters. That may come as no surprise to many people, but my next statement may. The

people causing the problem are primarily the married students and commuters.

2   Let's discuss married students first. I have lived in Lakewood Terrace and Normal Hall, so I have firsthand knowledge of the situation these students face. Married parking spaces are numbered, which creates a problem because if just one car—be it a married student or not—parks out of place, it causes a chain reaction.

3   Forget the parking ticket deal. It has been proven that tickets are not a deterrent. But has anyone ever seen an illegally parked car underneath those little black signs that read, "Tow Away Zone"? Put one of those signs under the sign reading "Zone M" and watch the problem be solved.

4   Another group, one of which I am a part, that causes a parking problem for themselves is the commuters. Picture this scene. You arrive on campus 30 minutes early for class. You check each commuter lot, and there is no space to be found. After two more trips through each commuter parking lot, you finally discover a single empty space tucked away in the back of the lot. You drive quickly to the spot only to have your hopes smashed because one of those huge "land yachts" from the '60s is parked diagonally across two spaces.

5   I see this problem every day I am on campus. Yet when I call the Office of Public Safety, they do nothing. They tell me that there is a commuter lot over by the city park. Apparently my idea of a commuter (one who drives from home directly to school) and the OPS's idea of a commuter (one who drives halfway to school, parks in a field and then walks half a mile to class) are different.

6   So if the OPS won't help solve these problems, then who will? How about the groups that are causing a lot of the problems?

7   I realize that there is still a problem with regular students taking up spaces that aren't theirs. But it is even more frustrating to see individuals from one of the two groups discussed cause the problem because they should know better.

8   Married students and commuters should unite to solve this problem. OPS has proven by their past actions (and inaction) that they don't give a damn. We must.

Activity 6.4

Read Conley's argument again and, working alone or in small groups, consider the following questions:

1. What techniques does Conley use to establish a tone of voice that sounds reasonable and friendly?

2. What details show that Conley has personal knowledge of the situation?

3. What possible solutions does Conley offer for these particular parking problems?

4. What alternative solutions does Conley mention and then reject? What are his reasons for rejecting them?

5. Like any good argument, Conley's is clearly organized. What are his major points? Why do you think he uses the order he does?

6. What transitional markers does Conley use to lead readers through his argument?

Activity 6.5

In 1982, while she was a sophomore at Southern Illinois University, Rachel Jones wrote an essay that was eventually published in *Newsweek*. Jones, who is black, argues that black English, in addition to its positive values, can cause problems for its speakers. She especially objects to the discrimination she has experienced because she herself most often does not speak black English. This has led to what she calls "my 'white pipes' problem."

After giving several examples of personal difficulties she has had because she "talks white," she asks just what this term means and why her speech has caused a strange kind of discrimination. Read these closing paragraphs of her essay, and then answer the questions that follow.

1   [This is] a question I've wanted an answer to for years: how does one "talk white"? The silly side of me pictures a rabid white foam spewing forth when I speak. I don't use Valley Girl jargon, so that's not what's meant in my case. Actually, I've pretty much deduced what people mean when they say that to me, and the implications are really frightening.

2   It means that I'm articulate and well-versed. It means that I can talk as freely about John Steinbeck as I can about Rick James. It means that "ain't" and "he be" are not staples of my vocabulary and are only used around family and friends. . . . As a child I found it hard to believe that's what people meant by "talking proper": that would've meant that good grades and standard English were equated with white skin, and that went against everything I'd ever been taught. Running into the same type of mentality as an adult has confirmed the depressing reality that for many blacks, standard English is not only unfamiliar, it is socially unacceptable.

3   James Baldwin once defended black English by saying it had added "vitality to the language," and even went so far as to label it a language in its own right, saying, "Language is a

political instrument" and "a vivid and crucial key to identity." But did Malcolm X urge blacks to take power in this country "any way y'all can"? Did Martin Luther King Jr. say to blacks, "I has been to the mountaintop, and I done seed the Promised Land"? Toni Morrison, Alice Walker and James Baldwin did not achieve their eloquence, grace and stature by using only black English in their writing. Andrew Young, Tom Bradley and Barbara Jordan did not acquire political power by saying, "Y'all crazy if you ain't gon vote for me." They all have full command of standard English, and I don't think that knowledge takes away from their blackness or commitment to black people.

4   I know from experience that it's important for black people, stripped of culture and heritage, to have something they can point to and say, "This is ours, *we* alone can speak it with a soulful flourish." I'd be lying if I said that the rhythms of my people caught up in "some serious rap" don't sound natural and right to me sometimes. But how heartwarming is it for those same brothers when they hit the pavement searching for employment? Studies have proven that the use of ethnic dialects decreases power in the marketplace. "I be" is acceptable on the corner, but not with the boss.

5   Am I letting capitalist, European-oriented thinking fog the issue? Am I selling out blacks to an ideal of assimilating, being as much like whites as possible? I have not formed a personal political ideology, but I do know this: it hurts me to hear black children use black English, knowing that they will be at yet another disadvantage in an educational system already full of stumbling blocks. It hurts me to sit in lecture halls and hear fellow black students complain that the professor "be tripping dem out using big words dey can't understand." And what hurts me most is to be stripped of my own blackness simply because I know my way around the English language.

6   I would have to disagree with [noted linguist William] Labov in one respect. My goal is not so much to acquire full control of both standard and black English, but to one day see more black people less dependent on a dialect that excludes them from full participation in the world we live in. I don't think I talk white, I think I talk right.

1. What does Jones finally decide that most people mean when they use the term "talk white"?

2. Why does she say that the implications (that is, the unspoken messages that people imply by this term) are frightening?

3. What authorities on language does Jones refer to? How does she use these experts in her argument?

4. The writer also mentions a number of examples of black people who have successfully used standard English: Malcolm X, Martin Luther King Jr., Toni Morrison, Alice Walker, Andrew Young, Tom Bradley, and Barbara Jordan. Can we consider these "examples" to be implied "authorities" as well? Why or why not?

5. How does Jones anticipate and deal with possible opposition to her argument?

6. Where does Jones use emotional appeal? Is it effective? Why or why not? Do you think she should have used more? Why or why not?

Writing Assignment

Choose a campus problem that you feel you understand and for which you think you might have a solution. Write a persuasive article (such as Cary Conley's) that might appear in the campus newspaper. In your article try to persuade your readers that (1) you have examined this problem thoughtfully, (2) your analysis of the problem is correct, and (3) after careful consideration you have a workable solution. You may have few or no statistics or authorities, so make especially good use of examples. Remember that your own image as a reasonable, trustworthy writer is an important tool of persuasion.

Writing Assignment

Write an essay in which you examine some personal opinion and try to persuade readers of its value. You can mention examples, refer to authorities, use emotional appeal, or employ any of the methods of persuasion you have seen in this chapter. If you are arguing a point that many of your readers may not at first agree with (as Rachel Jones is doing), be sure to anticipate the readers' objections and try to deal with them.

In this chapter you have seen several successful pieces of persuasive writing. The writers used patterns and techniques that you have seen elsewhere in this book, but they used them to persuade rather than just to give information. They supported their opinions with illustrations, statistics, and the ideas or research of authorities on the subject. They also worked to win sympathy and agreement by appealing to their readers' emotions.

During your college years you may use persuasion in themes, research papers, essay exams, and reports. Beyond college you may find yourself using the same tools in preparing business and professional reports, recommending the purchase of a particular product or piece of equipment, or even proposing a particular solution to a problem in the workplace. As we said at the beginning of the chapter, persuasion is everywhere; and it, perhaps more than any other type of writing, demands sound thinking, careful planning, and clear writing.

CHAPTER 7

Developing and Linking Paragraphs

Paragraphs are the building blocks of essays and other types of writing. This chapter will emphasize two points: (1) stating a main idea clearly in the topic sentence of a paragraph and (2) providing specific support in logical order. It will give you practice with several different types of paragraph order and then turn to ways of linking the sentences within paragraphs to achieve unity and coherence.

IDENTIFYING PARAGRAPHS

A **paragraph** is a block or unit of writing that can stand alone or be linked to other paragraphs to build a longer piece of writing. Many basic or transitional writing classes concentrate on practicing paragraph writing because learning to build good paragraphs is a necessary part of learning the whole writing process.

Paragraphs can be identified simply by their appearance: each paragraph begins on a new line, and the first word is indented. When the paragraph ends, you move to the next line before starting the next paragraph. There is little use in talking about the length of a paragraph because the number of words may vary widely depending on the paragraph's purpose. The effectiveness of a paragraph depends more on whether it is *complete* than on whether it is short or long. A look at the reading selections in this text will give some idea about how paragraphs look and how different they are in length.

The example that follows shows, however, that not all sentences grouped together into a unit actually compose a good paragraph. These

90

sentences do not develop one consistent subject and therefore do not make a successful paragraph.

> Being a secretary can be frustrating or even infuriating. Some bosses expect their secretaries to be their personal servants. Good secretaries are difficult to find. The secretary's pay is usually below that of blue collar workers. Being a secretary has been shown to be a high-stress job. Secretarial training is available at many colleges and universities in night classes for nontraditional students.

Even though all the sentences are about secretaries, they do not develop the main idea of the paragraph: that being a secretary can be frustrating or infuriating. The second sentence seems to explore one reason that the secretary's job is so frustrating, but the third sentence moves away from the subject entirely, and the last sentence is unrelated to any of the others. There is no unity created by the details that are used to develop the topic.

IDENTIFYING TOPIC SENTENCES

It is necessary for all the sentences within a paragraph to be related to one central or core idea. This idea is the topic of the paragraph, and writing about this one idea creates unity. Often, this central or core idea is stated within the paragraph in one sentence, called the **topic sentence**. It is a good idea when you read to look for the topic sentence of paragraphs to help you understand them. It is also a good idea when you write to use a topic sentence, usually near the beginning of the paragraph, to help your readers understand the main idea.

Activity 7.1

Read the following paragraphs, and identify the topic sentence of each. After you have picked out the topic sentence, reread the paragraph to see how each sentence in it is related to the main topic. Remember that a topic sentence need not be the first sentence in the paragraph. Compare your ideas about the relationship of the sentences with the ideas of other students in the class.

> *PARAGRAPH 1*
>
> The most important thing in football is the ball. The object of all the activity is to get possession of the ball, for without it

a team cannot score. The ultimate aim is to ground the ball on or beyond opponent's goal line (for a touchdown), but the vast size of the playing field makes that impossible without small interim gains to move the ball within striking distance of the goal. Meanwhile the defensive team is devoting all its efforts to blocking such progress by halting the offensive team in its tracks or best of all, getting the ball away and heading for the opposite line.   (Betty Lehan Harragan, *Games Mother Never Taught You*)

PARAGRAPH 2

As the weeks went by the chimpanzees became less and less afraid. Quite often when I was on one of my food-collecting expeditions I came across chimpanzees unexpectedly, and after a time I found that some of them would tolerate my presence provided they were in fairly thick forest and I sat still and did not try to move closer than sixty to eighty yards. And so, during my second month of watching from the Peak, when I saw a group settle down to feed I sometimes moved closer and was thus able to make more detailed observations.   (Jane van Lawick-Goodall, "First Observations")

PARAGRAPH 3

A friend of mine used to teach at Fairview Hospital and Training School, one of the centers for retarded children in Oregon. Because the teachers were aware that some of the kids could not see, they used special funds to buy eyeglasses for them. After a while, however, the staff just gave up; the kids simply would not wear the glasses. The inability to see was in the brain and not in the eyes.   (Svea J. Gold, *When Children Invite Child Abuse*)

PARAGRAPH 4

By the age of eleven, Mindy no longer had a peer group into which she could retreat; she was alone in an adult world. In fact, she had been so well programmed that she did not want to retreat. Instead, she wanted to be included in her parents' complete social calendar, and she became furious and unmanageable if she was not. Because she had been conditioned to consider their life also hers, she interpreted any failure on the part of her parents to include her in their activities as an overt rejection. It was not loneliness but rebellion and despair that brought Mindy to my office.   (Murray Kappelman, *Raising the Only Child*)

Activity 7.2   Read the following paragraphs in the "Reader" section of this text. Working in small groups, identify the topic sentence in each paragraph.

page 174, paragraph 6	pages 212–213, paragraph 1
page 182, paragraph 15	page 233, paragraph 2
page 194, paragraph 14	page 239, paragraph 9
page 203, paragraph 1	pages 258–259, paragraph 2

As the selections in the activities show, the topic sentence is not always the first or second sentence in the paragraph. There is no rule of writing that says this must be the case. The topic sentence can be *suggested* by the sentences of the paragraph but never actually be stated at all, or it can be withheld until the end of the paragraph. These cases, however, are not the general rule. It is usually wise to look for the topic sentence early in the paragraph when you are reading and to include it there when you are writing, especially while you are developing your reading and writing skills.

Activity 7.3   Read the following groups of sentences. Working in small groups, decide what the main idea is in each collection of sentences, and write a topic sentence for it. Compare the topic sentences written by your peer group with those written by others.

PARAGRAPH 1

My roommate Greg and I never make our beds. Greg also leaves his clothes scattered all over the floor. I manage to pick up my clothes, but I often have a pile of empty pizza boxes, potato chip bags, and soft drink cans on my desk. Since my desk is covered by this debris, my books and notes are stacked (sort of) in a corner by our one closet. Inside the closet . . . No, I don't think there are words to describe the closet.

PARAGRAPH 2

Most people who come to Burger Quick are there because they are in a hurry. They don't want to stop and chat, but they expect me to be friendly and courteous—even when they are not. Younger kids, however, like to talk about what they're ordering. Sometimes they just put their money on the counter and ask me what it will buy. Older customers, especially those that are retired, like to talk briefly, and they are happy when I remember their names or recall that I served them day before yesterday. They often seem to be more interested in seeing other people than in eating.

PARAGRAPH 3

Every day Professor Anderson begins by reviewing the major points he covered the day before. This might be a good idea if he didn't repeat himself, but he does—always using exactly the same words. Next he gives a brief introduction to the artists in today's assignment. Then the lights go off, and he drones on. Slide after slide flashes almost unnoticed on the screen while Professor Anderson's voice, flat and unchanging, washes over the 100 plus students sitting in the dark, warm classroom. Twenty minutes into the period, most of the class has gone to sleep, and those of us still awake wish desperately that we could join them.

PARAGRAPH 4

Before one tall front window was an ornamental fig tree. An umbrella plant stood before the other, looking rather exotic in the late afternoon light. Three large Boston ferns sat on plant stands near the smaller side windows, and vines and flowering plants covered the tops of tables that had been arranged to catch the light, not to be useful to anyone who happened to be in the room. In the middle of this green clutter sat the frail, white-haired man, looking with pleasure at the small pots of African violets that bloomed on a table near his chair.

DEVELOPING PARAGRAPHS

General to Particular

Ideas may be made more specific within the paragraph to explain the writer's meaning and make it clearer. For example, a sentence may state:

The shot clock makes college basketball more exciting.

The reader is aware of the writer's opinion about the use of the shot clock but does not know why the writer holds this opinion. A reader unfamiliar with basketball may not even understand what procedure is being discussed. One or two more sentences would explain the general sentence by providing more specific information:

> Using a forty-five-second shot clock makes college basketball more exciting. The team with the ball must post up and take a shot within forty-five seconds. The players are not allowed to hold the ball and slow down the pace of the game.

With the addition of these two sentences, the writer is well on the way to developing a short paragraph on the use of the shot clock in college basketball.

An idea is made more specific when it is developed by examples, illustrations, or other types of explanations that clarify the wording and make the writer's intention clearer. Often, whole paragraphs are developed by stating a general idea and then making it more specific.

Activity 7.4

The following paragraphs in the "Reader" section of this text are developed from general to particular. Working in small groups, identify the topic sentence in each paragraph, and see how the specific details are related to that general statement. Is there anything in the paragraph that you feel does not belong there?

page 184, paragraph 1	page 233, paragraph 4
pages 203–204, paragraph 2	page 251, paragraph 25
pages 216–217, paragraph 22	page 276, paragraph 10
page 219, paragraph 8	page 282, paragraph 13

Writing Assignment

Practice using specific support in paragraphs by supplying details for one or more of the following topic sentences. When you have added the needed information, the paragraphs will be examples of general-to-specific paragraph development. Working with a partner, read the paragraphs to see that each specific detail is clearly related to the topic sentence.

1. A person cannot depend on the quality of products anymore. I recently bought a _____ and immediately started having trouble with it.

2. I heard a scream for help. I knew someone was in serious trouble.

3. Running for public office requires a candidate to be completely open about his or her past.

4. Television advertising is truly creative.

5. That salesperson must have thought I was a real sucker.

Time Order

Another method of development that works for some writing topics is called time order or chronological development. The details that the writer uses to make the topic clear and interesting to the reader are written in the order in which they occurred, with an emphasis on the time or the sequence of the events. Words that commonly indicate time are used to link the sentences together and help the reader follow the time order easily.

There is often no topic sentence in this type of paragraph, so it is important for the writer to be logical and consistent with time references and to avoid confusing the reader by giving details out of order. Consider the following example:

> I woke up in the middle of the night with the strange feeling that something was wrong. Maybe it was just a bad dream that had waked me, but I really didn't think that was the case. I had the feeling, though I couldn't say why, that some noise had startled me awake. I threw back the covers and quietly swung my feet to the floor. I crept to the door of my room. Also I had put on my bedroom slippers before I got up from the side of the bed. My soft-soled slippers kept my footsteps from being heard as I passed through the doorway and into the hall where I saw the flashlight beam of the robber who was silently emptying the contents of my silver chest into a bag.

The writer's actions are described in the exact order in which they occurred throughout most of this paragraph, making the incident easy to picture. There is, however, one exception: *Also I had put on my bedroom slippers before I got up from the side of the bed*. The paragraph would be better if this detail had been reported when it occurred in the series and not inserted, with the help of "also," as an afterthought.

Time order can also help the writer clearly report information covering a much longer time span than the one in the previous example. Look for references to time that give unity and order to the following paragraph about growing up:

> I was born January 21, 1944, on a military base in Oscoda, Michigan. I was in and out of foster homes almost from the moment of my birth. My formal education: I never com-

pleted the sixth grade. At age nine I began serving long
stints in juvenile detention quarters. At age twelve I was sent
to the Utah State Industrial School for Boys. I was "paroled"
once for about sixty days, then returned there. At age eighteen I was released as an adult. Five or six months later I was
sent to the Utah State Penitentiary for the crime of "issuing a
check against insufficient funds." (Jack Henry Abbott, *In the
Belly of the Beast*)

The author guides you from the year of his birth to age eighteen by focusing
on important events that shaped his life. These are easy to follow through
the eighteen-year span because the author refers often to his age and the
references are kept in correct time order. Notice that again there is not a
topic sentence.

*Writing
Assignment*

Using time order, write a paragraph about some event in your own life that
occurred over several months or years. Before you start to write, make a list
of the parts of the incidents that you want to include. Then check the list to
see that the incidents are in the correct order. When you start to draft the
paragraph, remember to include words to show the reader *when* this part of
the event occurred. When you have finished writing, exchange paragraphs
with a partner and read to see if the time order is clear and logical.

Space Order

Just as writers use time to help them give order to the details of a paragraph, so they use space to show where items are placed or how they are
arranged. They describe what is seen by looking from left to right, from floor
to ceiling, from sky to ground, from building to building along a street, from
inside to outside, and so on. The writer must let the reader know the direction he or she is using, and then follow that direction faithfully throughout
the entire paragraph. The reader will then be able to picture the scene from
the cues the writer gives. Often, paragraphs developed using space order do
not have topic sentences.

The following paragraph illustrates how this method of ordering
works:

From my mother's balcony I could see the neighborhood
where I grew up. The school, the library, the stores, and
many of the buildings are still there, but formerly Jewish
streets are now Puerto Rican. The Forward Building is
owned by Chinese investors. I could also follow the skyline,
beginning at the Empire State Building, going west and

south until stopped by the new, twin towers of the World
Trade Center. They stand shoulder to shoulder like huge
rectangular thugs.   (Leonard Michaels, "New York, New York")

The first sentence makes it clear that the New York neighborhood is being
viewed from above. The speaker is looking down on the school, library,
stores, buildings, and streets that he mentions. Then he begins to look along
the skyline, and to make the order clear, he states that his gaze starts at the
Empire State Building and continues west and south to the World Trade
Center. The paragraph is about the change that has occurred in the neighborhood, and the writer uses a description of the streets and buildings to
show what the change is. The use of space order helps the reader to see the
changes.

This final example uses space order to arrange a description of the
shocking destruction after the atomic bomb was dropped on Hiroshima:

It was when I crossed Miyuki Bridge that I saw Professor
Takenaka, standing at the foot of the bridge. He was almost
naked, wearing nothing but shorts, and he had a ball of rice
in his hand. Beyond the streetcar line, the northern area was
covered by red fire burning against the sky. Far away from
the line, Ote-machi was also a sea of fire.   (Jonathan Schell,
The Fate of the Earth)

The reader's view is guided from near to far, from the foot of the bridge and
Professor Takenaka to the distant fire at Ote-machi.

*Writing
Assignment*

Choose a scene with which you are well acquainted, one that you can see in
your mind. Decide how you can best describe that scene to a reader. Choose a
direction to order the details you plan to use to describe the scene. Write a list
of these details in the order in which you plan to use them. Then check the
list to see if you have been careful to keep a consistent space order. While you
are writing, remember to use words to show the reader where the parts of
the scene are. When you have finished, exchange paragraphs with a partner
and read to see if the space order is clear and reasonable.

Analysis

One way to begin to understand analysis as a method of paragraph
development is to compare it to analysis that takes place in a chemistry labo-
ratory. A student in a lab might be given a beaker of liquid and asked to
analyze it. The student would know to identify the various elements mixed
together in the liquid in order to understand the parts and their characteris-

tics as well as their additional characteristics when combined. To analyze water, H_2O, you would separate it into two parts hydrogen and one part oxygen and describe the characteristics of the individual elements as well as their characteristics when combined, such as freezing and boiling points.

When you analyze an idea, you must also break it into its parts and consider their characteristics and features, both individually and in combination. The thinking skill involved is critical examination; the goal is improved understanding of the idea or concept being analyzed. The writer who uses analysis as a method of paragraph development performs the breakdown and examination for the reader, making clear the idea that is being presented.

Here is an example:

> But I did not want to shoot the elephant. I watched him beating his bunch of grass against his knees, with that preoccupied grandmotherly air that elephants have. It seemed to me that it would be murder to shoot him. At that age I was not squeamish about killing animals, but I had never shot an elephant and never wanted to. (Somehow it always seems worse to kill a *large* animal.) Besides, there was the beast's owner to be considered. Alive, the elephant was worth at least a hundred pounds; dead, he would only be worth the value of his tusks—five pounds, possibly. But I had got to act quickly. I turned to some experienced-looking Burmans who had been there when we arrived, and asked them how the elephant had been behaving. They all said the same thing: he took no notice of you if you left him alone, but he might charge if you went too close to him.   (George Orwell, "Shooting an Elephant")

The topic sentence of the paragraph states the author's decision that he does not want to shoot the elephant. The text of the paragraph analyzes this decision to help the reader understand Orwell's reasons for it. First, there is the description of the elephant as "grandmotherly"; this feeling may have led Orwell to conclude that it would be murder to kill the animal. He explains this reaction further by saying that he is not squeamish but that he did not like the thought of killing large animals. Next, Orwell considers the value of the elephant both dead and alive. Of course, the animal is worth more alive. These thoughts lead to the conclusion that he must act quickly to avoid the killing.

As this paragraph illustrates, analysis breaks a complex idea into at least some of the individual thoughts that compose it so the reader can better understand the author's meaning. Analysis may also be used to show the process that must be followed to make or do or accomplish something. Or it may be used to list the reasons for doing or thinking something. It may even break some whole into its parts so that the reader will better understand the whole.

Clearly, analysis is a more complex method of paragraph order than the others considered in this chapter. You must think carefully and make decisions before writing. And you must understand the idea thoroughly yourself before you can make it clear to a reader.

In another but very different paragraph about elephants, a writer analyzes how a magic trick might have been performed by the world-famous magician Houdini:

> . . . On January 7, 1918, Houdini had a ten-thousand-pound elephant led onto the bright stage of the Hippodrome in New York City. A trainer marched the elephant around a cabinet large enough for an elephant, proving there was space behind. There was no trap door in the floor of the Hippodrome, and the elephant could not fly. Houdini ushered the pachyderm into the cabinet and closed the curtains. Then he opened them, and where the elephant stood there was nothing but empty space. Houdini went on with his program, which might have been making the Hippodrome disappear, for all the audience knew. A reporter for the *Brooklyn Eagle* noted: "The program says that the elephant vanished into thin air. The trick is performed fifteen feet from the backdrop and the cabinet is slightly elevated. That explanation is as good as any." After Houdini stopped making elephants disappear, nineteen weeks later, the trick would never be precisely duplicated. (Daniel Mark Epstein, "The Case of Harry Houdini")

After the author carefully explains the details of the disappearing elephant trick, he then gives a reporter's account of the trick. The reporter's comment that the explanation about vanishing into thin air is "as good as any," and the following information that the trick was never duplicated suggest that no one really knows how the trick was performed. The analysis here is to inform about an amazing feat of magic and to leave the reader impressed by the abilities of Houdini.

Writing Assignment

Here are some activities that can be analyzed in a paragraph: making a foul shot, returning a punt, throwing a curve ball, scrambling eggs, fixing a burger in a fast food restaurant, sorting laundry, selecting good tomatoes in a market, chopping oriental vegetables, buying a pair of shoes, painting a floor, killing insects. You may add to this list if you wish.

Pick one subject, write a topic sentence for your paragraph, and then analyze the process, breaking it down into its individual steps. Be sure you keep the steps in clear and reasonable order. When you have finished, exchange papers with a partner. Read the paragraph to see if the process is clearly explained.

Other Types of Paragraph Order

There are other methods of paragraph development besides those discussed here. Some are simple variations of the ones presented. For example, a general-to-particular order can become particular to general if you withhold the topic sentence until the end of the paragraph and give the supporting details first. You may open a paragraph with a question that you intend to answer within the body of the paragraph. Or you may even end the paragraph with a question. These methods are not used as often as the four described earlier, but they can be useful. When you become comfortable writing the basic general-to-particular paragraph, you will soon learn to handle variations when you want to include them.

Activity 7.5   The following paragraphs in the "Reader" section of this text are developed by several of the methods you have studied. Working in small groups, identify the topic sentence (if any) in each paragraph, and examine the supporting details. Identify the type of development in each paragraph.

page 181, paragraph 12	page 238, paragraph 1
page 185, paragraph 5	page 248, paragraph 5
page 197, paragraph 37	page 251, paragraph 22
page 219, paragraph 6	page 276, paragraph 7

SPECIAL-PURPOSE PARAGRAPHS

There are also paragraphs that serve special purposes within an essay. The introduction of an essay is clearly a separate paragraph, but often it does not have the usual characteristics of one. The same is true of the concluding paragraph. Sometimes, you will notice a very brief paragraph that simply summarizes one idea and introduces another, moving the reader from one part of the essay to the next. It is called a "transitional paragraph," and it too lacks the usual features of paragraphs. Introductions, conclusions, and transitional paragraphs are special types of paragraphs that are useful tools for writers, but they may best be practiced and perfected after you are comfortable with basic paragraph writing.

LINKING SENTENCES
WITHIN PARAGRAPHS

So far in this chapter, you have been asked to devote your attention to how to arrange ideas within paragraphs, but correct and logical arrangement alone may not make a satisfactory paragraph that says what you want it to say. Look at the following example:

> I was really tired of going to school. I had already been a student for twelve years, and now my parents expected me to hit the books hard for four more years just to prove that a miner's kid from a dying coal town could do it. I was ready to rebel and quit. However, I could not deny the consequences of passing up the scholarship and disappointing my family.

The word *however* is an important transitional device in this paragraph. It shows that the last idea stated is a change from the other ideas expressed in the paragraph. This is clearly the other side of the issue, and the word signals the change. You can also show the way that ideas relate to one another with words like *however*, *therefore*, *moreover*, *consequently*, *nevertheless*, and *nonetheless*. Such words are not interchangeable; each has a very particular meaning of its own, but each does show the relationship between ideas.

Activity 7.6

Practice with transitional words that link up ideas by choosing either *however*, *therefore*, *moreover*, *consequently*, *nevertheless*, *nonetheless*, or a similar word for the following sentences. Explain the different meanings created as you choose different transitional words.

1. I had been brought up to believe that honesty is important and that a man's word can be counted on. _____, I was shocked and hurt when I learned that few in the business world shared my values.

2. Rob had just had a physical examination; _____ he was surprised but unconcerned about the pain in his chest.

3. I was out of money and discouraged; _____ I was not even sure I had a place to spend the night. _____ I decided not to take Sue's offer of a bus ticket home.

4. Most word processing programs allow you to move text from one place in a document to another. This makes revision easier to accom-

plish; _____, you still need to have a clear outline in mind or you will not be able to improve your report.

In addition to words such as these that serve as noticeable markers of transition, there are other writing methods that help to create coherence within paragraphs. These methods make the sentences "stick together"; this is what *coherence* means. Examine the following descriptive paragraph, which uses space order as a method of development:

> My hotel room was furnished with the most modern conveniences. The door was opened with a slender metallic card that activated a red light that flashed when the door could be opened. Just inside the door to the left was the kingsize bed covered by pastel sheets and a thermal blanket. Near the bed was a television set, but the casual visitor to the room would never suspect its presence. It was carefully hidden behind the doors of a cabinet that served double duty as a storage chest. The remote control on the stand beside the bed also served a double duty: it turned the TV on and off and it called up my hotel account so that I could view my room charges at any time. This was especially handy just before check-out time.

The paragraph is a simple description that is easy to follow because the space order is made clear by words and phrases that link sentence to sentence clearly. Pronouns are used to avoid the repetition of nouns, and they refer clearly and consistently to their antecedents. Note how the paragraph would come unglued without these devices:

> My hotel room was furnished with the most modern conveniences. The door was opened with a slender metallic card that activated a red light that flashed when the door could be opened. The kingsize bed was covered by pastel sheets and a thermal blanket. There was a television. The casual visitor to the room would never suspect its presence. The television was carefully hidden behind the doors of a cabinet. The cabinet served double duty as a storage chest. The remote control also served double duty: the remote control turned the TV on and off and the remote control called up my hotel account so that I could view my room charges at any time. Calling up my room charges was especially handy just before check-out time.

The paragraph is not only long and wordy; it is also hard to follow when the linking or transitional words and phrases are omitted. *Just inside the door, to the left, near the bed*, and *on the stand beside the bed* are phrases that link the sentences together and help the reader to see where objects are in the room. The word *but* is also a linking word because it shows a contradiction: the television is there *but* a visitor cannot see it. Even pronouns like *it* and *this* are linking devices because they call to mind ideas already stated. These linking or transitional devices are used to help the reader move from one sentence to another and to understand how one sentence relates to another.

Activity 7.7   Look at the following groups of paragraphs in the "Reader" section of this text. Working alone or in small groups, identify the transitional words and phrases and other linking devices (such as the clear use of pronouns) that help to improve coherence within and between paragraphs. See what happens to the meaning of the paragraphs when these links are left out.

page 174, paragraphs 5, 6

pages 180–181, paragraphs 4–8

page 188, paragraphs 3–5

pages 212–213, paragraphs 1, 2

page 214, paragraphs 7–9

pages 220–221, paragraphs 18–24

page 241, paragraphs 1, 2

pages 258–259, paragraphs 1, 2

Learning to write good paragraphs is an important, basic skill for the writer. It is worth practice and careful attention. Remember, you are writing to clarify and support your ideas. You can choose the right kind of paragraph order and the right amount of support for the topic. You always need to check and recheck what you have written to make sure that you have not included ideas that are unrelated to the main topic. You also need to use transitional words and phrases that will link up the sentences in the paragraph and help the reader to move easily from one idea to another.

CHAPTER 8

Building Better Sentences

To communicate your ideas to your readers, you must depend on sentences. These are perhaps the most important units of writing. You always need to think about individual words and about the organization of paragraphs, but writing will often succeed or fail at the sentence level. In this chapter you will look at basic sentence structure and note several ways to avoid sentence errors. You will also work with combining short, often underdeveloped sentences into more complex ones that can communicate more interestingly and effectively.

Simply stated, a **sentence** is a unit of writing that contains at least a subject and a verb and that expresses a complete thought. The shortest possible sentence is one word long. If you see someone about to cross the street in the path of an oncoming car and you shout "Stop!" you have used a sentence. In exclamations like "Stop!" or "Wait!" the subject *you* is understood even though it is not spoken or written. So "Stop!" actually contains a subject and a verb: *[you] stop*. It is also complete. Thus, it is a sentence. The same is true in the case of commands ("Start now") or requests ("Please don't smoke"). These are also sentences with the subject *you* understood.

Most sentences are longer than one word, but it is not length that determines whether they are complete or not. Consider the following conversation:

INSTRUCTOR: In order to enroll in this course, you should have completed two prerequisites, Psychology 154 and Education 207, but you haven't taken either of them; consequently, you will have to postpone taking my course until you have taken the other two—unless, of course, you get special permission to enroll from the department chair.

STUDENT: I see.

Although the first statement contains over fifty words and the second contains only two, both are sentences. They have at least a subject and a verb, and they express complete thoughts.

SENTENCE PROBLEMS

Sentence Fragments

We often see sentences that are not complete. We may understand what they say, but grammatically they are not really sentences. They are called **fragments** because they are only pieces of sentences.

In written advertising you will often find sentence fragments along with complete sentences:

Advertisers like using short groups of words.

Like this.

Because they catch your attention.

And they don't require you to concentrate.

Or think much about the meaning.

See?

Only the first group of words is a true sentence. "Like this" is a modifier; the phrase makes clear the kind of "groups of words" you are talking about. "Because they catch your attention" is a subordinate or dependent clause. It does have a subject (*they*) and a verb (*catch*), but it cannot stand by itself because it begins with the subordinating conjunction *because*. "And they don't require you to concentrate" also has a subject (*they*) and a verb (*do [not] require*), but this fragment is actually another part of the subordinate clause that begins with *because*. "Or think much about the meaning" does not even have a subject. It belongs with *concentrate* in the phrase *to concentrate or think*. Finally, "See?" is just part of the verb in a sentence that is not written fully: "Do you see?" To turn this advertising language into good college writing, we would use only two sentences:

> Advertisers like using short groups of words like this because they catch your attention and don't require you to concentrate or think much about the meaning. Do you see?

Even now this is not a great piece of writing, but it would be acceptable in most college composition classes.

As a reader you do not stop to analyze each group of words to determine if it is a complete sentence. You should know how to do so, however, especially in your own writing. No rule of writing says you can never use a fragment. Professional writers use them; they can sometimes be effective and attention-catching. The "rule" is that you must be able to tell the difference between complete and incomplete sentences so that if you use a fragment, you know when you have done so and why.

Fragments are rarely used in college writing because the chief purpose of such writing is to communicate ideas clearly to readers. If you had to read many bits and pieces like those in the advertising examples, you would soon find yourself losing interest and probably patience. When you are reading and trying to follow ideas in logical order, you expect the writer to be clear and complete and to help you move smoothly through from one sentence to another. When you are writing, you owe your readers the same consideration.

Activity 8.1

The following groups of words are all sentence fragments. Rewrite them so that they are complete sentences. Compare your sentences with those of your classmates to see some of the variety possible in sentence construction.

1. Lying on the white sand and listening to the Beach Boys.
2. Whether Juanita is able to go to New York or not.
3. Since I washed the dishes yesterday.
4. Terrified of taking an advanced course in calculus.
5. To be ready for next week's launch.
6. Considering his courtroom record in dealing with minorities.
7. Although my garden was washed out by the April rains.
8. Forgotten by all but his very oldest friends.
9. Because traffic on the freeway is so bad at 5:00.
10. Before you decide which pair of jeans to buy.
11. If she enjoyed visiting Cancun last summer.
12. The tall man who walked his dog on Delancy Avenue.
13. Left to run the deli for a week.
14. Having drunk six cans of beer in half an hour.
15. However you want to organize these files.

16. People who try to get ahead by holding others back.

17. For as long as I have lived in Lubbock.

18. Even though the rent was two months overdue.

19. Which is exactly why I do not like to go to ballgames with him.

20. Like trying to get water from a rock.

Activity 8.2

Some of the following groups of words are complete sentences; others are fragments. Determine which are complete. When you find a sentence fragment, try to determine why it is one. Is it missing a subject or a verb? Is it actually a subordinate clause or other sentence part that is not complete by itself? Rewrite each fragment to make it a complete sentence.

1. My brother once found a snake in a hen's nest.

2. Even though the weather is warm and the sun is shining.

3. Being the youngest child in a family of four girls and three boys.

4. We were starved, so we sent out for pizza.

5. To be sure that all the doors and windows were locked and the house was secure for the night.

6. The ambulance speeding toward the hospital with its siren screaming and red lights flashing.

7. The morning newspaper folded neatly beside her coffee mug.

8. Ricardo finishes work at 5:00, but he rarely gets home before 6:30.

9. Clean up that mess.

10. When Alice learned that her cousin had twins and needed someone to help her for a few weeks.

11. Wishing she were back home in Kansas.

12. He likes to help with housework on Saturday.

13. The frozen waffles that we had for breakfast this morning.

14. The couple danced in the dark corner.

15. The couple dancing in the dark corner.

16. The movie that Tom and I watched last night.

17. Because of the weather, Gene missed class for two days.

18. The portable radio that Frank left out in the rain all night.

19. Frank left the portable radio out in the rain all night.

20. Dr. Angela Winters, who graduated at the head of her class.

Activity 8.3

In the following paragraphs there are again groups of words that are complete sentences and others that are fragments. Rewrite the paragraphs, locating the fragments and making them complete sentences. Often, the fragments can be corrected by combining them with sentences that are already complete. For others you will need to add missing subjects or verbs. You may work alone or in small groups.

PARAGRAPH 1

(1) My friend Rob's mom claims to be clairvoyant. (2) Which means she can predict the future. (3) Once, using a special deck of cards that her grandmother gave her years ago. (4) She predicted that I would get a B on my geometry exam and Rob would get a C −. (5) She was exactly right. (6) Sometimes reads tea leaves in the bottom of a cup. (7) I think this is even stranger than predicting with cards. (8) Whenever Rob and I want to know ahead of time about our success on a test. (9) We just ask his mom to predict our futures. (10) Unfortunately, she not always right.

PARAGRAPH 2

(1) Many nontraditional students find that their most difficult task is not keeping up in their classes but trying to balance their college work and their responsibilities at home. (2) Single women or men with young children have an especially difficult time. (3) Because they often cannot find or afford good day care. (4) A problem that government and the colleges and universities have been slow to deal with. (5) Some single parents who attend college have formed "care pools" so that they can trade child-care time with others in their group. (6) A good plan, but doesn't work for everyone. (7) Others depend on relatives. (8) This too is only a partial solution. (9) Since many of the student-parents do not live near their families. (10) Until a better solution is found, many single parents who want to continue their education will have to remain full-time parents and only part-time students.

PARAGRAPH 3

(1) Reading crime novels at bedtime is one of my favorite pastimes. (2) I like best those written during the 1930s.

(3) And also in the 1940s. (4) Mostly the ones set in England. (5) Often I can figure out "whodunit." (6) But not always. (7) Even when I think I know who the murderer is, I keep on reading because a good mystery writer can often fool his or her readers. (8) Revealing the real killer only in the last three or four pages. (9) I probably won't learn anything useful from these novels, but I don't consider reading them a waste of time. (10) If they clear the day's problems from my head and help me go to sleep.

Activity 8.4   Exchange recently written papers with one or more of your classmates. See if you can find any sentence fragments, and if you do, decide how best to rewrite them so that they are complete.

Fused Sentences

Even though fused sentences are quite different from sentence fragments, the two problems have one thing in common: both occur because writers do not recognize what belongs inside sentence boundaries. Fragments are incomplete. Fused sentences are more than complete. **Fused sentences**, as the name implies, occur when two complete sentences are run together or "fused" without any word or punctuation mark to show where they are joined.

Suppose you have written these two sentences:

My father had to quit school and go to work at thirteen.

I've been lucky enough to finish high school and start college.

These sentences are closely related in meaning and similar in structure; it would be logical to put them together. But if there is nothing to indicate where they are joined, where one ends and the next begins, the result is a fused sentence:

My father had to quit school and go to work at thirteen I've been lucky enough to finish high school and start college.

One complete thought ends with the word *thirteen*, and another begins with *I've*. With nothing to mark the joining point, the sentence is fused.

If you want to combine the two sentences into one, there are at least four ways of doing so. (We will examine these in detail later.)

My father had to quit school and go to work at thirteen; I've been lucky enough to finish high school and start college.

My father had to quit school and go to work at thirteen, but I've been lucky enough to finish high school and start college.

While my father had to quit school and go to work at thirteen, I've been lucky enough to finish high school and start college.

My father had to quit school and go to work at thirteen; however, I've been lucky enough to finish high school and start college.

The key to dealing with fused sentences is understanding sentence boundaries. If you have a problem with them, you should start looking at each sentence you write to see how many independent or main clauses it contains. If you have written more than one, you need to indicate where the two (or more) are joined.

Activity 8.5

The following are all fused sentences. First, decide where they run together; then rewrite them. Sometimes, it may be best to separate a fused sentence into two or more sentences. If the thoughts seem to belong together, however, you may join them using any of the techniques shown above or others that you may know.

1. It has been raining for three days the river is above its banks.

2. From my window I can watch the birds in my yard several robins are looking for seeds.

3. Yesterday I spent $75 at the grocery where the rest of this week's money went I don't know.

4. Ellen needed eye surgery Dr. Chang was her immediate choice.

5. Sam is allergic to cats he had to give his Siamese to his cousin.

6. My brother is a top auto mechanic he takes special training courses several times each year.

7. Telephone salespersons interrupt me often they usually seem to call just at mealtime.

8. Sandra wanted to work in the library last night it closed early the air conditioning system broke down.

9. Most of my friends said the movie was terrible I wanted to see for myself if they were right.

10. Maria has been accepted by three law schools she is checking to see which one has the best program in tax law.

Activity 8.6   Some of the following sentences are correctly written; others are fused. Working alone, in pairs, or in small groups, decide which sentences are fused and how you might rewrite them. Use the methods of rewriting suggested in Activity 8.5.

1. Some of my courses in marine biology are very difficult I enjoy them anyway.

2. Joining a study group in American history proved to be a good idea.

3. To quit my job now is to admit that my ex-girlfriend was right about me.

4. Economists frequently predict a recession most of the time they are wrong.

5. Friends at the office where my mom used to work often ask when she's coming back she usually says not until the baby is two or three.

6. I was not able to get tickets for the Erotic Nightmares concert even though I got in line six hours before the box office opened.

7. I could hear the voices of the children playing in the street below my open window I could not concentrate on my work.

8. My roommate and his girlfriend cut their afternoon classes to watch TV during the entire two weeks that Dr. Lance was curing four hundred cases of plague on *City Hospital.*

9. Deciding on the topic for an essay usually isn't hard for me actually writing the paper sometimes is.

10. Jane decided long ago to major in social work her own early life made her want to help others.

Activity 8.7   In the following paragraph some sentences are correct and some are fused. Correct the fused sentences using any of the methods in Activity 8.5. You may work alone or in small groups.

(1) When Allen and Vickie opened their first paint and wall-paper shop, they were excited but worried they weren't sure they would be successful. (2) They had both quit good jobs and put most of their savings into the shop. (3) They knew if they failed, it would take years to recover financially however owning their own business had been a longtime dream. (4) Vickie now says she was so nervous when the shop opened

that she couldn't eat normal meals she lost seven pounds in the first four weeks. (5) Allen had the opposite problem he nibbled all the time and gained weight. (6) After the first few weeks, they had several well-satisfied customers, and the reputation of their shop began to spread. (7) By the end of the first year, they felt confident of success. (8) In fact, within two years they decided to open a second store in a nearby mall. (9) They now have three shops and will open their fourth one in a few weeks their investment has paid off and they are financially secure. (10) Still, as the next opening date comes closer Vickie is beginning to lose weight and Allen is beginning to gain they are as nervous about their fourth shop as they were about their first.

Activity 8.8   Exchange recently written papers with one or more of your classmates. See if you can find any fused sentences, and if you do, decide how best to rewrite them.

Comma Splices

A **comma splice** occurs when two sentences are improperly joined or "spliced" with a comma. In most cases the function of a comma is to separate, not to join. There are a few exceptions, but for now it is safer always to follow this guideline: a comma cannot join two independent clauses or two complete sentences.

Look again at the fused sentence we examined earlier:

> My father had to quit school and go to work at thirteen I've been lucky enough to finish high school and start college.

Suppose the writer realized immediately that she had fused two sentences and punctuated by adding a comma after the word *thirteen*. The sentence would then look like this:

> My father had to quit school and go to work at thirteen, I've been lucky enough to finish high school and start college.

The writer has now exchanged one problem for another. She has eliminated a fused sentence but has created a comma splice.

A recent survey of a wide and varied group of well-educated readers—including teachers, business executives, and other professionals—shows that most believe the comma splice is not as serious a problem as the fused sentence. They notice but sometimes choose to ignore the comma splice; they view the fused sentence as a sign of an untrained writer. There is no reason, however, why writers should settle for a "smaller error" when learning how to eliminate both errors is rather simple.

To review: *My father had to quit school and go to work at thirteen* is a complete thought; it is an independent clause. It is followed by another complete thought, also an independent clause: *I was lucky enough to finish high school and start college.* These two independent clauses can be separated by a period and written as two separate sentences, or they can be joined into a single sentence in any of the ways shown on page 110. They cannot, however, simply be spliced together with a comma.

The most important thing to remember in deciding how to punctuate sentences like this one is the sentence structure. Look for independent clauses that have their own subject and verb and can stand as complete thoughts. Look also for independent clauses joined by coordinating conjunctions (*and, but, or, yet, so, for*) and for dependent clauses that begin with subordinating conjunctions such as *after, because, if, when.* Both these types of clauses may require a comma for separation, not for joining. We will examine sentences like these in detail later in this chapter.

Activity 8.9

All of the following sentences contain comma splices. Correct them by rewriting. Then, working in small groups, compare revised sentences to see how different ways of rewriting a sentence can give slightly different shades of meaning.

1. The federal budget seems to be out of control, our elected officials seem unwilling to do anything about it.

2. Whenever I vacation in the mountains, I like to spend a few days fishing, I may soon stop because some of my favorite trout streams are showing signs of pollution.

3. The fence we built keeps us from seeing our awful neighbors, we still have to listen to them.

4. If the Lady Bobcats win tonight's game, they are guaranteed a spot in the tournament, even if they lose, they will probably be given an invitation.

5. Chad spends hours getting a dark tan, he says he's willing to risk wrinkles and dry skin when he's older and no longer concerned about his good looks.

6. Mrs. Gardone often brings her customers' meals herself, and she always says one word, a hearty "Enjoy," this personal service makes her restaurant a friendly, very special place.

7. My class in Roman mythology is always interesting, today we read the story of Vulcan catching Venus and Mars committing adultery.

8. My brother-in-law, who was once a Navy pilot, now flies for a commercial airline, he likes his work, but he sometimes suffers from stress.

9. Dr. Vincent's veterinary practice is very specialized, he treats only gerbils and hamsters.

10. This may be your idea of a good time, it certainly isn't mine.

Activity 8.10   Some of the following sentences are punctuated correctly; others contain comma splices. Decide which contain splices and correct those sentences by rewriting them.

1. Whenever Eve feels depressed, she orders a pizza with onions and anchovies.

2. A good friend of ours recently moved to California, she is teaching in a small college and raising almonds.

3. Only thirty people showed up for our tenth class reunion, most were unable to attend.

4. My husband is happy to help me fix meals and clean up the kitchen, but he hates doing laundry.

5. Susan has a terribly fear of spiders and crawling insects, her sister often threatens to catch them and put them in her bed.

6. The Sado-Masochists canceled their concert, so refunds must be sent to all 20,000 ticket holders.

7. Although he has worked at Southwest Printing Services for only eight months, Carlos has already been promoted to word processing supervisor.

8. These data were collected in a small random sample, they may not be representative.

9. My roommate and I stayed up until 2:30 watching a slasher movie on TV, then I couldn't go to sleep, that's why I missed the math test this morning.

10. If I go to the ball game with my cousin, I'll have to take the bus home, the subway isn't safe at night.

Activity 8.11   In the following paragraph some of the sentences are punctuated correctly; others contain comma splices. Rewrite the paragraph, eliminating the comma splices.

(1) During my first week at college I was often confused, but I suppose that is to be expected. (2) My first problem was housing, someone must have mistaken my name "Francis" for "Frances," and I was assigned to a room with three girls. (3) I was willing to overlook this error, my mother was not. (4) I also had a bit of trouble with the orientation lectures, several of them were dull, I let my mind wander and probably failed to hear some important information. (5) Then I missed a tour of the campus, I couldn't find the building where the tour started. (6) Registering for classes was not as bad as I feared, but I still worried about getting to the right class at the right time. (7) I soon learned that other first-time students had many of the same concerns, that made me feel better.

Activity 8.12   Exchange recently written papers with one or more of your classmates. See if you can find any sentences with comma splices, and if you do, decide how best to rewrite them.

COMBINING SENTENCES

If you can avoid fragments, fused sentences, and comma splices, you have mastered some basic principles of sentence construction. Now you can turn your attention to the ways in which writers build more complex structures. You already write sentences like most of those we will examine. That means you can focus attention not so much on *what* you are writing as on *how* and *why*.

COORDINATION

Coordination joins sentence elements of like kind. The prefix *co-* indicates equality, as in *co*chairs, *co*inventor, or *co*habit. *Ordination* suggests rank or degree. (Notice the *ord-* in *ord*er and *ord*erly.) Thus, when you coordinate two or more things, you give them equal rank or importance.

In English we coordinate sentence elements with **coordinating conjunctions**. (A conjunction is simply a word that joins one element with another. Note the *co-*, as explained in the previous paragraph, and *junction*, the same as in highway junction or railroad junction.) The most common coordinating conjunctions are *and, but, or, yet, so,* and *for*. Less often used is *nor*, which is simply the negative form of *or*. You may find it helpful to remember them as a rhyme: *and, but, or / yet, so, for.*

These conjunctions are used to coordinate words, phrases, or clauses.

WORDS

Tom *and* Jerry, bread *and* butter, running *and* jumping

slow *but* certain, small *but* strong, handsome *but* dumb

wet *or* dry, hot *or* cold, you *or* I, neither you *nor* I

PHRASES

over the river *and* through the woods, in one ear *and* out the other

not on the floor *but* in the closet, well planned *but* poorly executed

in the basement *or* in the attic, too much *or* too little, neither at home *nor* in the office

CLAUSES

Carla thought we should complain to the manager, *and* I agreed.

She knew several phrases in English, *but* I knew no Chinese at all.

You can pump gas yourself, *or* you can have full service.

Frank was no longer willing to work in the mines, *nor* did he want his sons working there.

All of us thought we knew the answer, *yet* in fact not even one of us did.

The market was out of fresh dill, *so* I will make the Scandinavian fish appetizers some other time.

Sarah has decided to postpone her trip to France, *for* her father-in-law is very ill.

Each of the preceding independent clauses could stand by itself as a **simple sentence**. When you join two or more independent clauses with coordinating conjunctions, combining them into a single structure, you have written a **compound sentence**. This is a common and effective way of building sentences, so long as it is not overused.

Before you practice with coordination, notice the punctuation in compound sentences. In all the preceding examples there is a comma before the coordinating conjunction. Though there may occasionally be exceptions, you should play it safe by always placing a comma before a coordinating conjunction when that conjunction joins two independent clauses.

Activity 8.13   Combine the following pairs (or trios) of sentences into single sentences using coordination. Check your punctuation carefully.

1. The sweater Angela gave me for my birthday is awful.
   It matches the awful skirt she gave me last year.

2. The fog is heavy on the hills this morning.
   The sunlight is unable to get through.

3. You may go to the grocery and buy something for dinner.
   You may watch the baby while I go.

4. Jim and Ruth both have high-paying jobs.
   They always seem to be in debt.

5. Jo skipped dinner and spent all evening studying math.
   She had a test at 8:00 the next morning.

6. I can't finish reading these books by the due date.
   I'll have to pay another big library fine.

7. I hate helping my younger brother clean his room.
   He keeps bugs, spiders, and all kinds of disgusting things there.

8. Late in the afternoon the noise of the traffic dies down.
   I can hear the voices of children playing in the park.

9. Rob plans to work this summer at McDonald's.
   He'll have extra money for school in the fall.

10. Alicia is as good a basketball player as her brother.
    He got a scholarship.
    She got a job typing in the athletic office.

Activity 8.14   For each of the following five sentences, make up a sentence of your own that will go with the one in the text. Then combine the five pairs using coordinating conjunctions. Remember to place a comma before the conjunction. You may work alone or in small groups.

1. Maria wanted to spend the summer with her grandmother in Rome.

2. Sam's father keeps a large herd of dairy cattle.

3. By 4:00 the snow had stopped.

4. The black Trans Am was clocked at 85 mph.

5. Bits of dialogue from the afternoon soap operas drifted into the kitchen.

SUBORDINATION

Another method of joining sentence elements is subordination. Unlike coordination, subordination joins clauses of unequal rank. The prefix *sub-* indicates that one part is below the other in rank or degree. (Notice the prefix in *sub*way, *sub*set, and *sub*marine.) Though this sentence structure may indicate that one idea in the sentence is less important than the other, this is not always the case. It is more important to remember that the inequality is mainly grammatical. The subordinate or dependent clause is so named because it cannot stand by itself and make complete grammatical sense. This combination of one independent clause and one or more dependent clauses makes a **complex sentence**.

Among the most common subordinate clauses are **adverb clauses**. They cannot stand alone because they are introduced by **subordinating conjunctions**. These words join sentence elements by making one of them dependent on the other. Consider the following example:

> Whenever there is a violent thunderstorm, our cat and dog hide together under a bed.

Notice that only the second part of the sentence (after the comma) can make complete sense by itself. Try it. *Our cat and dog hide together under a bed.* We do not know when or why they do this, but we certainly are clear about what they do. Now try the first part of the sentence: *Whenever there is a violent thunderstorm.* This is obviously incomplete. In fact, it is one kind of sentence fragment.

Here is a partial list of common subordinating conjunctions:

after	because	though
although	before	unless
as	even if	until
as if	even though	when
as soon as	if	whenever
as though	since	while

At the beginning of a clause, any of these words will make that clause subordinate or dependent.

You must use extra care in punctuating complex sentences. When the subordinate clause comes *before* the main clause, a comma separates them. (This is what happens in the sentence you just read.) No punctuation is needed if the subordinate clause comes *after* the main clause. (Look at the last sentence you read; you will see there is no internal punctuation.)

Activity 8.15   Combine the following pairs of sentences using subordinating conjunctions. You may reverse the order of the clauses or change the wording slightly if you wish. Remember the formulas for punctuation: (1) subordinate clause + *comma* + main clause *but* (2) main clause + subordinate clause. You may work alone or in small groups.

1. You want to be at the airport by 1:30.
   You had better leave now.

2. Len got A's on the first three unit tests.
   He will not have to take the final exam.

3. I dreaded helping my cousin study English.
   He was a very quick learner.

4. You get some dimes and quarters for the machines.
   I will sort the laundry.

5. It gets dark.
   Fireflies begin to flicker in the empty lot next door.

6. Mona decided not to go to her ballet class.
   She hurt her ankle jogging.

7. Paul graduates from college in May.
   He will be the first member of his family to do so.

8. This course is required of all students.
   I might as well get it over with during my first semester.

9. Pete wanted to buy a designer sweater.
   He didn't have enough money.

10. You need to buy a new toothbrush.
    You had better do it before the pharmacy closes at 6:00.

Activity 8.16   Write your own sentences with subordinate clauses using the following models. Use the subordinating conjunctions in the positions that are given, and punctuate where necessary. When you have finished, you and another student may wish to exchange papers and check the work.

1. _____ unless _____.

2. Even though _____.

3. _____ as soon as _____.

4. Before _____.

5. Since _____.

6. _____ because _____.

7. Whenever _____.

8. Although _____.

9. _____ while _____.

10. _____ even if _____.

SEMICOLONS AND ADVERBIAL CONJUNCTIONS

Another easy way to join two clauses into a single sentence is by using a semicolon. Look at the following examples:

> Five crates of fossils from Tibet arrived at the museum today; seven more are due next week.

> Ed supports the National Rifle Association's position on gun registration; I do not.

> Susan is a Capricorn; Jennifer is a Libra.

> If you enjoy danger, drink and drive; if you enjoy life, don't.

Notice that the semicolon joins only independent clauses. In this way, it acts like a coordinating conjunction. Notice also that clauses joined by semicolons should be closely related in meaning. Consider the following example:

> Susan is a Capricorn; I enjoy astrology.

This sentence is technically correct, but it does not make sense. Finally, notice that clauses joined by semicolons are often set in contrast to each other. This is true in three of the first four examples.

Activity 8.17 Write five sentences of your own using semicolons. Remember to join only independent clauses that are closely related in meaning. In some of your sentences, try joining clauses that offer contrasts. When you have finished, you and another student may wish to exchange papers and check the work.

Sentence combinations can also be made using semicolons in connection with **adverbial conjunctions**. These words and phrases are so named because they are adverbs that can be used as conjunctions. (In fact, they are also called "conjunctive adverbs." You may use either name you wish.) Among the most commonly used adverbial conjunctions are *however, moreover, nevertheless,* and *therefore.* Other examples are *as a result, consequently, conversely, on the other hand, furthermore,* and so on. When used as conjunctions (rather than as simple adverbs), they are always preceded by a semicolon and followed by a comma.

Here are some examples:

> Janet hopes to be promoted to a high management position with Toyota; *therefore,* she has enrolled for Saturday classes in Japanese language and culture.

> The instructor proudly announced that 90 percent of his advanced physics class made passing grades; *however,* he didn't mention that only ten students were enrolled.

> Roberto Lopez says his new film on migrant workers will win an award as Best Documentary; *moreover,* he predicts it will be a commercial success.

> Senator Smithers fears that the scandal in his personal life may attract more attention than his excellent political record; *nevertheless,* he intends to run for a fourth term.

Inexperienced writers often avoid adverbial conjunctions because these words may seem unfamiliar or too formal. Yet these conjunctions can be quite effective when used wisely. Because they are less frequently used than other conjunctions, they are more likely to catch a reader's attention. They are also more emphatic than other conjunctions. It is as if the semicolon plus the adverbial conjunction gives double weight.

We can show this by repeating the sentences just used as examples and using coordinating conjunctions instead of adverbial conjunctions. For example:

> Janet hopes to be promoted to a high management position with Toyota, *so* she has enrolled for Saturday classes in Japanese language and culture.

> The instructor proudly announced that 90 percent of his advanced physics class made passing grades, *but* he didn't mention that only ten students were enrolled.

> Roberto Lopez says his new film on migrant workers will win an award as Best Documentary, *and* he predicts it will be a commercial success.

> Senator Smithers fears that the scandal in his personal life
> may attract more attention than his excellent political record,
> *yet* he intends to run for a fourth term.

The rewritten sentences have less emphasis; the statements are less determined. Thus, adverbial conjunctions are useful when you want to give slightly increased importance to the clause that follows. They are not generally used for simple connections.

Activity 8.18   Write five sentences of your own using adverbial conjunctions. Remember to punctuate with a semicolon before the conjunction and a comma after it. When you have finished, substitute coordinating conjunctions and read the sentences aloud. Notice the difference in emphasis. You may work alone or in two-person teams with partners writing different versions of the five sentences.

RELATIVE PRONOUNS

Another useful tool in building sentences is the group of words called **relative pronouns**: *who, whose, whom, which,* and *that. Who, whose,* and *whom* are used to refer to humans. *Which* refers to nonhumans. *That* may refer to either.

Adjective Clauses

Relative pronouns (sometimes called simply "relatives") are used to form **adjective clauses**, which work in sentences the same way single-word adjectives do. Here are some examples:

> Nicholas Bass, *who began his concert career at age 9*, made his
> first tour of Europe when he was only 13.
> (The clause modifies the subject, *Nicholas Bass.*)

> My mother, *whose maiden name was Corelli*, is proud of her
> Italian ancestry.
> (The clause modifies the subject, *mother.*)

> My Uncle Sol, *whom I have never met*, asked me to visit him in
> Cincinnati.
> (The clause modifies the subject of the sentence, *Uncle Sol.*
> The relative *whom* is the object of its own clause.)

Potassium, *which is necessary for good health*, is plentiful in bananas.
(The clause modifies the subject, *Potassium*.)

Dogs *that run loose in the neighborhood* are a terrible nuisance.
(The clause modifies the subject, *Dogs*.)

Restrictive and Nonrestrictive Clauses

There is one further distinction to be made between types of adjective clauses. Some give essential information about the word they modify. These are called **restrictive clauses** because they actually restrict the identification or limit the meaning of the noun being modified. These clauses are not marked by punctuation. Others give information that may be helpful but is not essential. These are called **nonrestrictive clauses**, and they are set off from the rest of the sentence by being enclosed in commas. Notice that adjective clauses introduced by *that* are usually restrictive. Those introduced by *which* are usually nonrestrictive.

Here are some examples of restrictive and nonrestrictive clauses:

RESTRICTIVE

Anyone *who likes slasher films* will enjoy *The Minnesota Machete Murders*.

A student *whose test scores are as high as yours* should be in the advanced math class.

The old lady *whom Sarah took care of for many years* left her $50,000.

Books *that are over 14 inches tall* are shelved in the Oversize Section of the library.

NONRESTRICTIVE

Maya Angelou, *who is perhaps best known as a writer*, is also a fine actress and lecturer.

JoAnne, *whose boyfriend works in the box office*, always gets discount tickets.

Alex Gory, *whom you may have seen in The Minnesota Machete Murders*, has left Hollywood to run for political office.

Grandfather's will, *which we all thought was in the safe deposit box*, is missing.

Distinguishing Restrictives and Nonrestrictives

Though it is sometimes tricky to decide whether an adjective clause is restrictive or nonrestrictive, it is important to do so. There are times when the punctuation can affect the meaning of a sentence. Consider these two examples:

My cousin *who lives in Portland* was arrested for public intoxication.

My cousin, *who lives in Portland*, was arrested for public intoxication.

In the first sentence it a specific cousin—the one who lives in Portland—who was arrested. We know exactly which cousin is being referred to. In the second sentence we know the arrested cousin lives in Portland, but whether he or she is the only one living there is unclear. In the first example the clause is restrictive; in the second it is not.

Look at one more example:

The minister, *who preached on the Eighth Commandment last week*, was arrested for shoplifting.

The minister *who preached on the Eighth Commandment last week* was arrested for shoplifting.

This time the adjective clause in the first sentence is nonrestrictive; it simply gives additional information about the subject—the minister. In the second sentence the restrictive adjective clause indicates specifically which minister was arrested: it was the one who preached on the Eighth Commandment, not some other minister who may have preached on the Seventh or the Tenth Commandment.

Activity 8.19

Using the relatives *who, whose,* and *whom,* write two sentences with each, one sentence with a restrictive adjective clause and the other with a nonrestrictive adjective clause. Also write one sentence with a restrictive clause introduced by the relative *that* and another with a nonrestrictive clause introduced by *which.* Remember that nonrestrictive clauses are enclosed in commas, but restrictive clauses are not. When you have finished, you and another student may wish to exchange papers and check the work.

Noun Clauses

The same relatives that are used in adjective clauses can also form **noun clauses**. These clauses function in sentences in the same way simple nouns do. For example:

> I knew *who he was* as soon as I heard his voice on the telephone.
> (The clause is the direct object of the verb, *knew*.)

> When Janice learned *whose car was parked in her space*, she immediately called a tow truck.
> (The clause is the direct object of the verb, *learned*. The whole structure is part of the adverb clause introduced by the subordinating conjunction, *When*.)

> Mitch's friends can't find out *from whom he received that letter written on purple, perfumed stationery*.
> (The clause is the direct object of the verb, *find out*. Within the clause, *whom* is the object of the preposition *from*.)

> *Which students most deserve the scholarship* is the toughest question we will have to answer all year.
> (The clause is the subject of the sentence.)

> Erika said she was afraid to fly in a small commuter plane, but the truth is *that she simply didn't want to go on vacation with her sister*.
> (The clause is a complement following the linking verb, *is*.)

Activity 8.20   Write sentences using the relatives *who*, *whose*, *whom*, *which*, and *that* to introduce noun clauses. Try to vary your sentence structure so that you use noun clauses in at least two ways: as subject and as direct object. You may wish to experiment with other noun functions, especially the complement. You may work alone or in small groups.

SENTENCE VARIETY
AND SENTENCE LOGIC

Working with the various methods of combining sentences, we are studying the *how* of sentence building. That leaves the matter of *why* we do it. There are at least two reasons. The first is variety. Read through the following paragraph:

> Yesterday started off badly for me. I had set my clock wrong.
> I woke up late. I finally got to class at 9:15. Everyone was
> working on a test. I had forgotten about it. I couldn't just
> leave again. I sat down and quickly got to work. I didn't have
> much time. That didn't matter. I didn't know many answers.

There is nothing "wrong" with this paragraph; it is just boring. It is composed of eleven simple sentences, all of which have the same basic structure: subject + verb. In most cases there is not even an object or complement. Eight of the eleven sentences begin with the pronoun *I*. No reader can be expected to remain interested in this sort of writing for very long.

Now see how applying a few of the techniques we have examined in this chapter can add variety:

> Yesterday started off badly for me. I had set my clock wrong,
> so I woke up late. When I finally got to class at 9:15, every-
> one was working on a test that I had forgotten about. I sat
> down and quickly got to work. I didn't have much time, but
> that didn't matter because I didn't know many answers.

This paragraph still will not leave a reader breathless for more, but it is certainly more readable than the first version. Writers try to vary their sentence structure to avoid boredom and to keep readers reading.

Sentence structure is also related to sentence logic. This point has already been suggested in one or two places, but now it can be stated directly. The structure of a sentence can help the reader understand the thought that the sentence contains.

Consider ways of combining these two sentences:

> I want to succeed.
> I will.

They can be combined with a coordinating conjunction:

> I want to succeed, *and* I will.

The connection indicates that both ideas are equal, and the sentence suggests the writer's simple determination. The two sentences can also be combined with a subordinating conjunction:

> *If* I want to succeed, I will.

This says something quite different. The first clause is dependent, and the conjunction *if* sets a condition for success. The sentence is still positive, but not so positive as the first version.

Here is another pair to experiment with:

Ernie loves professional wrestling.
His wife hates it.

One possibility is a compound sentence:

Ernie loves professional wrestling, but his wife hates it.

The coordinating conjunction *but* gives the ideas equal weight while signaling the contrast between them. The sentence could also be made complex:

Although Ernie loves professional wrestling, his wife hates it.

The contrast still exists, but Ernie's love of the sport is now a subordinate idea. The main idea is that his wife hates it. Of course, his wife's feelings could be put in the subordinate clause.
There are other possibilities:

Ernie loves professional wrestling; however, his wife hates it.

This sentence is rather formal sounding. Unless the writer has some good reason for wanting such a formal and emphatic structure for these ideas, he or she would probably reject this version. The writer could try a relative:

Ernie loves professional wrestling, which his wife hates.

This may be acceptable, but it is not a very good sentence. Loosely connected *which* clauses often lead to vagueness. The simplest, and probably the best, combination can be made with a semicolon:

Ernie loves professional wrestling; his wife hates it.

This one sentence contains two statements that are short, clear, and absolutely opposite.

Activity 8.21   Following are five pairs of sentences. Join each pair in the five ways covered in this chapter: with a coordinating conjunction, a subordinating conjunction, a semicolon, an adverbial conjunction, and a relative. If your instructor wishes, you can work on this exercise in small groups and compare results. When you have finished, read the combined sentences aloud. What are the shades of difference in meaning? Are some combinations more successful than others? If so, why?

1. Mayor Edwards lost the last election.

   He had been in office for twelve years.

2. The Weird Sisters remain a highly popular rock group.

   They have been jailed four times on drug charges.

3. My grandmother rarely leaves her house.

   She knows all the gossip in town.

4. Uncle Elliot claimed he never liked women.

   He was married seven times.

5. I wanted to go to Barbados for my vacation.

   I could barely afford a nearby national park.

Activity 8.22   Reread some of your recent writing assignments, looking for short, under-developed sentences and combining them to improve your composition. If your instructor wishes, you may work in small groups, exchanging papers with other students.

> *This chapter contains much material, but the skills it stresses are important for all writers. Well-built sentences are essential for success, while poorly built sentences almost guarantee failure. The first priority, of course, is to write complete sentences rather than accidental fragments. Then you need to avoid fused sentences and comma splices. But most important, you should practice various ways of building sentences to maintain your readers' attention and to guide them logically through your thinking.*

CHAPTER 9

~~~~~~~~~~~ *Writing Standard English Correctly*

This chapter is mostly about the rules by which standard written English works. These guidelines for writing correctly are not new to you, of course. Many college-age writers have seen and heard them—but have failed to learn and use them—for a number of years. One reason is that they see no need for such rules. But there certainly is such a need, and writers who continue to disregard widely accepted standards are taking risks they may not even be aware of.

The simplest method of dealing with the topic of writing standard English correctly would be to say: "Here is a set of rules; learn them and use them." We are not doing that for two reasons. First, it wouldn't work. Second, and more important, it gives a wrong idea about language. Language is so complex, so changeable, and so closely tied to the people who use it that we cannot say simply: "If you write this, it is always right; if you write that, it is always wrong." Before we can understand what such terms as "right" and "wrong" really mean in relation to English, we need to look more closely at how the language has developed and is still developing.

THE CHANGING LANGUAGE

Over many centuries all written languages have developed certain patterns of grammar, usage, and punctuation. For example, users of English accept that an -s added to the end of a noun indicates that the noun is plural, while an -s added to the end of a verb indicates that the verb is singular. Users have also accepted that these nouns and verbs must agree in number, either singular or plural, and we follow this as a rule of standard English. Thus, we can correctly write *a dog barks* or *dogs bark* but not *a dog bark* or *dogs barks*.

Some of the rules of grammar have existed for as long as English has been spoken and, in fact, existed long before that in the older languages from which English developed. Other rules have changed over the years. In the fourteenth century Geoffrey Chaucer could say about one of his characters: "There was not nowhere no man so virtuous." In the sixteenth century William Shakespeare could describe one of Julius Caesar's stab wounds by saying: "This was the most unkindest cut of all." By today's rules these sentences by two of the greatest writers in English would both be grammatically incorrect.

The rules of punctuation are even more flexible. Early English was often written with no punctuation at all, and for centuries writers punctuated more or less as they wished. It is only in fairly modern times that the rules we now use were commonly agreed upon. And the guidelines for using commas, to take one example, have changed within recent years and are still changing. Forty years ago most writing textbooks insisted on a comma before *and* in a phrase such as "apples, oranges, and grapes." Recently, that comma has been deemed optional. Now some textbooks do not mention it at all.

The point is that English, both spoken and written, is very much alive. The ways in which we speak and write change, and over time the rules change to reflect what we do. Who, then, determines what is correct and incorrect at any given time? The majority of educated speakers and writers do. The conventions or customs followed by this majority set the standard.

STANDARD AND NONSTANDARD ENGLISH

Often, we use such terms as "correct and incorrect" or "right and wrong" because they are convenient. To be more accurate, however, we should describe grammar, usage, punctuation, and so forth as **standard** or **nonstandard**. Standard English is that variety or dialect of English used by the majority of educated speakers and writers. Language that does not follow the conventions of standard English is considered nonstandard.

Here is an example. As you know, singular verbs go with singular nouns. Thus, in standard English we write "He doesn't (= does not) want any milk" but not "He don't (= do not) want any milk" because *he* and *does* are singular while *do* is plural. "He don't" is nonstandard.

Here is another common illustration. The infinitive form of a verb (such as *be*) has no number; it is neither singular nor plural. Thus, in standard English we write "She is living at home" but not "She be living at home." We might say that "She be living at home" is wrong, but we would be more exact if we called it nonstandard.

The best-known example may be *ain't*. For years teachers insisted, "There is no such word as *ain't*," and many complained when the word was first printed in college dictionaries. This is not a sensible approach. *Ain't* was first recorded in written English almost three hundred years ago, and it probably existed in speech long before that. Of course the word exists. So do other "nonexistent" words such as *hisself* and *theirselves*. They exist, but they are now, and always have been, nonstandard. They are not ordinarily used by the majority of educated writers and speakers.

Activity 9.1

Check the front pages of your college dictionary to see how it treats grammar and usage. Look for such headings as "Grammar," "Usage," "Usage Labels," or "Nonstandard English." Look up a few words like *ain't*, *his'n*, *hisself*, or *their-selves* to see how your dictionary describes their use.

There are many dialects in American English, and they all share many or most of the characteristics of standard English. Yet they also have their own distinctive characteristics; that is what makes them identifiable as dialects. Some are primarily ethnic. Groups of speakers and writers who are black, Hispanic, Chinese, Jewish, and so forth often share patterns of language that are not common to other groups. Other dialects, such as rural southern or Appalachian or southwestern, are regional. There can even be combinations. Northern black English, for example, is in some ways different from southern black English. All of these groups have language patterns that are considered standard and others that are not.

CHOOSING THE APPROPRIATE DIALECT

By now it should be clear that nonstandard English is not automatically "wrong." When people label it "wrong," they usually mean it is unsuitable for the particular situation in which it is found. In Chapter 1, when we talked about planning writing, we identified three questions that writers must be able to answer:

1. What do I want to write?

2. For whom am I writing?

3. How am I going to write it?

The answers to these questions, particularly questions 2 and 3, determine what dialect a writer will use.

There are times, especially when you are writing description or narration, when nonstandard English is more effective than standard English. Let's look at two examples from American literature. In 1885 Mark Twain published *Adventures of Huckleberry Finn*. Here is the opening paragraph of that novel:

> You don't know about me, without you have read a book by the name of "The Adventures of Tom Sawyer," but that ain't no matter. That book was made by Mr. Mark Twain, and he told the truth, mainly. There was things which he stretched, but mainly he told the truth. That is nothing. I never seen anybody but lied, one time or another, without it was Aunt Polly, or the widow, or maybe Mary. Aunt Polly—Tom's Aunt Polly, she is— and Mary, and the Widow Douglas, is all told about in that book—which is mostly a true book; with some stretchers, as I said before.

The second example is from Alice Walker's *The Color Purple*, another American classic published almost one hundred years after Twain's:

> Sofia would make a dog laugh, talking about those people she work for. They have the nerve to try to make us think slavery fell through because of us, say Sofia. Like us didn't have sense enough to handle it. All the time breaking hoe handles and letting the mules loose in the wheat. And how anything they build can last a day is a wonder to me. They backward, she say. Clumsy and unlucky.

Activity 9.2

Working in small groups, reread these passages together and pick out examples of nonstandard English. Why do you think the authors wrote in nonstandard dialects? Is their nonstandard English convincing?

Next, as a group, try rewriting the passages in standard English. (Choose one person as a recorder to write down your new version.) Share the results with other groups to see how similar or different your rewritten versions are. What would be the result if your standard versions were used in place of the originals?

THE NEED FOR STANDARD ENGLISH

Consider the following sentences:

> It don't matter how much money you got; ain't nobody no better than nobody else.

> I reckon I'll stay here this weekend cause I ain't got no ride home.

If you and your friends or families feel natural and comfortable with sentences like these, then this textbook will not insist that you should speak or write differently when you are communicating casually. At such times this type of language may be entirely appropriate among people who speak and write the same way.

Other situations, however, call for a different dialect or type of language. For academic and business writing, standard English is expected. When you are working on a test or paper for a college class, a resume for your personnel file, a letter of application, a request for credit, a report for your supervisor, a memo to the workers you supervise, or any one of dozens of common writing tasks, then you need to be in firm command of standard English. It is the language appropriate for these situations.

Some writers do not want to conform to the conventions of standard English because, they feel, doing so would cause them to give up their own dialect and thus give up some of their own freedom and individuality. That need not happen. Adopting one way of writing does not mean giving up another. It means that we can learn to write in more than one way.

Activity 9.3

Here are two more passages from Mark Twain and Alice Walker, both written in standard English. Working in small groups, read these paragraphs and compare them to the passages in Activity 9.2. In addition to the clear differences in word choice and grammar, what other differences do you find between standard and nonstandard written English? Why do you think the writers chose standard English for these paragraphs? What do you think their purposes are in these passages and in the earlier ones?

So, by and by, I ran away. I said I would never come home again till I was a [river boat] pilot and could come in glory. But somehow I could not manage it. I went meekly aboard a few of the boats that lay packed together like sardines at the long St. Louis wharf, and humbly inquired for pilots, but got only a cold shoulder and short words from mates and clerks. I had to make the best of this sort of treatment for the time being, but I had comforting day-dreams of a future when I should be a great and honored pilot, with plenty of money, and could kill some of these mates and clerks and pay for them. (Mark Twain, *Life on the Mississippi*)

How was the creativity of the black woman kept alive, year after year and century after century, when for most of the years black people have been in America, it was a punishable crime for a black person to read or write. And the freedom to paint, to sculpt, to expand the mind with action did not exist. Consider, if you can bear to imagine it, what might have been the result if singing, too, had been forbidden by law. Listen to the voices of Bessie Smith, Billie Holiday, Nina Simone, Roberta Flack, and Aretha Franklin, among others, and imagine those voices muzzled for life. Then you may begin to comprehend the lives of our "crazy," "Sainted" mothers and grandmothers.   (Alice Walker, "In Search of Our Mothers' Gardens")

WRITING STANDARD ENGLISH IN COLLEGE AND BEYOND

The introduction to this chapter mentioned the risks of not following widely accepted rules of standard English. These risks are real and may sometimes be serious. When you allow nonstandard forms to slip into your academic writing (essays, tests, research papers, and so on), you run the risk of receiving a poor grade. When you use nonstandard forms in business or professional writing, the risks are just as great—maybe greater. Jean Sherman, an assistant editor of *Working Woman* magazine, advises that "while the literary merits of your documents aren't crucial, your grammar and spelling are. Don't rely on your secretary or subordinates to do it for you. Your name is going on the memo and, with it, your communication reputation."

The hazards of using nonstandard English in situations where it is not appropriate may even go beyond your educational or career objectives. The people with whom we all deal daily—teachers and students, employers and employees, colleagues and coworkers, doctors, lawyers, sales clerks, receptionists, loan officers, local government officials, and so on—often make judgments about us based on the way we use English. They may judge our social, economic, educational, intellectual, or cultural level by our language. Often they are not even aware that they are doing so. Such judgments may seem unfair, but they are made anyway. Rightly or wrongly, using standard English is one of the best guards against being underestimated or misjudged on first impressions.

For some students writing well becomes a source of enjoyment and personal satisfaction. For others it remains a survival skill. Whichever category you belong in, you are taking this class to improve your composition skills; and learning standard sentence structure, grammar, usage, and punctuation is an important part of learning to write well.

In the pages that follow, you can review some of the basic conventions of the grammar and punctuation of standard English and practice them briefly. You should know that these guidelines are not intended to be complete; they simply cover the areas with which inexperienced writers often have the most difficulty.

Reviewing Standard Written English

REVIEWING VERBS

Principal Parts of Verbs

A verb has three basic forms or principal parts from which other parts can be built. The first, the *present tense* form, indicates action or existence at the present time. The second, the *past tense* form, indicates action or existence in the past. The third, the *past participle*, is not used by itself as a verb; it is used with auxiliary or helping verbs to form the present perfect, past perfect, and future perfect tenses.

Many English verbs are regular; the past and past participle are both formed by adding *-d* or *-ed*. For example, the principal parts of *stop* are:

Present	*Past*	*Past Participle*
stop	stopped	stopped

Since the final two forms are alike, you will probably not make a mistake in using them. Both *I stopped smoking* and *I have stopped smoking* are correct.

Other verbs, often very common ones, are irregular; they change one or more letters in forming the past and past participle. For example, the principal parts of the verb *to go* are:

Present	*Past*	*Past Participle*
go	went	gone

To indicate present action, we write *I go to college*. To indicate past action, we write *I went to college*. But in standard English we cannot write *I gone to college*. We can, however, add auxiliary or helping verbs and write *I have gone to college* (present perfect), *I had gone to college* (past perfect), or *I will have gone to college* (future perfect).

The last point is worth repeating: the past participle form cannot stand alone as the main verb in a sentence or clause. If you write that way, the result is nonstandard English. *I tore my shirt* and *I have torn my shirt* are both standard; *I torn my shirt* is not.

Irregular Verbs

For quick reference, here are the principal parts of some common irregular verbs:

Present	Past	Past Participle
am (base = to be)	was	been
begin	began	begun
bite	bit	bitten
bleed	bled	bled
blow	blew	blown
break	broke	broken
buy	bought	bought
catch	caught	caught
choose	chose	chosen
come	came	come
do	did	done
draw	drew	drawn
drink	drank	drunk
drive	drove	driven
eat	ate	eaten
fall	fell	fallen
feel	felt	felt
fight	fought	fought
find	found	found
fly	flew	flown
forget	forgot	forgotten
get	got	gotten
give	gave	given
go	went	gone
grow	grew	grown

Present	*Past*	*Past Participle*
have	had	had
hide	hid	hidden
hold	held	held
keep	kept	kept
know	knew	known
lay	laid	laid
lead	led	led
leave	left	left
lie ("lie down")	lay	lain
lose	lost	lost
ride	rode	ridden
ring	rang	rung
rise	rose	risen
run	ran	run
seek	sought	sought
shake	shook	shaken
shrink	shrank	shrunk
sing	sang	sung
sleep	slept	slept
speak	spoke	spoken
spring	sprang	sprung
steal	stole	stolen
strike	struck	struck (stricken)
swear	swore	sworn
swim	swam	swum
take	took	taken
teach	taught	taught
throw	threw	thrown

Present	Past	Past Participle
wake	woke (waked)	waked (woken)
weep	wept	wept
wind	wound	wound
write	wrote	written

Regular Verbs

The majority of English verbs are regular; that is, they form their past and past participle forms by adding -d if the verb ends in a vowel or -ed if the verb ends in a consonant. Often, the final consonant is doubled. Here are a few examples:

Present	Past	Past Participle
bounce	bounced	bounced
form	formed	formed
lie ("tell a lie")	lied	lied
march	marched	marched
occur	occurred	occurred
refer	referred	referred
stop	stopped	stopped
swat	swatted	swatted
travel	traveled	traveled
work	worked	worked

Though you do not need a long list of regular verbs, you may need a reminder about spelling their past and past participle forms. Many speakers do not sound the -d in the past tense. Instead of saying, "On the way home yesterday I *stopped* to buy bread," they say, "On the way home yesterday I *stop* to buy bread." Be very careful that this habit of speaking does not transfer into writing. When you *write* the past or past participle of a regular verb, the -d or -ed tense marker must always be included whether you regularly *say* it or not.

One final comment on principal parts. There are many irregular verbs that are not included in the list given earlier. There are also regular verbs that add -*d* or -*ed* while changing the spelling (for example, *pay, paid, paid* or *say, said, said*). A few verbs do not change form at all (for example, *let, let, let* or *shed, shed, shed*). If you are uncertain about a verb that is not given here, consult your dictionary.

The Irregular Verb *to Be*

The verb *to be* is so irregular, at least in the present and past tenses, that you may need to review part of its conjugation. The following table shows how to conjugate *to be* in the various tenses.

PRESENT TENSE

	Singular	Plural
1st Person	I am	we are
2nd Person	you are	you are
3rd Person	he/she/it is	they are

PAST TENSE

	Singular	Plural
1st Person	I was	we were
2nd Person	you were	you were
3rd Person	he/she/it was	they were

FUTURE TENSE

	Singular	Plural
1st Person	I will be	we will be
2nd Person	you will be	you will be
3rd Person	he/she/it will be	they will be

PRESENT PERFECT TENSE

	Singular	*Plural*
1st Person	I have been	we have been
2nd Person	you have been	you have been
3rd Person	he/she/it has been	they have been

PAST PERFECT TENSE

	Singular	*Plural*
1st Person	I had been	we had been
2nd Person	you had been	you had been
3rd Person	he/she/it had been	they had been

FUTURE PERFECT TENSE

	Singular	*Plural*
1st Person	I will have been	we will have been
2nd Person	you will have been	you will have been
3rd Person	he/she/it will have been	they will have been

Activity 9.4   Decide which form of the verb should go in the blank in each sentence. The base forms are given in parentheses.

Example: I _____lost_____ my wallet yesterday. It must ___have fallen___ out of my pocket when I _____went_____ to the gym to play racquetball. (lost / fall / go)

1. I _____ saving money for college when I was only twelve years old. (begin)

2. I don't think you will ever _____ a fish with that lure you _____. (catch / buy)

3. If Ava _____ when Dr. Cross _____ the as-

signment for today, she would _____ there was a test.

(listen / give / know)

4. Jason _____ down to rest for a few minutes before he

_____ studying. When he _____, it was

nearly midnight. (lie / start / wake)

5. When the wind _____ from the southwest, we often

_____ rain. (blow / have)

6. I _____ to my uncle about a loan, but he never

_____ my letter. (write / answer)

7. Have you ever _____ tequila? I _____ it

when I was in Mexico, but I _____ not like it very much.

(drink / try / do)

8. By the time you get this message, I _____ home. (go)

9. Don can certainly _____ this job well; he

_____ similar work for many years. (do / do)

10. Theresa now _____ the same youth group that her

mother _____ many years ago. (lead / lead)

11. When Andy _____ the old clock in the middle of

campus _____ 10:00, he _____ he

_____ through the beginning of his math class. (hear /

strike / realize / sleep).

12. As the jeep _____ through the rough fields, small ani-

mals _____ out of the way and flocks of birds

_____ into the air. (bounce / spring / fly)

13. Every time Ricardo _____ his famous fastball, his young

son _____ loudly from the stands. (throw / cheer)

14. Anne now _____ her keys _____ in her

coat pocket when she _____ home last night, but I

_____ she _____ them at the office again.

(swear / be / come / think / leave)

15. Debbie's bike _____ not in the garage. Do you think

someone _____ it? (be / steal)

Subject-Verb Agreement in the Present Tense

You were reminded earlier in this chapter that subjects and verbs must agree in number; that is, both must be singular or both must be plural. For example, the singular noun *flower* goes with the singular verb *blooms*; the plural noun *flowers* goes with the plural verb *bloom*. Likewise, the singular pronoun *she* takes the singular verb *sings*; the plural pronoun *they* takes the plural verb *sing*.

Notice that in these examples the verbs are all in the present tense. Those ending in *-s* are also in the third person, singular—the one we indicate in conjugation by using *he/she/it*. This is the only form that may cause you an agreement problem. In standard English almost all verbs add an *-s* in the third person, singular, present tense. No other endings for verb number are left in modern English.

Activity 9.5

In the following sentences choose the verb form from those in parentheses that agrees with the singular or plural subject.

1. I usually (agree / agrees) with the president, but most of the time my father (doesn't / don't).

2. My history instructor (come / comes) to class late every day.

3. Those cigarettes (isn't / aren't) mine; maybe they (belongs / belong) to my roommate.

4. My Uncle Luigi (tries / try) to lose weight by running, but that only (seem / seems) to make him eat more.

5. When I get home at 3:30, I always (hopes / hope) the kids will say, "Hi, Mom, glad you're back." Instead, I usually (hear / hears), "We (wants / want) a snack!"

Agreement After an Intervening Phrase

You should not be misled by a phrase that comes between the subject and the verb. Look, for example, at this sentence:

Usually the members of the city council *vote* with the mayor.

The subject is the plural noun *members*; therefore the verb *vote* must be plural as well. Do not be misled by the word *council* that comes just before the verb. It is not the subject. It is, in fact, an object of the preposition and cannot be the subject of the sentence.

Another example:

> Only one member of the three committees *is* really qualified.

Here the subject is the singular noun *member*, which takes the singular verb *is*. Do not be misled by the plural *committees*, which is the object in a prepositional phrase.

Agreement with Compound Subjects

Two or more singular subjects joined by the conjunction *and* are considered plural and take a plural verb:

> Jose and his father *spend* most Sunday afternoons building model ships together.

Two or more singular subjects joined by *or* or *nor* are considered singular and take a singular verb:

> A white wine or perhaps a rosé *goes* best with this chicken casserole.

If a singular and a plural subject are joined by *or* or *nor*, then the verb agrees with the closer subject:

> Neither the soldiers nor their sergeant *is* able to explain the strange events of that night.

Agreement with Indefinite Pronouns

Pronouns such as *either, neither, each, anybody, somebody, nobody,* and so forth are singular and take a singular verb. (These pronouns are listed on page 151.)

> *Either is* a good choice for secretary.

> *Each pays* her half of the rent and *buys* her own food.

> *Anybody* who lives in a one-room apartment with five Persian cats *is* likely to have furry-looking clothes.

In the last example do not be misled by the intrusive adjective clause *who lives in a one-room apartment with five Persian cats*. The singular subject *anybody* takes the singular verb *is*.

Other indefinite pronouns such as *both* and *several* are plural:

> *Both waste* too much money at the arcade.

> *Several are* leaving before the class is over.

Agreement After the Introductory Word *There*

It is fairly common to begin sentences with the word *there*. Remember, however, that *there* is not the true subject of the sentence; the subject will come later. Here is an example:

> There *are* seven *students* in the class with averages of B or above.

The true subject is *students*, which takes the plural verb *are*. But consider this example:

> There *is* no *reason* why we cannot clean up this mess later.

Here the subject is *reason*, and the verb is the singular *is*.

Agreement with Relative Pronouns

The most common relative pronouns are *who, whose, whom, which,* and *that*. (See Chapter 8, pages 123–126.) In clauses they can be either singular or plural depending on the number of the word the clause modifies. For example, consider this sentence:

> I know many people *who like* to sleep late on Saturday morning.

The pronoun *who* is related to the plural noun *people*. Therefore *who* is considered plural and so takes the plural verb *like*. Notice the difference in the following sentence:

> I know only one person *who likes* to sleep in the nude.

Here *who* is related to the singular noun *person* and so takes the singular noun *likes*.

Here is another pair of examples:

Lisa wants a job that *pays* at least $30,000 a year.

Lisa has two part-time jobs that together *pay* less than $15,000 a year.

Activity 9.6   In the following sentences choose the verb form from those in parentheses that agrees with the singular or plural subject.

1. Any one of Hemingway's novels (are / is) OK for your book report.

2. Maxine Hong Kingston and Jade Snow Wong (is / are) sometimes linked together because they are Chinese-American women writers, but each (has / have) her own very special style.

3. There (was / were) two major aftershocks following the quake; either of them (was / were) strong enough to cause the additional damage to my house.

4. One of the five men who (performs / perform) together as the Sabbatini Brothers (is / are) really an Englishman named Cecil Smythe.

5. There (has been / have been) more false rumors spread about me than about any candidate who (has / have) run for this office before.

6. My opponent, whom neither I nor anyone else (respect / respects) because of his dirty political tricks, (have / has) started most of these stories himself.

7. (Do / Does) the three of you want to have lunch with me?

8. These books, which (was / were) brought from Poland by my grandfather, (is / are) among my mother's favorite possessions, even though she (is / are) unable to read one word of them.

9. Allen and Ellen, the twins who (live / lives) next door, (was / were) recent contestants in the Cutest Kids in Columbus Contest.

10. Either a vase of carnations or an arrangement of mixed flowers (make / makes) a nice gift on Valentine's Day. Both (is / are) cheaper than roses.

REVIEWING PRONOUNS

A pronoun, as its name suggests, stands for (*pro-*) something else. Specifically, it substitutes for a noun or other pronoun known as its antecedent. There are two primary problems with using pronouns: clear pronoun reference and pronoun-antecedent agreement.

Pronoun Reference

Pronouns make a language easier to write and read. Consider this sentence:

> Sarah told *her* father *she* needed $500 for books and supplies, but *he* strongly suspected that *she* had inflated *her* estimate in order to redecorate *her* dorm room.

If it were not for pronouns, the sentence would read:

> Sarah told Sarah's father Sarah needed $500 for books and supplies, but Sarah's father strongly suspected that Sarah had inflated Sarah's estimate in order to redecorate Sarah's dorm room.

Vague Reference: Pronouns with Unclear Antecedents

Just a few sentences like the previous one would drive both writers and readers mad. It is almost as maddening, however, when readers cannot be certain what a pronoun refers to. Here is an example:

> Alicia's mother says *she* needs to lose ten pounds.

Who needs to lose ten pounds—Alicia or her mother? The reader cannot tell. Here are two possible solutions:

> Her mother says Alicia needs to lose ten pounds.

> Alicia's mother says she herself needs to lose ten pounds.

Vague Reference: Pronouns Without Antecedents

Another problem occurs when the pronoun has no antecedent at all:

> Mark is an excellent trombone player, but he doesn't enjoy *it*.

The pronoun *it* doesn't refer to *player*; in fact, it doesn't refer to anything. A bit of revising will make the sentence clearer:

> Mark is excellent on the trombone, but he doesn't enjoy playing.

Vague Reference: Indefinite Use of
You and *They*

One other reference problem is very common. It occurs most often in very informal writing when we use *you* and *they* without antecedents:

> Instructors always seem to schedule big tests on Monday when *you* had planned to party all weekend.

> In Florida *they* lost much of their citrus crop in a late freeze.

Who is *you*? Who are *they*?
Revision can clear up these sentences:

> My instructors always seem to schedule big tests on Monday when I had planned to party all weekend.

> Instructors always seem to schedule big tests on Monday when their students had planned to party all weekend.

The sentence about citrus might be revised this way:

> Florida citrus growers lost much of their crop to a late freeze.

Activity 9.7

Rewrite the following sentences to make certain all pronouns refer clearly to antecedents. There will often be more than one way to revise.

1. Scott's father said he had to leave the house by 6:00 in order to catch his plane.

2. Representative Rocca's press secretary said she was amazed at how little criticism she had received after the speech in favor of the new immigration bill.

3. In parts of Alaska they say temperatures may stay below zero for weeks at a time.

4. The celebration of Martin Luther King's birthday has gained wide acceptance; only a few states don't do it.

5. Bethany's younger sister was excited about her wedding plans.

6. In her rear view mirror, Jeana spotted the red Honda Civic she had seen earlier; she was sure he was following her.

7. For many years I have been interested in the Pueblo Indians and their wonderful dwellings. I always like to see pictures of them.

8. According to this do-it-yourself book, building a deck is easy. They give you step-by-step instructions.

9. By the end of the day, the tables in Ma's Old Fashioned Restaurant are so dirty it almost makes you sick.

10. Six-year-old Ed and four-year-old Ted won the Cute Kids of Columbus Contest so many times that he was almost as unbearable as his brother.

Pronoun-Antecedent Agreement

We have already seen that subjects and their verbs must agree in number; both must be either singular or plural. The same is true of pronouns and their antecedents. But some pronouns must also agree in other ways as well. We shall first review some common pronouns and then look at agreement.

Personal Pronouns

Personal pronouns are unusual among English pronouns because they change form to indicate person, number, case, and gender. Let's review these basic terms.

There are three persons: *first*, indicating the person(s) speaking (*I/we*); *second*, indicating the person(s) spoken to (*you*); and *third*, indicating the person(s) or thing(s) spoken about (*he/she/it/they*).

There are two numbers: *singular* (*I*) and *plural* (*we*).

There are three cases. The *subjective case* is used when the pronoun is the subject of a sentence or clause:

> *He* scored 27 points.

The *possessive case* indicates ownership or close association:

> That is *her* favorite sweater because it has the colors of *her* country's flag.

The *objective case* is used when the pronoun is an indirect object, a direct object, or an object of the preposition:

> Tony gave *her* the gold and diamond bracelet Saturday night. She thanked *him* and put it on, but she kept telling herself she should not accept such an expensive gift from *him* on their second date.

There are also three grammatical genders in the third person, singular: *masculine* (*he*), *feminine* (*she*), and *neuter* (*it*).

The following table shows the various forms of personal pronouns.

SINGULAR

	Subjective Case	Objective Case	Possessive Case
1st Person	I	me	my/mine
2nd Person	you	you	your/yours
3rd Person	he (masculine)	him	his
	she (feminine)	her	her/hers
	it (neuter	it	its

PLURAL

	Subjective Case	Objective Case	Possessive Case
1st Person	we	us	our/ours
2nd Person	you	you	your/yours
3rd Person	they	them	their/theirs

Indefinite Pronouns

Another group of pronouns is called *indefinite* because the pronouns do not refer to specific antecedents. Here are the more common ones:

Singular	Plural	Singular or Plural
each	few	all
one	both	any
anyone	several	most
someone		some
everyone		
no one		
anybody		
somebody		
everybody		
nobody		
either		
neither		

The pronouns in the first column are always singular; those in the second are always plural. Those in the third depend in number on their antecedents.

> *Singular:* A small area of the playground has dried, but *most is* still too wet for the children to play on.

> *Plural:* Some of my friends really enjoy their jobs, but *most are* interested only in the money.

The indefinite pronouns are all considered third person. They do not show case or gender.

Relative Pronouns

The relative pronouns, as we have seen before, are few. Only one changes its form: *who* is subjective, *whom* is objective, and *whose* is possessive. The other common relatives are *which* and *that*.

The number of a relative pronoun depends on the number of its antecedent:

> *Singular:* Increasing taxes is one subject *that is* certain to send legislators running for cover.

> *Plural:* My aunt and uncle, *who are* now visiting us, lived for many years in Kenya.

Principles of Agreement

Pronouns should agree with their antecedents in person, number, case, and gender. As we have seen, not all types of pronouns show all of these characteristics, but we must be aware of those that do. To review: (1) personal pronouns show person, number, case, and gender; (2) indefinite pronouns are considered third person and show number; (3) relative pronouns may show case and take their person, number, and gender from their antecedents.

Determining Gender in Third Person, Singular

Do not forget that third person, singular, personal pronouns have three gender forms. If you know the gender of the singular antecedent, you can select the correct pronoun with no trouble:

The *boy* rode *his* bicycle through the flower bed.

The *girl* ran *her* leg of the relay in record time.

The cracked *egg* oozed from *its* shell.

If, however, you are uncertain whether the gender is masculine or feminine, either use both forms of the personal pronouns or switch to plural where there are no separate gender forms:

A *student* cannot do *his or her* best work if *he or she* is tired.

Students cannot do *their* best work if *they* are tired.

Be especially careful when personal pronouns take indefinite pronouns for their antecedents:

Everyone going to the rally should bring *his or her* own sign.

All people going to the rally should bring *their* own signs.

Most writers now use the plural rather than struggle with gender forms. Sometimes, however, this is not possible or even desirable. When singular antecedents are used, careful writers generally choose *he or she* and *his or her* for agreement, even if the resulting sentence is somewhat awkward.

Sometimes writers, even those who know better, opt for sentences like these:

A *student* cannot do *their* best when *they* are tired.

Everyone going to the rally should bring *their* own sign.

Even if these sentences sound right to you, a quick look will show you they are illogical. *Their* and *they* (both plural) cannot agree in number with *student* (singular). Neither can *their* (plural) agree with *everyone* (singular).

If you are caught in a writing situation where you cannot comfortably shift to the plural number but are not satisfied with the way the singular sounds, it is still better to be awkward than illogical.

Activity 9.8

In the following sentences choose pronouns that agree with their antecedents in number and, when necessary, in case and gender. You may change third person, singular antecedents to plural if you wish.

1. Everybody should have _____ work finished by 3:00.

2. My older brother got _____ first car when he was 19; my

    sister got _____ when she was only 17. I hope to get

    _____ even sooner.

3. My Siamese cats are jealous of each other, so each has

   _____ own food and water bowls.

4. My grandparents still make _____ own wine, just as

   _____ did in Spain.

5. Louisa and Nick, whose apartment is right above _____,

   left their baby with my husband and me for the weekend.

6. Neither of the Haywood sisters has saved enough money to start

   _____ own business.

7. "Men," said the coach, "we can hold our lead if everyone on the team

   does _____ job out there."

8. We can finish our class project on schedule if everyone does

   _____ job.

9. Meg Merrill, _____ advice I usually follow, told me not

   to invest in junk bonds. I wish I had listened to _____.

10. A person who wants to keep _____ good health should

    exercise regularly and watch _____ diet.

11. A senator needs to keep in touch with _____ constitu-

    ents, but the public should not have to pay the postage bill.

12. _____ summer trip to Canton did not give the students

    as much opportunity to practice _____ Chinese as

    _____ had hoped.

13. During the tornado most of the Civic Sports Center was blown off

    _____ foundation.

14. I am a person who values _____ privacy.

REVIEWING BASIC PUNCTUATION

Punctuation is not as simple as sometimes claimed. There is a certain amount of personal choice in punctuation, and some writers can use (or misuse) punctuation to create effects that are part of their writing style. There are certain basics, however, that nearly all writers agree on, and those are the topics covered here.

The Period and Other End Marks

Do not forget that each sentence must end with a mark of punctuation. Use a *period* at the end of a sentence that simply makes a statement:

The woman in the picture is my Aunt Francis.

Use a *question mark* at the end of a sentence that asks a question:

Have you seen my tennis racquet?

Do not use a question mark, however, with an indirect question:

He asked me if I had seen his tennis racquet.

Use an *exclamation point* or *exclamation mark* at the end of a sentence that expresses strong feeling:

This is a complete disaster!

You may also use it after a single word that expresses strong feeling, such as *Ouch!* Sentences with imperative verbs frequently end with this mark as well:

Don't act stupid!

Be careful not to overuse the exclamation mark; it soon loses its effectiveness.

The Comma

Use a comma to separate items in a series:

Gloria has dated an animal trainer, a martial arts instructor, a suspected mass murderer, and an accountant.

The final comma before the conjunction (*and*) is optional. Do not use a comma, however, if there are only two items joined by a conjunction:

Lenny ordered steak and fries.

Use a comma before the coordinating conjunction in a compound sentence:

I'll wash the dishes, and you can give the baby her bath.

Do not use a comma to join two sentences if there is no conjunction; the result is a comma splice. (For more information and practice sentences, see Chapter 8, pages 113–116.)

Use commas to set off nonrestrictive clauses:

> Jon's brother, who was once an alligator wrestler, likes to vacation in the Everglades.

(For more information and practice sentences, see Chapter 8, pages 124–125.) You may also use commas to set off other restrictive elements:

> The pilot, reaching for the coffee the flight attendant had brought him, felt a sharp pain in his lower back.

> The children, tired and hungry, began to complain about everything.

Use commas after a word, phrase, or clause that introduces a sentence:

> Remarkably, he won the game in only a dozen moves.

> Of all the movies I've seen this year, *Grand Rapids Gimlet Murders, Part 8* is my favorite.

> If you want to travel with the group to Chicago, you will need to turn in your $250 deposit by next Friday.

The Semicolon

Use a semicolon to join two closely related independent clauses that are not already linked by a coordinating conjunction:

> You scrub the potatoes; I'll peel the carrots.

Use a semicolon with an adverbial conjunction to combine independent clauses. Remember to put a comma after the adverbial conjunction:

> Reba was horribly tired; nevertheless, she sat down at her terminal and went to work again.

(For more information and practice sentences, see Chapter 8, pages 121–123.)

You may sometimes use a semicolon instead of the usual comma before a coordinating conjunction if there are other commas in the sentence that might cause confusion:

> Jackson won the county election by more than 10,000 votes, a feat his opponent had thought was impossible; but then his

opponent had not considered how many days, nights, and $100 dollar bills Jackson would spend campaigning.

The Apostrophe

Use an apostrophe followed by an -*s* to form the possessive of nouns that do not already end in -*s:*

> Loretta's mother, a man's jacket, Professor Chang's class, the vice president's office, a day's work, a nickel's worth

Do *not* use an apostrophe before the -*s* that indicates the plural of nouns or the third person, singular, present tense of verbs:

> two coats of paint, *not* two coat's of paint; he moves slowly, *not* he move's slowly

Also use an apostrophe followed by an -*s* to form the possessive of most singular indefinite pronouns:

> someone's money, everybody's responsibility, no one's fault, anyone else's toothbrush

Do *not* use an apostrophe to form the possessive of personal pronouns:

> theirs, *not* their's; ours, *not* our's

Use an apostrophe alone to form the possessive of nouns that already end in -*s:*

> my friends' parents, members' wishes, students' worst fears, Cincinnati Reds' manager

Use an apostrophe to indicate where letters are omitted in contractions:

> can't, won't, aren't, I'll, you're, it's

Be especially careful about *it's*, which is the contraction of *it is*. Do not confuse it with *its*, which is the possessive form of the neuter pronoun.

REVIEWING USAGE

One of the characteristics of good standard written English is proper usage. Writers, especially those with limited writing experience, make errors in usage for several reasons: they confuse two words that look or sound alike, they treat words as the wrong part of speech, or they simply use words that are not considered part of standard English. The list that follows contains many, but certainly not all, of the common troublemakers. For convenience, they are arranged alphabetically.

ACCEPT, EXCEPT   *Accept* is a verb meaning "to receive, allow, or agree to." *Except* is a preposition meaning "excluding" or a verb meaning "to exclude."

> I *accept* the responsibility for the error.

> She seems to like everyone *except* me.

> We cannot *except* him merely because he is dull.

AFFECT, EFFECT   *Affect* is a verb meaning "to change or influence." *Effect* is a noun meaning "result" or a verb meaning "to cause or bring about."

> Your attendance in class will *affect* your grade.

> Your attendance in class will have an *effect* on your grade.

> A strong antibiotic will quickly *effect* a cure for your ear infection.

ALL READY, ALREADY   *All ready* means all the things being talked about are finished or prepared. *Already* is an adverb meaning "by now or by a certain time."

> The letters for the out-of-state members are *all ready*.

> We are *already* two days late in mailing them.

ALL RIGHT, ALRIGHT   *All right* means "entirely correct or acceptable." *Alright* (a word modeled on *already*) is not accepted in standard English. It is usually considered a misspelling or is branded "not a word."

A LOT, ALOT, LOTS   Except in the most informal writing, these words are better avoided. If you do use *a lot*, however, make certain it is written as two words; in standard English *alot* is a nonword.

> Nonstandard: I like her *alot*.

> Informal: I like her *a lot*.

> Informal: I like her *lots*.

> Preferred: I like her *very much*.

AS, AS IF, LIKE   Careful writers use *as* and *as if* to introduce dependent clauses. They use *like* as a preposition (or, of course, a verb).

Do *as* I say, not *as* I do.

When I arrived at the party, my ex-girlfriend acted *as if* she had never seen me before.

Like many other New Englanders, I am used to cold winters.

BAD, BADLY *Bad* is an adjective meaning "not good, "sick," or sometimes "severe." *Badly* is an adverb meaning "not well" or in some cases "greatly or much." (Compare **good, well**.)

Today has been a *bad* day.

I need to lie down because I feel *bad*.

Sam has a *bad* cold.

Because she was so nervous, Susan auditioned *badly*.

My car is *badly* in need of a paint job.

COULD OF This phrase is nonstandard, an error for *could have*. It occurs because it sounds like the contraction *could've*, which is used only in the most informal writing.

GOOD, WELL *Good* is an adjective which has a number of meanings. *Well* is most frequently an adverb meaning "skillfully, competently, satisfactorily" and so forth. *Well* is an adjective, however, when it is used to mean "in good health." (Compare **bad, badly**.)

This is *good* ice cream.

I feel *good* today.

The Hawks played a *good* game last night.

The Hawks played *well* last night.

You always do everything *well*.

She left the hospital looking *well*.

HISSELF This form is nonstandard. Use *himself*.

ITS, IT'S *Its* (without the apostrophe) is the third person, singular, neuter personal pronoun. *It's* (with the apostrophe) is the contraction of the verb phrase *it is*.

Your plan has *its* good and bad points.

It's almost time to leave.

It's too bad your St. Bernard shed most of *its* fur just before the annual dog show.

LIE, LAY   *Lie* means "to recline" or "to remain in place." It is an intransitive verb, which means it cannot take an object. The principal parts are: *lie, lay, lain*. *Lay* means "to place." It is a transitive verb; it can take an object. The principal parts are: *lay, laid, laid*.

> Grandmother likes to *lie* down and rest after lunch.

> Todd *lies* on the beach almost every day; yesterday afternoon he *lay* there for three hours.

> The ship *had lain* for centuries at the bottom of the bay.

> Will you please *lay* the baby on the changing table?

> Last week I *laid* the foundation for my new storage building.

> Yvonne was sure she *had laid* her books on her desk.

NOWHERES   This form is nonstandard. Use *nowhere*.

PASSED, PAST   *Passed* is the past tense and past participle of the verb *pass*. *Past* can be a noun, adjective, or preposition but never a verb.

> I *passed* several hitchhikers on the highway.

> Sharon *passed* French last term; she hopes to pass again.

> Many survivors of the Holocaust work to keep the *past* alive.

> He hopes to be forgiven for his *past* offenses.

> She walked quickly *past* the empty buildings.

RISE, RAISE   *Rise* means "to get up or go up." It is an intransitive verb, which means it cannot take an object. The principal parts are: *rise, rose, risen*. *Raise* means "to lift or move something up." It is a transitive verb; it can take an object. The principal parts are: *raise, raised, raised*.

> Cindy usually *rises* at 6:00 A.M.

> Ramon *rose* quickly through the military ranks.

> The sun *had risen* hours before I woke up.

> Please *raise* your hand before you speak.

> Barbara *raised* three children before she returned to school.

> I *have raised* beef cattle for several years now.

SET, SIT   *Set* means "to put or place." The principal parts are: *set, set, set*. *Sit* means "to take a seat" or "to put in a sitting position." The principal parts are: *sit, sat, sat*.

Please *set* the table for dinner.

Myra *set* her coffee mug on the floor beside her.

Dr. Plotkin *has set* 70 as the passing score on the test.

Please *sit* near the front so you can hear.

The teacher stopped the fight and *sat* the boys beside her desk.

I *sat* next to a disgusting drunk on the subway.

Ray and Marlene *have sat* through this film six times.

SHOULD OF This phrase is nonstandard, an error for *should have*. It occurs because it sounds like the contraction *should've*, which is used only in the most informal writing.

SOMEWHERES This form is nonstandard. Use *somewhere*.

THAN, THEN *Than* is a conjunction frequently used in making comparisons. *Then* is an adverb indicating time.

My chocolate fudge is much richer *than* hers.

No one's checking account could be lower *than* mine.

Denise is better in accounting *than* I.

She watched the speedometer move past 75; *then* she heard the siren.

Go ahead *then*.

THERE, THEIR, THEY'RE *There* is an adverb indicating place or a word that starts a sentence with a delayed subject. *Their* is the possessive form of the third person, plural, personal pronoun. *They're* is the contraction of the verb phrase *they are*.

My grandfather was born *there*.

There are too many of us to go in one car.

Their record last season was 12-4.

They're the only tickets still available.

They're ready to eat *their* lunch now. Do you want them to sit *there*?

THEIRSELF, THEIRSELVES These forms are nonstandard. Use *themselves*.

TO, TOO, TWO *To* is a preposition or part of the infinitive form of a verb. *Too* is an adverb meaning "in addition, also, excessively." *Two*, of course, is a number.

Return this cassette *to* your Spanish teacher.

It's hard *to get* from here *to* there.

Make a sharp turn *to* the right.

My test scores are *too* good *to be* true.

Rhonda wants to go *too*.

This is *too* much work for one day.

If you're still hungry, you can have my sandwich *too*.

My younger brother doesn't act *too* smart.

Two of my friends are going *to* the concert *too*.

USE TO   This form is nonstandard because the past tense marker (*-d*) is missing from the verb. The proper form is *used to*.

WHOSE, WHO'S   Whose is a relative pronoun in the possessive case. *Who's* is the contraction of the verb phrase *who is*.

Whose socks are these?

He looks like a person *whose* luck has run out.

He looks like a person *who's* out of luck.

Who's going to clean up after the party?

WOULD OF   This phrase is nonstandard, an error for *would have*. It occurs because it sounds like the contraction *would've*, which is used only in the most informal writing.

YOUR, YOU'RE   *Your* is the possessive form (both singular and plural) of the second person personal pronoun. *You're* is the contraction of the verb phrase *you are*.

Would you turn down *your* stereo, please?

You're still not ready for a solo flight.

You're lucky *your* medical insurance will pay for the surgery.

PART TWO

The Reader

~~~~~~~~~~~~~ Some Advice on Reading

This textbook stresses the idea that writing, reading, and thinking are interrelated skills, each of which strengthens the other two. In this part of the book, the emphasis is on reading, but the other skills must be used as well.

There are whole books—in fact, whole college courses—that can teach you how to improve your reading skills. In these few pages we will not attempt anything very complicated or detailed, but we will offer some advice about reading the selections that follow. These suggestions are general. You can change them to fit your own reading and studying style, but you should try to do everything you are asked.

LOOK OVER THE
READING ASSIGNMENT

Each reading selection is accompanied by several aids that should make your job easier. If you skip everything else and jump immediately into paragraph 1 of the reading selection, you are ignoring the help that has been provided for you.

Before you begin, pick up a pencil or pen. If you are going to combine writing with your reading, you need something to write with. After you have looked at the title of the selection and the name of the author, read the short introduction called "First Thoughts." This will tell you what the subject of the selection is, and it may suggest some of the main points as well.

Next look through the vocabulary list. You may already know some of the words. When there are words you do not know, look at the definitions. Then locate the words in the paragraphs where they occur and underline or circle them. That way, when you are reading through a paragraph and come to a marked word, you may recall its definition. If not, you can go directly to the word list to look again.

Look though the whole reading selection. Just turn the pages. There may be nothing much to see, but you will sometimes find subheadings or other markers that help you understand how the piece is organized or what ideas the writer wants to emphasize.

Read through the questions in the section called "Thinking It Through." You will not answer those questions now, of course, but they may give further hints about main ideas or suggest important writing techniques that you can watch for.

READ THE SELECTION

Be sure your pen or pencil is still handy. One of the best study habits you can develop is marking what you read. Be practical, however. Some students underline or highlight so much of the text that the important parts don't really stand out. Think *while* you read, and think *before* you mark.

Some reading specialists suggest that underlining is not nearly as effective as making marks or notes in the margin. You may want to combine these techniques, underlining or highlighting just a few words or phrases and depending more on your marginal notes.

Many readers develop their own set of marks or symbols to help them remember what they read. If you do not have your own marks, you might use these:

M   Underline *main ideas* and mark "M" in the margin.

S   Mark "S" in the margin to indicate illustrations, quotations, or other evidence that gives *support* for main ideas.

Sum   Mark "Sum" in the margin when you read a sentence that gives a *summary* of a point.

V   Circle words that you need to define but that are not in the "Word List." Mark "V" in the margin (for *vocabulary*). Sometimes, you can figure out what a word means from the way it is used. Other times, you will need a dictionary. You have already marked the words defined in the "Word List."

?   Place a question mark in the margin beside sentences or paragraphs that are not clear to you and that you may want to ask your instructor about.

In addition to using these marks, write notes in the margins. You can compare a point the author makes in one place with one he or she makes elsewhere. You can note when you agree or disagree with the author. If you think of questions you would like to ask or discuss in class, write them down. You can even jot down short summaries of your own. Remember that writing something down often helps you to clarify it and remember it later. A sample page, marked and noted, follows.

1   A rise of less than two feet in sea level might inundate 27 percent of Bangladesh, displacing 25 million people. Egypt could lose 20 percent of its productive land, the United States, between 50 and 80 percent of its coastal wetlands. A 6-foot rise could wipe out the 1,190-island Maldivian archipelago. *Where?*

2   If the Arctic and the Antarctic glaciers were to melt, sea levels would rise nearly 300 feet, flooding many major world cities and all ports.

3   Average global temperatures may rise by 4.5 degrees centigrade by the year 2030. To understand the magnitude of this occurrence, one only must realize that the planet's climate has not varied by more than 2 degrees centigrade over the past 10,000 years and that during the last Ice Age global temperatures averaged some 5 degrees colder than now.

4   A six-foot sea level rise, dramatic as that might be, would be among the milder consequences of a global warming. Agriculture would be hardest hit. Wheat production would have to move north, where depleted soils could result in crop reduction. The production of rice—crucial to the diets of 60 percent of the world's population—would suffer in a drier world. Dust bowls, dying forests, unbearably hot cities, more frequent storms, forest fires and outbreaks of pestilence and disease would also occur.

WHY IS THE EARTH WARMING UP?

m – cause of greenhouse effect

5   Carbon dioxide—mainly released by the burning of coal, oil and other fossil fuels—and other industrial gases are trapping heat in the atmosphere and warming the Earth as if it were a greenhouse. . . .

6   At the end of March 1988, American, British and Soviet scientific data showed that the decade of the 1980s has been the warmest in over a century. The warmest year on record

was 1987, according to the Climatic Research Unit at the
University of East Anglia in the United Kingdom.

different opinions

7   Some scientists (attribute) this to the "greenhouse effect." ∨
Others prefer to wait and see if the pattern (persists) into the ∨
next decade before deciding. Tom Wigley, head of the British research unit, told *The New York Times* that if "the next 10
years are as warm or warmer, it would be very hard to deny
the greenhouse effect," adding "it is very hard to deny now."

m   8   Little has been done to tackle this problem which is, in
many ways, a more serious issue than ozone loss.

9   For the United Nations Environment Programme
(UNEP), which pioneered studies on the subject in the early

Sum   1970s, its reality is no longer at issue: the only questions remaining are when the effects will occur and to what degree.
With ozone loss widely acknowledged as a major threat in
need of urgent solution, the "greenhouse effect" is moving to
the top of UNEP's agenda.

LOOK AT THE QUESTIONS

Look again at the questions in "Thinking It Through." You previewed
these earlier. Now you should be able to give possible answers to them. In
most cases there will be several answers or at least several ways of expressing
one answer. Your instructor may ask you to write out answers for some of
these questions. If not, think through them anyway, and be ready to discuss
them in class.

As you work through these questions, return to the reading selection
whenever necessary to refresh your memory or look for information. The
more you reread, the better you should remember.

REVIEW THE ASSIGNMENT

Before you consider yourself finished, take just a few minutes to look
back over the entire assignment. Look quickly at "First Thoughts." Do you
see how the ideas mentioned there are connected to the reading selection?
Skim the word list. Try to recall how the words were used. You will encounter
many of them again, and you may find some appearing in your own writing.

If the selection is brief, you may not need to reread it. Look at what you
have underlined, however, and read your notes in the margin.

Look quickly at the questions. Are your answers still firm in your mind?

CONNECT IDEAS

If you are assigned several selections in one unit, they will all be on one general topic—success, TV, and so forth. When you find that two essays agree or disagree, add a note about that in the margin. Notice how the ideas contained in several related selections are connected with one another and how different writers express their ideas in different ways.

Some of you may already follow these or similar suggestions about reading. To others, it may seem that you are asked to do a great deal of work for what is sometimes a short piece of writing. You will find, however, that following this simple preview-read-review formula is much more efficient than reading quickly and then finding later that you do not recall or understand much of what you have read.

Success

Nothing succeeds like success.
—French proverb

Nothing succeeds like the appearance of success.
—Christopher Lasch

College Pressures

WILLIAM ZINSSER

First Thoughts   William Zinsser argues that college students too often struggle for high grades just to be accepted into the careers they have chosen. Their belief that all success is material or financial drives them to seek careers above all else and to avoid exploring and taking risks during their college education.

Zinsser organizes his essay by discussing the four types of pressure to succeed that he sees daily in the lives of the students with whom he works. Follow the organization of the essay by noticing which paragraphs make up the introduction and which are devoted to the discussion of each category Zinsser creates. Notice also how the author maintains the unity of the essay as he moves from point to point.

Word List   SUPPLICANTS (paragraph 1):   people seeking help

LADEN (paragraph 1):   loaded

BALM (paragraph 1):   a salve that heals

PRIVY TO (paragraph 3):   to have private information

SAVOR (paragraph 5):   enjoy

NAIVE (paragraph 6):   unsophisticated

VENERATED (paragraph 6):   honored

POTENT (paragraph 6):   powerful

CONFIRMED (paragraph 8):   proved to be true

INTANGIBLE (paragraph 8):   cannot be known through the senses

MATRICULATES (paragraph 9):   enters

EXHILARATE (paragraph 11):   delight

TENACITY (paragraph 14):   determination

FACULTIES (paragraph 19):   abilities

SYNTHESIZE (paragraph 19):   combine

PRESUMABLY (paragraph 20):   appears to be true

VACILLATES (paragraph 21):   wavers

FURTIVELY (paragraph 21):   secretly

CODIFIED (paragraph 27):   arranged

BLITHE (paragraph 29):   cheerful

CIRCUITOUS (paragraph 31):   roundabout

Dear Carlos: I desperately need a dean's excuse for my chem mid-term which will begin in about 1 hour. All I can say is that I totally blew it this week. I've fallen incredibly, inconceivably behind.

Carlos: Help! I'm anxious to hear from you. I'll be in my room and won't leave it until I hear from you. Tomorrow is the last day for . . .

Carlos: I left town because I started bugging out again. I stayed up all night to finish a take-home make-up exam & am typing it to hand in on the 10th. It was due on the 5th. P.S. I'm going to the dentist. Pain is pretty bad.

Carlos: Probably by Friday I'll be able to get back to my studies. Right now I'm going to take a long walk. This whole thing has taken a lot out of me.

Carlos: I'm really up the proverbial creek. The problem is I really bombed *the history final. Since I need that course for my major I . . .*

Carlos: Aargh! Trouble. Nothing original but everything's piling up at once. To be brief, my job interview . . .

Hey Carlos, good news! I've got mononucleosis.

1   Who are these wretched supplicants, scribbling notes so laden with anxiety, seeking such miracles of postponement and balm? They are men and women who belong to Branford College, one of the twelve residential colleges at Yale University, and the messages are just a few of the hundreds that they left for their dean, Carlos Hortas—often slipped under his door at 4 A.M.—last year.

2   But students like the ones who wrote those notes can also be found on campuses from coast to coast—especially in New England and at many other private colleges across the country that have high academic standards and highly motivated students. Nobody could doubt that the notes are real. In their urgency and their gallows humor they are authentic voices of a generation that is panicky to succeed.

3   My own connection with the message writers is that I am master of Branford College. I live in its Gothic quadrangle and know

the students well. (We have 485 of them.) I am privy to their hopes and fears—and also to their stereo music and their piercing cries in the dead of the night ("Does anybody ca-a-are?"). If they went to Carlos to ask how to get through tomorrow, they come to me to ask how to get through the rest of their lives.

4   Mainly I try to remind them that the road ahead is a long one and that it will have more unexpected turns than they think. There will be plenty of time to change jobs, change careers, change whole attitudes and approaches. They don't want to hear such liberating news. They want a map—right now—that they can follow unswervingly to career security, financial security, Social Security and, presumably, a prepaid grave.

5   What I wish for all students is some release from the clammy grip of the future. I wish them a chance to savor each segment of their education as an experience in itself and not as a grim preparation for the next step. I wish them the right to experiment, to trip and fall, to learn that defeat is as instructive as victory and is not the end of the world.

6   My wish, of course, is naive. One of the few rights that America does not proclaim is the right to fail. Achievement is the national god, venerated in our media—the million-dollar athlete, the wealthy executive—and glorified in our praise of possessions. In the presence of such a potent state religion, the young are growing up old.

7   I see four kinds of pressure working on college students today: economic pressure, parental pressure, peer pressure, and self-induced pressure. It is easy to look around for villains—to blame the colleges for charging too much money, the professors for assigning too much work, the parents for pushing their children too far, the students for driving themselves too hard. But there are no villains; only victims.

8   "In the late 1960s," one dean told me, "the typical question that I got from students was 'Why is there so much suffering in the world?' or 'How can I make a contribution?' Today it's 'Do you think it would look better for getting into law school if I did a double major in history and political science, or just majored in one of them?'" Many other deans confirmed this pattern. One said: "They're trying to find an edge—the intangible something that will look better on paper if two students are about equal."

9   Note the emphasis on looking better. The transcript has become a sacred document, the passport to security. How one appears on paper is more important than how one appears in person. A is for Admirable and B is for Borderline, even though in Yale's official system of grading, A means "excellent" and B means "very good." Today, looking very good is no longer good enough, especially for students who hope to go on to law school

or medical school. They know that entrance into the better schools will be an entrance into the better law firms and better medical practices where they will make a lot of money. They also know that the odds are harsh. Yale Law School, for instance, matriculates 170 students from an applicant pool of 3,700; Harvard enrolls 550 from a pool of 7,000.

10   It's all very well for those of us who write letters of recommendation for our students to stress the qualities of humanity that will make them good lawyers or doctors. And it's nice to think that admission officers are really reading our letters and looking for the extra dimension of commitment or concern. Still, it would be hard for a student not to visualize these officers shuffling so many transcripts studded with As that they regard a B as positively shameful.

11   The pressure is almost as heavy on students who just want to graduate and get a job. Long gone are the days of the "gentleman's C," when students journeyed through college with a certain relaxation, sampling a wide variety of courses—music, art, philosophy, classics, anthropology, poetry, religion—that would send them out as liberally educated men and women. If I were an employer I would rather employ graduates who have this range and curiosity than those who narrowly pursued safe subjects and high grades. I know countless students whose inquiring minds exhilarate me. I like to hear the play of their ideas. I don't know if they are getting As or Cs, and I don't care. I also like them as people. The country needs them, and they will find satisfying jobs. I tell them to relax. They can't.

12   Nor can I blame them. They live in a brutal economy. Tuition, room, and board at most private colleges now comes to at least $7,000, not counting books and fees. This might seem to suggest that the colleges are getting rich. But they are equally battered by inflation. Tuition covers only 60 percent of what it costs to educate a student, and ordinarily the remainder comes from what colleges receive in endowments, grants, and gifts. Now the remainder keeps being swallowed by the cruel costs—higher every year—of just opening the doors. Heating oil is up. Insurance is up. Postage is up. Health-premium costs are up. Everything is up. Deficits are up. We are witnessing in America the creation of a brotherhood of paupers—colleges, parents, and students, joined by the common bond of debt.

13   Along with economic pressure goes parental pressure. Inevitably, the two are deeply intertwined.

14   I see many students taking pre-medical courses with joyless tenacity. They go off to their labs as if they were going to the dentist. It saddens me because I know them in other corners of their life as cheerful people.

15   "Do you want to go to medical school?" I ask them.

16   "I guess so," they say, without conviction, or "Not really."

17   "Then why are you going?"

18   "Well, my parents want me to be a doctor. They're paying all this money and . . . "

19   Poor students, poor parents. They are caught in one of the oldest webs of love and duty and guilt. The parents mean well; they are trying to steer their sons and daughters toward a secure future. But the sons and daughters want to major in history or classics or philosophy—subjects with no "practical" value. Where's the payoff on the humanities? It's not easy to persuade such loving parents that the humanities do indeed pay off. The intellectual faculties developed by studying subjects like history and classics—an ability to synthesize and relate, to weigh cause and effect, to see events in perspective—are just the faculties that make creative leaders in business or almost any general field. Still many fathers would rather put their money on courses that point toward a specific profession— courses that are pre-law, pre-medical, pre-business, or, as I sometimes heard it put, "pre-rich."

20   But the pressure on students is severe. They are truly torn. One part of them feels obligated to fulfill their parents' expectations; after all, their parents are older and presumably wiser. Another part tells them that the expectations that are right for their parents are not right for them.

21   I know a student who wants to be an artist. She is obviously an artist and will be a good one—she has already several modest local exhibits. Meanwhile she is a growing well-rounded person and taking humanistic subjects that enrich the inner resources out of which her art will grow. But her father is strongly opposed. He thinks that an artist is a "dumb" thing to be. The student vacillates and tries to please everybody. She keeps up with her art somewhat furtively and takes some of the "dumb" courses her father wants her to take—at least they are dumb courses for her. She is a free spirit on a campus of students—no small achievement in itself—and she deserves to follow her muse.

22   Peer pressure and self-induced pressures are also intertwined and they begin almost at the beginning of freshman year.

23   "I had a freshman student I'll call Linda," one dean told me, "who came in and said she was under terrible pressure by her roommate, Barbara, who was much brighter and studied all the time. I couldn't tell her that Barbara had come in two days earlier to say the same thing about Linda."

24   The story is almost funny—except that it's not. It's systematic of all the pressures put together. When every student or every other student is working harder and doing better, the solution is

to study harder still. I see students going off to the library every night after dinner and coming back when it closes at midnight. I wish they would sometimes forget about their peers and go to a movie. I hear the clacking of typewriters in the rooms before dawn. I see the tension in their eyes when exams are approaching and papers are due: "Will I get everything done?"

25   Probably they won't. They will get sick. They will get "blocked." They will sleep. They will oversleep. They will bug out. Hey, Carlos, help!

26   Ultimately it will be the students' own business to break the circles in which they are trapped. They are too young to be prisoners of their parents' dreams and their classmates' fears. They must be jolted into believing in themselves as unique men and women who have the power to shape their own future.

27   "Violence is being done to the undergraduate experience," says Carlos Hortas. "College should be open-ended: at the end it should open many, many roads. Instead, students are choosing their goal in advance, and their choices narrow as they go along. It's almost as if they think that the country has been codified in the types of jobs that exist—that they've got to fit into certain slots. Therefore, fit into the best-paying slot.

28   "They ought to take chances. Not taking chances will lead to a life of colorless mediocrity. They'll be comfortable. But something in the spirit will be missing."

29   If I have described the modern undergraduate primarily as a driven creature who is largely ignoring the blithe spirit inside who keeps trying to come out and play, it's because that's where the crunch is, not only at Yale but throughout American education. It's why I think we should all be worried about the values that are nurturing a generation so fearful of risk and so goal-obsessed at such an early age.

30   I tell students that there is no one "right" way to get ahead—that each of them is a different person, starting from a different point and bound for a different destination. I tell them that change is a tonic and that all the slots are not codified nor the frontiers closed. One of my ways of telling them is to invite men and women who have achieved success outside the academic world to come and talk informally with my students during the year. They are heads of companies or ad agencies, editors of magazines, politicians, public officials, television magnates, labor leaders, business executives, Broadway producers, artists, writers, economists, photographers, scientists, historians—a mixed bag of achievers.

31   I ask them to say a few words about how they got started. The students assume that they started in their present profession and

knew all along that it was what they wanted to do. Luckily for me, most of them got into their field by a circuitous route, to their surprise, after many detours. The students are startled. They can hardly conceive of a career that was not pre-planned. They can hardly imagine allowing the hand of God or chance to nudge them down some unforeseen trail.

Thinking It Through

1. Where does Zinsser state or at least suggest the main idea of the essay? Restate that thesis in your own words.

2. The introduction of Zinsser's essay is longer than usual. Describe the type of information used to develop this introduction.

3. Zinsser divides or classifies the types of pressure that college students struggle with into four categories. He then says that the pressures can be seen as two intertwined pairs. Look again at paragraphs 13 and 22. Explain how economic pressure and parental pressure are related. Then explain how peer pressure is related to self-induced pressure.

4. Working to get good grades is generally considered a positive trait. Why does the author view it as negative and destructive?

5. How does meeting successful men and women help students to gain a healthier perspective?

6. Zinsser's essay was written several years ago. Are any of the pressures described here no longer of concern to students? Are there additional pressures driving students today that are not described here? What are they? Give an example that illustrates the point.

Thinking and Writing

What motivates students currently taking college courses to work hard for good grades? Examine your own behavior first. List the pressures or other strong motivations you feel to perform well in the courses you take. Then think of other students you know; what pressures them to succeed in class? Make another list of pressures that you believe affect others. Combine the two lists and eliminate duplication. If possible, share the combined list with your classmates, and make whatever changes you wish as a result of your discussion.

Choose three or four of the strongest pressures to succeed in college and write your own essay in which you explain what you believe motivates students currently in college to struggle to succeed. Remember to give examples and illustrations to make your points clear and interesting to the reader.

Dress for Success

JOHN T. MOLLOY

First Thoughts

John T. Molloy describes himself as a "wardrobe engineer." He conducted considerable research in the mid-seventies to learn how certain items of clothing affect the way a person is accepted and believed by others. He used the results of this research to teach people how to dress to project the most successful image for business and personal relationships. This excerpt first briefly describes his research techniques and then describes the process by which Molloy determined the impressions made by black and beige men's raincoats. Examine the steps in the process to see if they seem clear and logical.

Word List

METHODOLOGY (paragraph 1):   a system of procedures

SUBSTANTIATE (paragraph 1):   support

HYPOTHESIS (paragraph 1):   theory

FRUGAL (paragraph 2):   thrifty

VALIDITY (paragraph 2):   reliability

JARGON (paragraph 3):   words familiar to a particular group

SOCIOECONOMIC (paragraph 4):   both social and economic

CREDIBILITY (paragraph 4):   believability

INTUITIVELY (paragraph 5):   instinctively

ASCERTAIN (paragraph 6):   learn

VARIABLES (paragraph 7):   factors that could influence results

HYPOTHESIZE (paragraph 9):   theorize

INTRINSIC (paragraph 9):   natural

PREDOMINANCE (paragraph 9):   great importance

NONDESCRIPT (paragraph 15):   ordinary

1   *Dress for Success* is intended as a practical tool, not as an academic exercise. I am not (and you are not) interested in theory for its own sake. We will leave that to the educators. If I were to describe the methodology and results of all my experiments, surveys and tests in order to substantiate every statement in this

book, it would run several thousand pages and be absolutely useless. I will spare you that, but for those with backgrounds in research, I should state that I followed standard research techniques with several exceptions. There was virtually no review of the literature in the field, since there is no literature in the field. At the stage of creating a hypothesis, I refrained from making a researcher's prediction unless it had to be included in the formal statement of the hypothesis (these predictions can become self-fulfilling prophecies, I believe).

2   When designing the data-gathering instrument, I often had to limit my objective since I found that corporations were unwisely frugal when appropriating funds for this essential work. But I can state that I never undertook a new project without testing and retesting the reliability of the testing instrument, and the only validity I considered adequate was predictive validity. While this is the validity measure that is least often used in the social disciplines, it is by far the best. Naturally, I ran pilot projects when needed and set up control groups whenever possible.

3   I am now going to present a few examples of my research in a way that will make them clear to any reader who will bear with me, and will offer no more technical jargon.

THE PROOF: WHAT WORKS AND WHAT DOESN'T

4   Since I had very early on discovered that the socioeconomic value of a man's clothing is important in determining his credibility with certain groups, his ability to attract certain kinds of women and his acceptance to the business community, one of the first elements I undertook to research was the socioeconomic level of all items of clothing.

5   Take the raincoat, for example. Most raincoats sold in this country are either beige or black; those are the two standard colors. Intuitively I felt that the beige raincoat was worn generally by the upper-middle class and black by the lower-middle class.

6   First I visited several Fifth Avenue stores that cater almost exclusively to upper-middle-class customers and attempted to ascertain the number of beige raincoats versus black raincoats being sold. The statistical breakdown was approximately four to one in favor of beige. I then checked stores on the lower-middle-class level and found that almost the reverse statistic applied. They sold four black raincoats to each beige raincoat.

7   This indicated that in all probability my feeling was correct, but recognizing that there were many variables that could discredit such preliminary research, I set the second stage in motion. On rainy days, I hired responsible college students to stand

outside subway stations in determinable lower-middle-class neighborhoods and outside determinable upper-middle-class suburban commuter-stations, all in the New York area. The students merely counted the number of black and beige raincoats. My statistics held up at approximately four to one in either case, and I could now say that in the New York area, the upper-middle class generally wore beige raincoats and the lower-middle-class generally wore black ones.

8   My next step was to take a rainy-day count in the two different socioeconomic areas in Chicago, Los Angeles, Dallas, Atlanta and six equally widespread small towns. The research again held up; statistics came back from the cities at about four to one and from the small towns at about two-and-a-half to three to one. (The statistics were not quite that clear cut, but averaged out into those ranges.)

9   From these statistics I was able to state that in the United States, the beige raincoat is generally worn by members of the upper-middle class and the black raincoat generally worn by members of the lower-middle class. From this, I was able to hypothesize that since these raincoats were an intrinsic part of the American environment, they had in all probability conditioned people by their predominance in certain classes, and automatic (Pavlovian) reactions could be expected.

10   In short, when someone met a man in a beige raincoat, he was likely to think of him as a member of the upper-middle class, and when he met a man in a black raincoat, he was likely to think of him as a member of the lower-middle class. I then had to see if my hypothesis would hold up under testing.

11   My first test was conducted with 1362 people—a cross section of the general public. They were given an "extrasensory perception" test in which they were asked to guess the answers to a number of problems to which the solutions (they were told) could only be known through ESP. The percentage of correct answers would indicate their ESP quotient. Naturally, a participant in this type of test attempts to get the right answer every time and has no reason to lie, since he wants to score high.

12   In this test, among a group of other problems and questions, I inserted a set of almost identical "twin pictures." There was only one variable. The twin pictures showed the same man in the same pose dressed in the same suit, the same shirt, the same tie, the same shoes. The only difference was the raincoat—one black, one beige. Participants were told that the pictures were of twin brothers, and were asked to identify the most prestigious of the two. Over 87 percent, or 1118 people, chose the man in the beige raincoat.

13   I next ran a field test. Two friends and I wore beige raincoats for one month, then switched to black raincoats the following month. We attempted to duplicate our other clothing during both months. At the end of each month, we recorded the general attitude of people toward us—waiters, store clerks, business associates, etc. All three of us agreed that the beige raincoat created a distinctly better impression upon the people we met.

14   Finally, I conducted one additional experiment alone. Picking a group of business offices at random, I went into each office with a *Wall Street Journal* in a manila envelope and asked the receptionist or secretary to allow me to deliver it personally to the man in charge. When wearing a black raincoat, it took me a day and a half to deliver twenty-five papers. In a beige raincoat, I was able to deliver the same number in a single morning.

15   The impression transmitted to receptionists and secretaries by my black raincoat and a nondescript suit, shirt and tie clearly was that I was a glorified delivery boy, and so I had to wait or was never admitted. But their opinion of me was substantially altered by the beige raincoat worn with the same other clothes. They thought I might be an associate or friend of the boss because that is what I implied, and they had better let me in. In short, they reacted to years of preconditioning and accepted the beige raincoat as a symbol of authority and status while they rejected the black raincoat as such.

16   This study was conducted in 1971. And although more and more lower-middle-class men are wearing beige raincoats each year (basically because of improved wash-and-wear methods that make them much less expensive to keep clean), the results of the study remain valid and will continue to be for years to come. You cannot wear a black raincoat, and you must wear a beige raincoat —if you wish to be accepted as a member of the upper-middle class and treated accordingly (among all other raincoat colors, only dark blue tests as applicable).

Thinking It Through

1. Try to decide whom Molloy envisions as his reader. Try to state specifically how his choice of audience influences what he writes.

2. Does Molloy's description of his research techniques convince you that his conclusions are likely to be valid? Why or why not?

3. Molloy says that he used only research tools that had the ability to predict results accurately. What "tools" are described in paragraphs 6 and 7? Is this type of evidence convincing? Why or why not?

4. Molloy says in paragraph 3 that he "will offer no more technical jargon." Does he actually avoid words that are considered jargon by the general reader? If not, cite examples.

5. Locate the paragraph in which Molloy makes an inference about raincoats. (Inferences are discussed in Chapter 2.) From what observations is the inference drawn? Do you think there is enough evidence to declare the inference valid?

Thinking and Writing

Molloy says that "the socioeconomic value of a man's clothing is important in determining his credibility with certain groups, his ability to attract certain kinds of women and his acceptance to the business community . . ."

Is the same true of women? Does women's clothing have "socioeconomic value"—that is, does their clothing help create their image? Are women, especially professional women, judged successful or not partly by the way they dress? Write an essay that examines this question. You may draw on your own knowledge and experience; you may also want to check the library for recent information or to interview professional women on your campus or in your community.

Fear of Success

GAIL SHEEHY

First Thoughts   Gail Sheehy explains that both women and men have been trained to fear success in particular areas of their lives. If women are taught that their proper role is to please a man, they may subconsciously cause themselves to fail to achieve their potential because they fear the results of being successful. Men may also be afraid to express the parts of their personality that would allow them to show emotion and sympathy. Sheehy calls this "fear of softness." As you read, notice how Sheehy develops her explanations of these two general ideas by using analysis, specific details, and illustrations to make her points clear.

Word List   AMBIVALENCE (paragraph 1):   indecision, uncertainty

INHIBIT (paragraph 2):   restrict

DILEMMA (paragraph 3):   problem to which there is no satisfactory solution

THWARTED (paragraph 3):   prevented

AMUCK (paragraph 3):   out of control

VIRILITY (paragraph 4):   manliness

RENOUNCE (paragraph 4):   give up

CAUTERIZE (paragraph 4):   burn or sear

DEVASTATION (paragraph 5):   destruction

UNENCUMBERED (paragraph 6):   unburdened

INTROSPECTION (paragraph 6):   self-searching

FLUENCY (paragraph 6):   easy use

CUL-DE-SAC (paragraph 7):   dead-end street

1   The fear of success in women was first demonstrated by Matina Horner in 1968. As a doctoral student at the University of Michigan, she showed that the motive to achieve in women college students was complicated by ambivalence. To be tops in academic performance, particularly under competitive conditions, and most especially when the competition was with men, might result in a loss of love and popularity. The more competent the woman, the greater her conflict about achieving.

184

2   But there is more to it than the worry that no one will marry a woman if she's too successful and independent. We must remember that Horner's subjects were college freshmen. The evidence . . . collected here is that the combined fear of success and of failure can carry over even after a woman finds an encouraging mate . . . and often continues to inhibit women who have been married, either happily or miserably, for a decade or two.

3   The deeper psychological dilemma has to do with defying the inner custodian. A woman who was taught by her parents that her proper role is to please a man runs a great risk if she becomes too independent. Just as she is about to seize control of her own destiny, that inner custodian, thwarted by her disobedience, might run amuck. It might show its nasty tyrant side and make a fool of her. Or punish by causing her to fail: I told you so. In her darkest fantasies, she would be left stranded, lost, alone.

FEAR OF SOFTNESS

4   Boys too are invited to suppress certain aspects of their personalities, in particular, anything that might interfere with action and complicate the display of virility. Added to the demand that a boy renounce the primary attachment to mother, he learns that to please the traditional father and/or to gain approval in the world, he must cauterize many of his emotions. Men are to be strong, not soft.

5   One of the most useful defenses of the self is denial. When boys feel weak or fearful or about to cry, they are taught to deny the emotion, project it onto an outer obstacle, externalize it. When boys first scrimmage on the football field, they are not encouraged to admit any doubts about injury they might do to themselves or to empathize with the opposing players they leave in a heap of pain. And surely, no one in command of B-52 pilots in Vietnam encouraged those young men to think about the unseeable devastation they were leaving below. The B-52 may be the maximum technological expression to date of the militaristic man's continuing refusal to be human.

6   Although denial and externalization are immature defense mechanisms, they serve the young person's need to wall off inner doubts while the first major outer risks are run. Action is more easily possible when one is unencumbered by much introspection or empathy, even though this means that fluency with one's emotions is forfeited, at least in youth.

7   Until very recently in our culture, most men and women spent a good part of their twenties and thirties living one of two illusions:

that career success would make them immortal, or that a mate would complete them. (Even now, those illusions die very hard.) Men and women were on separate tracks. The career as an all-encompassing end to life turned out to be a flawed vision, an emotional cul-de-sac. But did attaching oneself to a man and children prove to be any less incomplete as life's ultimate fulfillment?

8   Each sex seemed to have half the loaf and was uncomfortable about the half they were missing. Did the missing halves even belong to the same loaf? Men had the credentials with which to barter for external advancement. Women had the perceptiveness to say: "What good is becoming president if you lose touch with your family and your feelings?"

9   The woman was jealous of the man's credentials. The man was disturbed by the woman's truth.

10   As men and women enter midlife, the tables begin to turn. Many men I interviewed found themselves wanting to learn how to be responsive. And a surge of initiating behavior showed up in most women. . . .

Thinking It Through

1. A gender stereotype is a commonly accepted idea of what the typical woman or man should be like. Using the details given in this essay, briefly describe the female and male American gender stereotypes.

2. Sheehy calls denial an "immature defense mechanism." What qualities do even mature men and women deny to defend their images of themselves?

3. In paragraph 7 Sheehy says that until recently "most men and women spent a good part of their twenties and thirties living one of two illusions." In your own words, what were these illusions? Do you know people who still have them?

4. Based on what Sheehy writes, how do you think an individual—man or woman—might find success as a *person*?

Thinking and Writing

Based on what Sheehy writes and your own knowledge of human behavior (perhaps from a psychology or sociology class you are taking), write an essay of several paragraphs in which you explain how certain kinds of childhood experiences contribute to gender stereotyping. You might consider the toys that children are given, the chores they are assigned, the games they are taught, or other experiences of this type as possible topics. Remember to give illustrations, as Sheehy does in paragraph 5, to show your reader how these experiences lead the person to accept a particular attitude.

A "Real" Man

ERIC FLAUGHER

First Thoughts   In this essay a nontraditional student describes how he developed into a stereotypical "real man," how that role became unsatisfactory, and what he finally did to break out of the mold. Notice the writer's various changes in attitude—toward himself, his family, and others—as the essay develops.

Word List   INNATE (paragraph 1):   native or inborn

EMPATHY (paragraph 4):   compassion or sympathy

ANIMOSITY (paragraph 6):   resentment or dislike

ARROGANCE (paragraph 9):   vanity

FARCE (paragraph 9):   a mockery, something foolishly false

AGGRESSOR (paragraph 12):   the attacker

1   Being the first born of three other children in my family has left me with empty answers about my role as the elder brother. At a very young age I would have to take charge of my younger brother and two sisters, when my parents were out. Quickly after the parents were gone, I became the authoritarian. When trouble broke out, I became Conan the Destroyer and showed the inferior sized family members that I was the strength to be dealt with. I don't know why I acted this way; maybe it was innate, or maybe it was conditioned by the influence of my peers and my uncles on my behavior.

2   My uncles were younger than my mother and only four to eight years older than I. They were my role models and had a great influence on my attitude about how a man is supposed to behave. For extra money, I worked side by side with my uncles in the tobacco, hay, or corn fields. Working with them, I saw that real men fought other men at the first sign of disagreement. Real men didn't wear shorts or ties. They had tanned backs, and those who didn't were sissies. I was conditioned to think that real men cussed when talking to other men, but never around a woman. Oh yes, they had to talk vulgar about women when there weren't any present. I can still feel my face turning red when they would tease me about losing my virginity.

3   As one can see, my uncles weren't very educated, but they had their skills and could outwork the handiest migrant worker. My stereotyped view of a real man was imprinted by my being hit on the head, punched in the shoulder, roughed around and taught their language.

4   This attitude was reinforced by my high school football team. The coach thought very highly of me when I was a freshman because of my scrappiness on defense. Before my junior year I became a leader on defense and gained respect by whipping a 210-pound lineman, just because he said he could handle me with ease. I should have been kicked off the team, but the coaches didn't like him anyway. So football supported my uncles' claim that real men hit hard and are relentless. Real men don't show pain or cry and have never heard the word "empathy."

5   But after high school reality of the world hit. After all, real men don't attend a university. They work! They have outdoor jobs and use their hands to make a living. Only sissies go to college, excluding athletes. After working at a welding job for a year, I noticed that I wasn't really satisfied with myself, and I began having some second thoughts about who I was and what I really wanted in life. I started to plan that spring to get back into football and school, without my uncles noticing my activities. Maybe they would think I was attending a vocational training school. Maybe it didn't matter.

6   So I started a workout program to help get myself into playing shape again. One day my workout buddy called to my attention that there was going to be a toughman contest in a nearby town. Maybe this was what I needed. I felt as if I were slipping because of my inactivity on the rough house scene. I was working with mostly thirty and forty-year-olds that seemed to respect each other and didn't try to dominate one another, as I was accustomed to seeing. Had I started to act like them? Surely not. Was I having what the teachers call an "identity crisis"? All I know is I didn't feel the same animosity toward people, and I didn't feel the security I once had in myself. Was I getting soft? My uncles didn't have much to say to me anymore; they probably didn't respect me for making a decision to return to school.

7   The two weeks before the contest were filled with hard work and a strict diet. My workout buddy gave me lots of encouragement and help during training. I didn't think about the contest much, just the respect I would receive when I won. Losing didn't even enter my mind. After all, I was nineteen, in shape, quick and had a background in scraps. My uncles and relatives would come by every now and then to watch me jump rope and ask if I were going to kick some tail at the contest.

8   My workout friend drove me to the contest, and for the first time I thought to myself that maybe, just maybe, I could lose. What if one of the contestants had a background in boxing? What if they had been training for months? Anxiety set in, and the butterflies were crowding my stomach.

9   The contestants were seated alone in the bleachers listening to the rules of the contest as I walked in. I knew I had to act like a real man and walk with an athletic stride that showed my arrogance and youth, even though I was nervous. The manager had us pick a name out of a hat and hand it to the fight organizer, but I knew this was a farce. They generally pick the best to fight the most unathletic looking in the early rounds.

10   Ten minutes before I started to put on my gear, I asked my friend to find some of my relatives in the crowd, but he couldn't see any. Oh, well. They probably got stuck doing something else. As I was waiting, I spoke to another contestant who told me he was fighting for the money ($1,500). He had recently divorced and needed it to pay the alimony he was behind on because of his unemployment. He asked me why I was here, but my mind went blank. He wished me good luck and thanked me for some of the pointers I gave him before he walked over to his metal chair.

11   I went to my corner of the ring where my friend started fitting me with 16-ounce gloves that felt like pillows and headgear that took him two minutes to put on because of his nervousness. I felt like a complete fool, but I had to gain back the respect that I had let slip away. As I looked across the ring, I saw my opponent. He was wearing brown socks with blue tennis shoes and had a pale, slender body that looked like Mr. Rogers or Pee Wee Herman. Man, I felt sorry for this guy. As he turned around, I noticed that he was the same one I was talking to earlier. I felt sorry for this guy who had huge bills and no prior experience in boxing or athletics.

12   The bell rang. I let him come to me and be the aggressor. What am I doing? I've always been the aggressor. I can't believe I'm actually feeling sorry for this guy who's trying to hit me. He came at me swinging wildly. I wanted the fight to be over to save him pain and to keep my uncles off my back about not being aggressive. So, I jabbed his nose with a left, then came down to the body with a left hook that buckled him and a right to the temple that made him fall to the canvas. He jumped to his feet quickly, with shaky legs, and made one last effort by head butting my chin. The referee quickly stopped the fight, and as I returned to the corner, I asked my friend to look at my chin because it hurt. What! I actually admitted feeling pain.

13   When I returned to the waiting room, I saw the guy I had just defeated trying to hide his tears, but for some reason I knew they weren't for himself. I went over to see what I could do. What! You mean I'm showing empathy now? He jumped up to congratulate me and said I was one hell of a fighter. I put my sweaty arm around his shoulder and pointed to my chin that was bleeding. He even apologized! I couldn't believe myself. Would people in the room think I was a faggot! I didn't even curse when I talked to him.

14   I went on to win the toughman contest after two more bouts, but the first fighter showed me what a real man was. My uncles and Dad never showed up and later admitted that they were afraid I might have lost and upset their many traditions.

15   Since that contest in 1982, I know that real men are people who care for others; they show empathy and respect for others. Real men also show character, responsibility, and do their best at whatever they choose to do in life. That slender man in the brown socks who fought his heart out against me showed me what class was all about. He was more of a real man than I ever thought about being.

ᐯᐯᐯᐯᐯᐯᐯᐯᐯᐯᐯᐯ

Thinking It Through

1. How is this essay organized? Can you think of another type of organization that would work as well?

2. Twice in this essay (in paragraphs 12 and 13) the writer suddenly shifts tenses. Why do you think he does this? Is it an effective technique? Why or why not?

3. What are the first signs that Flaugher is slightly uncomfortable with his family's concept of a "real man"? At what point does he actually begin to make a break with this tradition?

4. In your own words explain what Flaugher means in the last two sentences of his essay.

Thinking and Writing

Using yourself or someone you know as an example, write a paper showing what you believe a successful woman or man is. Begin your planning by listing everything about your model person that makes him or her a success as a man or woman. Then use these details to fill out your description. Of course, you will need to make a few general statements (notice Flaugher's last paragraph), but you should depend mainly on specific details and examples to make your ideas clear.

~~~~~~~~ Drugs

Just saying no doesn't cut it.
—Dr. Robert Millman

Children of the Night

JOHN ZACCARO, JR.

First Thoughts

In the summer of 1988, after this article was published, John Zaccaro, Jr., was sentenced to four months in prison and 300 hours of community service and fined $1,500 for selling drugs in 1986 while he was a student at Middlebury College in Vermont. John Zaccaro is the son of Geraldine Ferraro, former U.S. congresswoman and a candidate for the vice presidency of the United States. This article really tells two stories at once: one about John Zaccaro and one about the teenagers who try to survive on the streets.

Word List

BRAZEN (paragraph 4):   shameless, bold

WAIFS (paragraph 8):   children without homes

JEOPARDIZING (paragraph 19):   risking

PENDING (paragraph 19):   still to come

DEVASTATED (paragraph 20):   destroyed

NOTORIETY (paragraph 20):   bad reputation

CULINARY (paragraph 23):   having to do with cooking

AFFLUENT (paragraph 25):   rich

BRAVADO (paragraph 39):   a show of courage

1   It's one A.M., and the streets of New York are quiet now, the traffic stilled. Now it's the children's hour. Boys and girls, East Side, West Side, they're all around the town.

2   There's Susie, blue-eyed, hair the color of Kansas wheat, satin pants as tight as paint. Skittering in high heels, she sells sex to passing strangers in a neighborhood they call Hell's Kitchen.

3   Has she turned 16 yet? I see her every night as I drive by, riding an all-night van for Covenant House, a shelter for homeless and runaway youth. Sometimes I stop the van and we talk. Tonight she shoos me off with a flick of her hand. In the shadows her pimp is watching.

4   Downtown there's Marlene, strutting, tossing the dark mane of a new wig, inviting you to stare. Her spangled leotard is cut low

at the bosom and high at the thigh, flaunting everything, including a shock of pubic hair. We're in the meat-packing district, and this is TV (for transvestite) territory. Something is hidden after all. Marlene is really Marty, a brazen, confused 14-year-old boy.

5   Maybe this story should carry a warning label, like a medicine bottle or a pack of cigarettes. "Strong stuff. Could be hazardous to your peace of mind."

6   It should be said up front that at age 23 I have problems too. I have sleepless nights of my own. But my problems are nothing compared to the kids I see on the streets; when I ran into trouble, my family was there. I wait, we all wait, for the conclusion of my case. In the meantime I'm at school and working for the past year as a volunteer at the Covenant House. I've discovered a New York I never guessed at, and I've come to care about the kids who live in that shadow world. They've come to trust the white dove, the Covenant House symbol, on my shirt.

7   First let me explain Covenant House. Covenant House began on a cold, snowy night in 1968 with a midnight knock at the door of Father Bruce Ritter, a Franciscan priest working among the urban poor. Four boys and two girls stood there, shivering and sad-eyed, asking if they could sleep on the floor. He let them in. The next night there were more kids at the door. They had no place to go, and no existing social agency seemed ready or able to help these young street wanderers.

8   Father Bruce took them in also. Twenty years later some people—in and out of the church—still ask why he has given his life to these waifs. "I do what I do for God," he explains. "But sometimes God has a kid's face."

9   Today Covenant House operates seven shelters, in New York, Houston, Fort Lauderdale, New Orleans, Anchorage, Toronto (Canada) and Antigua, Guatemala. The shelters provide food and a place to sleep; health services and legal services; counseling to help some kids return home and others to make long-term plans for a different future; even a Rights of Passage program where older kids can finish their education, get job training and prepare for a successful life.

10   In the United States Covenant House touches 25,000 kids a year, more than any operation like it, but, for Father Bruce, still too few. A year ago the blue van began to roll, reaching out to the displaced kids who are too out of it or think they're too tough to knock on any door. They are white, black and Hispanic, poor and middle class. Is a teenage girl missing from your high school? Has the boy next door disappeared? I may have seen them on the streets.

11   On the West Side docks there's La Bamba, this week's street name for a homeless 18-year-old. My case made head-lines because of my parents, but, sadly, stories like his go unnoticed. He was pushed out the door three years ago, another throwaway kid, disposable as a tissue. He used to sell his body. Now he sells drugs. He's high on his own merchandise and full of street wisdom.

12   "What you see out here isn't real," he tells me. "It's fantastic. It's all plastic."

13   All over the city there are children like that, playing with sex and drugs. Most of them are good kids—living a bad life.

14   What everyone at Covenant House tries to do is pick up the pieces when they break. But there are so many of them. Most experts say there are more than a million homeless and runaway boys and girls. Some people think there could be as many as two million of these castaway kids.

15   Our van rolls around bringing sandwiches, on-the-spot counseling and a standing offer to help. "Go home," I want to tell them, but most of them can't. As many as two-thirds of them have no place to go—no home, no relative, no foster care, no institution, that will take them in.

16   Sometimes the police pick them up, but they're back the next day. I pour paper cup after cup of hot chocolate and try to talk them off the streets. I want to grab and take them someplace warm and safe. On a good night I might pull five or six in out of the cold.

17   On the street you learn not to ask for last names and nobody knows mine. I am just John, a friendly face in a blue van. Many of these kids pick up newspapers out of trash cans. If they read the stories about me and my family they don't make the connection.

18   And I'm glad of that. I'm proud of my family—my Mom for taking on a tough fight and my Dad . . . well, for going through a lot of grief in a gentle way that gives me a lot to imitate. But I didn't get to Covenant House as a "first choice" way of spending my time.

19   When I was arrested I was a senior and on the Dean's List at Middlebury College in Vermont. After my arrest I was allowed to finish my first semester but was told in no uncertain terms that I would not be permitted to finish my final semester and graduate without the school conducting its own internal hearing. I could not defend myself without jeopardizing my rights in the pending criminal action. So I withdrew. And then . . . well, things weren't easy. I tried to register at a college in New York to finish and get my degree. Two colleges turned me down because of the unre-

solved criminal matter in Vermont. Another would admit me but had a two-year residency requirement . . . which meant I would have to repeat two years of college when I needed only one semester to graduate. I decided to look for a job.

20   I've worked summers starting as a ball boy at the Forest Hills tennis tournament when I was 14. I've been a mail-room clerk, a bartender, a laborer on a construction site, a seaman on a merchant ship. I earned money and kept busy, and my parents wanted me to learn to do both. Now here I was, running up legal fees, growing impatient as the case dragged on and one employer after another turned me down. My Mom, who had helped so many college kids get jobs, was devastated by her inability to help me. "They don't want the notoriety of John Zaccaro working for them," she told me.

21   So after much discussion I decided to do volunteer work. Perhaps there was some group that needed my time and my energy. Perhaps there were some people who wouldn't care if I had no last name, who wouldn't close me out because of my prior actions, who wouldn't worry about their image if it somehow leaked that I was working for them.

22   And I found Covenant House. From the start it was special because they needed me as much as I needed them. When I told my parents, they were pleased. When I told my lawyers, they were not. They knew it meant my dealing with drug users. It would not be good for my image. I laughed. There were kids who needed help . . . kids without love, without homes, kids without hope. I've been lucky. These kids never had a fair chance.

23   At 8 P.M. Times Square is less crowded than earlier. The theatergoers are in their seats. The sex shops are just getting started. Three of us, two staff members and me, a volunteer, clean up the van and prepare the food. When I spent a college year studying in Italy, I also went to culinary school at night. I still enjoy cooking for my friends, but here I prepare a survival menu—baloney-and-cheese sandwiches, packs of donated cookies, gallons of Kool-Aid in the summer and hot chocolate in the winter.

24   By 10 o'clock we're cruising the downtown docks, mean and dark. We stop at one end to leave cards with the Covenant House address and telephone number in the wrecked cars that are abandoned here. Later tonight, kids will crawl into these hulks, and we want to tell them there is a safer place to sleep.

25   We pass a row of intact cars. I try not to think about what's happening in those back seats. The johns drive here from uptown and down, from the outer boroughs and the ring of affluent suburbs. Even after all the publicity about AIDS, the sex

business is still brisk. When these men drive home, what will they be bringing back to their wives and children?

26   We park at the end of a block. From out of the shadows, the kids come running, like innocent boys and girls chasing an ice-cream wagon. For some of these kids, we deliver their only food of the day. For others, we lend a willing ear to their problems.

27   They cluster around. Some straighten the clothes they've slept in. Some offer shy smiles and thank you's. Some put up brave fronts as they accept the sandwiches.

28   "Got one without mustard?" a young boy asks, hungry but picky. He's a runaway, begging for coins on the street, sleeping in an abandoned warehouse.

29   "Put some tomato on next time, John," a young girl laughs. "Think about my complexion." She shoplifts. She steals bread and milk, morning deliveries left in front of small groceries. Her stepfather lets her come home for Christmas and birthdays. On most nights she finds a parked bus at the terminal and sleeps there.

30   These kids survive by hiding their feelings. I have to go slow with them, trying to build a relationship. I offer cookies to show that someone cares. I try not to be disappointed when they don't take advantage of our help. I've learned that everyone deserves a second chance, or a third and fourth chance, however many it may take. . . .

31   It's past midnight and we're cruising Hell's Kitchen, driving slowly past the lineup of young girls. Susie waves to me. On the edge of a little park another girl stands, body rigid, face pale, eyes blank. She stares at the van and doesn't see it. When a trick touches her, she won't feel it. "Angel dust," my partner says. "With a crack chaser."

32   At the next corner two girls come to the van window for sandwiches. One of them keeps her head down, trying to hide the bruises on her face. These girls can earn $300 a night, and pimps get angry when they fall short. I push a card into her hand. "Keep this," I tell her. "Call us." . . .

33   The mobile phone rings and it's for me. "John, I want to talk." The voice is slurred and sleepy. "I've taken some pills . . ."

34   We find Christie in front of the place she works on Times Square. In the shop window, neon lights blink on—"nude dancing"—and off—"live sex shows." She's 17, pale, still baby-fat. "No hospital," she whispers. "I want to die."

35   Arm in arm, we walk up and down the street together. She has swallowed 30 pills. "Whatever was there. Some aspirin. Some downers. Some prescription stuff." Her eyes are closing. "But nothing special happened. Just the usual."

36   Finally she lets me coax her into the van, and we rush to Bellevue Hospital. One-third of all runaway girls try suicide. Another third threaten or think about it seriously. Christie is unconscious as we lift her body onto a stretcher. By the time my shift is over, maybe she'll be awake and we can talk some more.

37   It's almost 3 A.M., and we head for "the loop," the high-rent streets of the East Fifties. At night New York is a sexual department store, and somehow the shoppers know where to go. There are different streets for different drugs. The transvestites are in one place, the young girls in another. Here, the young boys are on sale.

38   We cruise slowly around the block to let everyone know we're here, and then we park, as usual on East 53rd. A dozen boys appear out of nowhere and then, in ones and twos, others come up to the van. "You're late," one of the regulars complains.

39   The boys are excited, full of high spirits and bravado. "Just hanging out," a skinny kid tells me. He does a little tap dance. "Just having fun with my friends."

40   They wait and it always happens. Two or three times a night a car slows down, "sometimes a limousine," the boy says, wide-eyed. Then he disappears for awhile, "on a date," as he puts it. When he comes back, his smile is a little dimmer, but he's $50 richer. "And sometimes more," he brags. He spends it as fast as he makes it, on hand-made shirts and designer drugs.

41   "Three months is a very long time on the streets," says Father Bruce. "Six months is literally forever. And in a year, it's over. Then they're just breathing, in and out, but dead inside. They become what they do. And they no longer care."

42   I hope he's wrong. That skinny kid has been out here for almost a year, and I can't give up on him. Yet it's going to take time to coax him off the only playground he knows. The dirty secret of the streets is that for some of these kids, staying there is exhilarating.

43   There are new faces out tonight. One of them looks shy, sleepy and about 14. I try but I can't make contact with him. Drugs are making his eyelids droop. "He's the youngest one out here," one of the regulars tells me, "and the johns are eating him up."

44   Another boy, thin, exhausted, about 18, is just off the bus from Washington, D.C. He was changing one city's streets for another's, but, earlier tonight, he was mugged. Four kids pulled him into a doorway and took everything he had, his wallet, his packet of drugs, even the $10 hidden in his sock.

45   "Do you mean it?" he asks. "Can you really give me a place to sleep? I'm trying to cut back on drugs," he says, rolling up a

sleeve, showing me heroin tracks that are healing. We can help with that too.

46   We drop him, shivering, feeling sick, at the shelter. We pass the Port Authority Bus Terminal, young boys and girls hugging the stone walls, trying to sleep on cardboard pallets. We make a last circle of the West Side streets. It's five in the morning but the girls, the johns, the pimps, are still doing business.

47   At dawn, we're back at the van headquarters. I call the hospital, but Christie is still asleep. "We saved a few kids," we tell each other. "It was a good night."

48   But I didn't see Bobby. He was one of the first street kids I met, a boy with gangly arms and dark eyes, big and round, like moon pies. He was 16, but pretending to be older.

49   I tried to talk him off the streets, but he wasn't ready. "I'm OK," he always grinned. He was surviving by selling his body to gay men and an occasional older woman.

50   I keep looking, but nobody has seen Bobby for two months. Maybe he has found an honest job. Maybe he has moved on to another city. Or maybe the wrong car slowed down at the curb, and Bobby disappeared into it.

51   He used to come running up to my van window for a sandwich and some lemonade. He'd tuck a second sandwich, "for later," into his pocket. "And some cookies," he'd always say. Chocolate chips were his favorites.

52   Bobby is missing. If you see him, tell him someone cares.

Thinking It Through

1. Numerous young people are briefly introduced by Zaccaro. Make several general statements based on the examples given in this essay that would accurately describe them all.

2. One way Zaccaro organizes his essay is by using references to the time of night. Why does he start at 1 A.M. and then move back to 8 P.M. several paragraphs later? Mention other devices he uses to help organize his material.

3. Look closely at paragraphs 19 and 20. What method of paragraph arrangement has Zaccaro used here? What transitional words does he use?

4. Zaccaro describes the young people sympathetically, as victims. At one point he writes: "Most of them are good kids—living a bad life." Do you accept this point of view? Why or why not?

5. Why do these young people often refuse to seek or even to accept help?

Thinking and Writing

Write a narrative about either the effect of drugs on someone's life or the process of running away. Use details from your knowledge of the circumstances to make the narrative vivid and interesting to the reader. Start by reviewing Chapter 4, "Writing Description and Narration," for advice about writing this type of essay. Then make a list of the parts of the situation that you want to include. Go over the list several times, and try to add to it each time you review it to help you recall specific details.

Make your first draft from this list, including as many of your details as you can. Keep in mind sentences like Zacarro's—"Downtown there's Marlene, strutting, tossing the dark mane of a new wig, inviting you to stare" or "On the edge of a little park another girl stands, body rigid, face pale, eyes blank"—that furnish interesting, realistic details.

If your instructor wishes, you can share this first draft in small groups with your classmates. They can suggest revisions to clarify the sequence of events or the description. Then you can revise your first draft until you are satisfied with it. Remember that first drafts are just that—first drafts. It is expected that they will be improved by revision.

Geraldine Ferraro: Just How Much Ought She Endure?

JOAN BECK

First Thoughts   Joan Beck, a columnist for the *Chicago Tribune*, expresses little sympathy for John Zaccaro, who himself writes so sympathetically of young drug users in "Children of the Night." Instead, Beck expresses sympathy for Zacarro's parents, especially his mother, Geraldine Ferraro, who stood by him through his trial and sentencing. She describes Zacarro's upbringing as one that should have prepared him to make better decisions. The Zacarro example leads Beck to ask questions about parents' responsibility for their children. When, if ever, does it end?

Word List   ENVIABLE (paragraph 1):   desirable, to be wished for

POIGNANT (paragraph 3):   emotional

BUFFERING (paragraph 5):   cushioning

ENTITLEMENT (paragraph 8):   right to something

EMPATHETIC (paragraph 9):   feeling as others feel

1   It's hard to feel much sympathy for John Zaccaro, Jr. He's no slum kid tempted to deal drugs as a way out of poverty for young men without the talents of Michael Jordan or William Perry. He is the privileged son of wealthy parents, bright enough to make it into and through a fine college. He had an enviable head start. And he wasn't just using cocaine because he couldn't resist peer pressure. He was pushing it.

2   What's sad is seeing his mother Geraldine Ferraro, walking in and out of court at his trial and at his sentencing last week, achingly supportive and obviously hurting.

3   The poignant pictures of Ferraro, whose son was sentenced to four months in prison along with 300 hours of community service and a $1,500 fine, point up how little guidance is available in one of the most difficult situations parents can face: What do you do when a young adult offspring gets into trouble?

200

4   Should you, like Ferraro and her husband, John Zaccaro, stand beside a 24-year-old guilty of selling illegal drugs? Claim that he was unfairly pursued and too harshly sentenced because of his family connections? Try to get him off with an appeal?

5   Or do you do more good by seeing that he faces up to the consequences of his behavior without your buffering? How much support and help can you give without sending the message that he is incapable of being a responsible adult or that his behavior isn't all that bad or that mommy and daddy will always be there to get him out of trouble, no matter what?

6   Or are some consequences—prison, for example—so devastating that you must help your grown-up child, whatever he has done? Do you owe him the chance to start over, to make up for his mistakes, to prove he learned his lesson? If you don't help him, what will happen to him?

7   There are no good answers, of course. *Money* magazine says an increasing number of parents have difficulty pushing adult offspring into successful independence. It's hard to break the habit of being supportive to a child, even when he's 23 or 28, and to wean him away from counting on his parents when the going gets rough.

8   *Money* points out that many youngsters now grow up with a sense of entitlement and fail to develop their own resources because they have always been handed whatever they need or want.

9   Be empathetic and supportive, *Money* advises. But give your grown-up child to understand that you won't help solve his problems with a check—or that if you do hand over help, you will expect certain results in return.

10   Yet, the parents of John Hinckley tried repeatedly to push him into being independent, on the advice of a psychiatrist. But that was the worst mistake he ever made, John's father said later, after the attempted assassination of President Reagan finally made it clear how seriously ill the young man was.

11   Often, parents can't be sure whether a young adult child is mentally ill, mixed up with drugs, acting out some normal adolescent rebellion, overly dependent, feeling a greedy sense of entitlement or simply being what one psychiatrist calls "bad."

12   And parents can't help telling themselves they could have caused the difficulty by making well-intentioned mistakes, by caring too much or too little.

13   I don't know the answers. It's easy to argue the issue when someone else's offspring is involved. But basically, I think parents never outgrow their long habit of picking up a hurting child (however old), and trying to make it all better—if not with a kiss, at least with cash.

14   And parents never outgrow the hope that if they just help this time, they will finally nudge their child into successful adulthood. I hope it turns out that way for Ferraro.

Thinking It Through

1. Joan Beck opens her *Chicago Tribune* article with the flat statement that "it's hard to feel much sympathy for John Zaccaro, Jr." She clearly *does* feel sorry for his mother, Geraldine Ferraro. Summarize the reasons Beck gives for not having sympathy for Zaccaro.

2. Beginning in paragraph 5, Beck generalizes about the experience with which many modern-day parents are faced. Beck balances her argument by mentioning one example that suggests an opposite point of view from the rest of the article. Explain what the example is and why she uses it.

3. Rethink the ideas presented in the essays by Zaccaro and Beck. Try to state in a sentence or two the main point that each writer makes. Clearly, these two writers present differing points of view, but restating their main points may show that they are writing about two different groups of people.

Thinking and Writing

Write an essay in which you state and support your opinion about the point Beck raises in her article about parental responsibility. When should parents expect their son or daughter to face their problems independently? Is there an age at which parents are justified in refusing to get involved in their childrens' problems? Why or why not? Recalling the details of John Zacarro's essay may help you think of different types of issues involved in the question.

After you have answered these questions so that you are sure of your own position on the topic, write the introduction to your essay. State your opinion on the topic as the main idea. Develop the essay by giving your reasons for believing as you do. Try to include examples from your personal experience or your reading to help the reader to understand your position clearly.

When you have finished your essay, examine each paragraph to see that it has a main idea and that the idea is clearly developed. Check to see if you have used enough transitional devices to link up the sentences of the paragraph. Do you also use clear pronoun references to help unify the paragraph?

Kids Who Sell Crack

JACOB V. LAMAR

First Thoughts   The three paragraphs that follow come from an article in *Time* magazine about the problem of children who become involved with drugs because of the quick, if dangerous, money they can make from selling them. Look at the arrangement of ideas in each paragraph to decide what type of paragraph development is used. Does each have a topic sentence?

Word List   DERIVATIVE (paragraph 1):   a substance obtained from another substance

TATTERED (paragraph 1):   torn

ENTICING (paragraph 1):   tempting

LURE (paragraph 1):   attraction

MANDATORY (paragraph 2):   required

UNIQUELY (paragraph 2):   one of a kind

RECYCLABLE (paragraph 2):   able to be used again

RESTRICTIVE CUSTODY (paragraph 2):   the legal right to limit or restrict a person's activities, often in an institution

APPRENTICE (paragraph 3):   someone learning a job

ENTERPRISING (paragraph 3):   inventive, ambitious

1   In the five years since crack first appeared in the U.S., this cheap, powerful cocaine derivative has virtually shredded what was left of the tattered social fabric of the ghetto. The driving force behind the drug epidemic is not just the highly addictive nature of crack; many young hustlers never touch the stuff. They are drawn by the more enticing lure of fast money. "They can make $1,000 a week dealing," says Blair Miller of the Adolescent Dual Diagnosis Unit in Detroit's Samaritan Health Center. "These kids have no other skills. It's very hard to resist." In some cities, the crack trade may be one of the bigger job programs for youngsters.

• • •

2   The thugs who founded the crack trade recognized early on that young teens do not run the risk of mandatory jail sentences that

courts hand out to older dealers. Because juveniles are rarely imprisoned for any great length of time, they provide a uniquely recyclable labor pool. "We have created a revolving door," says George Robinson, assistant district attorney for Fulton County, Ga., which covers Atlanta. "There is no provision under our law to mandate restrictive custody for these youths. They're selling drugs, and we're just spanking them on the hands."

•   •   •

3   Lookout is the entry-level position for nine- and ten-year-olds. They can make $100 a day warning dealers when police are in the area. Sometimes the pint-size apprentice is rewarded with the most fashionable sneakers, bomber jacket or bicycle. The next step up the ladder is runner, a job that can pay more than $300 a day. This is the youngster who transports the drugs to the dealers on the street from the makeshift factories where cocaine powder is cooked into rock-hard crack. Finally, an enterprising young man graduates to the status of dealer, king of the street. In a hot market like New York City, an aggressive teenage dealer can make up to $3,000 a day.

Thinking It Through

1. Paragraph 1 explains a serious problem that has developed in major cities. Restate the nature of the problem in your own words.

2. Describe the organization of the paragraph 1. You may need to review the discussion of paragraph organization in Chapter 7.

3. Paragraph 2 uses a cause and effect arrangement; the reader is led to understand how one thing brought about something else. What *cause* of the problem is discussed in this paragraph?

4. Describe the arrangement of specific details in paragraph 3. What transitional words help you to identify the pattern?

Thinking and Writing

1. Write a paragraph in which you summarize the reasons given in all three paragraphs for the problem of young children selling crack.

2. After you have summarized the problem, try to think of one way in which the problem might practically be solved. Write a paragraph proposing the solution. Begin with a topic sentence, and provide enough specific details to make the reader understand the idea you are proposing.

Shooting Up

ETHAN A. NADELMANN

First Thoughts Many people have argued that the sale and use of marijuana should be legalized. In "Shooting Up" Ethan Nadelmann extends this argument to say that all drugs should be legalized to eliminate the criminal activity associated with getting and using drugs. Nadelmann opens his essay by discussing four connections or links between drugs and crime. He makes frequent comparisons between the laws prohibiting drugs and the Prohibition of the 1920s when the sale and use of alcohol was illegal.

As you read, examine the organization of the essay to see if the connections on which Nadelmann bases his argument are clearly and convincingly presented. Consider also if the earlier Prohibition is a logical comparison to the present laws against drugs.

Word List INEVITABLE (paragraph 2): unavoidable

CONSEQUENCE (2): result

PROHIBITION (2): ban

ILLICIT (3): illegal

INHIBITIONS (3): restraints

UNLEASHING (3): letting loose

IMPONDERABLES (4): things that cannot reasonably be known

INHERENT (5): inborn

EQUIVALENTS (6): similar circumstances

SORDID (6): corrupt

FUTILE (7): useless

DISRUPTIVE (8): disturbing

ANALOGY (10): comparison

APT (10): appropriate

TAUTOLOGICAL (11): repetitive; saying the same thing in different words

1 Hamburgers and ketchup. Movies and popcorn. Drugs and crime.

2 Drugs and crime are so thoroughly intertwined in the public mind that to most people a large crime problem seems an

inevitable consequence of widespread drug use. But the historical link between the two is more a product of drug laws than of drugs. There are four clear connections between drugs and crime, and three of them would be much diminished if drugs were legalized. This fact doesn't by itself make the case for legalization persuasive, of course, but it deserves careful attention in the emerging debate over whether the prohibition of drugs is worth the trouble.

3   The first connection between drugs and crime—and the only one that would remain strong after legalization—is the commission of violent and other crimes by people under the influence of illicit drugs. It is this connection that most infects the popular imagination. Obviously some drugs do "cause" people to commit crimes by reducing normal inhibitions, lessening the sense of responsibility, and unleashing aggressive and other anti-social tendencies. Cocaine, particularly in the form of "crack," has earned such a reputation in recent years, just as heroin did in the 1960s and 1970s and marijuana did in the years before that.

4   Crack's reputation may or may not be more deserved than those of marijuana and heroin. Reliable evidence isn't yet available, but no illicit drug is as widely associated with violent behavior as alcohol. According to Justice Department statistics, 54 percent of all jail inmates convicted of violent crimes in 1983 reported having used alcohol just prior to committing the offense. The impact of drug legalization on this drug-crime connection is hard to predict. Much would depend on overall rates of drug abuse and changes in the nature of consumption, both imponderables. It's worth noting, though, that any shift in consumption from alcohol to marijuana would almost certainly reduce violent behavior.

5   The connection between drugs and anti-social behavior—which is inherent and may or may not be substantial—is often confused with a second link between the two that is definitely substantial and not inherent: many illicit drug users commit crimes such as robbery, burglary, prostitution, and numbers-running to earn enough money to buy drugs. Unlike the millions of alcoholics who support their habits for modest amounts, many cocaine and heroin addicts spend hundreds, maybe even thousands, of dollars a week. If these drugs were significantly cheaper—if either they were legalized or drug laws were not enforced—the number of crimes committed by drug addicts to pay for their habits would drop dramatically. Even if the drugs were taxed heavily to discourage consumption, prices probably would be much lower than they are today.

6   The third drug-crime link—also a byproduct of drug laws—is the violent, intimidating, and corrupting behavior of the drug

traffickers. Illegal markets tend to breed violence, not just because they attract criminally minded people but also because there are no legal institutions for resolving disputes. During Prohibition violent struggles between bootlegging gangs and hijackings of booze-laden trucks were frequent and notorious. Today's equivalents are booby traps that surround marijuana fields; the pirates of the Caribbean, who rip off drug-laden vessels en route to the United States; and the machine-gun battles and executions of the more sordid drug mafias—all of which occasionally kill innocent people. Most authorities agree that the dramatic increase in urban murder rates over the past few years is almost entirely due to the rise in drug-dealer killings, mostly of one another.

7   Perhaps the most unfortunate victims of drug prohibition laws have been the residents of America's ghettos. These laws have proved largely futile in deterring ghetto-dwellers from becoming drug abusers, but they do account for much of what ghetto residents identify as the drug problem. Aggressive, gun-toting drug dealers often upset law-abiding residents far more than do addicts nodding out in doorways. Meanwhile other residents perceive the drug dealers as heroes and successful role models. They're symbols of success to children who see no other options. At the same time the increasingly harsh criminal penalties imposed on adult drug dealers have led drug traffickers to recruit juveniles. Where once children started dealing drugs only after they had been using them for a few years, today the sequence is often reversed. Many children start using drugs only after working for older drug dealers for a while.

8   The conspicuous failure of law enforcement agencies to deal with the disruptive effect of drug traffickers has demoralized inner-city neighborhoods and police departments alike. Intensive crackdowns in urban neighborhoods, like intensive anti-cockroach efforts in urban dwellings, do little more than chase the menace a short distance away to infect new areas. By contrast, legalization of drugs, like legalization of alcohol in the 1930s, would drive the drug-dealing business off the streets and out of apartment buildings and into government-regulated, tax-paying stores. It also would force many of the gun-toting dealers out of business and convert others into legitimate businessmen. Some, of course, would turn to other types of criminal activities, just as some of the bootleggers did after Prohibition's repeal. Gone, though, would be the unparalleled financial gains that tempt people from all sectors of society into the drug-dealing business.

9   Gone, too, would be the money that draws police into the world of crime. Today police corruption appears to be more pervasive than at any time since Prohibition. In Miami dozens of law

enforcement officials have been charged with accepting bribes, ripping off drug dealers, and even dealing drugs themselves. In small towns and rural communities in Georgia, where drug smugglers from the Caribbean and Latin America pass through, dozens of sheriffs have been implicated in corruption. In one New York police precinct, drug-related corruption has generated the city's most far-reaching police scandal since the late 1960s. Nationwide, over 100 cases of drug-related corruption are now prosecuted each year. Every one of the federal law enforcement agencies with significant drug enforcement responsibilities has seen an agent implicated.

10   It isn't hard to explain the growth of this corruption. The financial temptations are enormous relative to other opportunities, legitimate or illegitimate. Little effort is required. Many police officers are demoralized by the scope of drug traffic, the indifference of many citizens, a frequent lack of appreciation for their efforts, and the seeming futility of it all; even with the regular jailing of drug dealers, there always seem to be more to fill their shoes. Some police also recognize that their real function is not so much to protect victims from predators as to regulate an illicit market that can't be suppressed but that much of society prefers to keep underground. In every respect, the analogy to Prohibition is apt. Repealing drug prohibition laws would dramatically reduce police corruption. By contrast, the measures currently being proposed to deal with the growing problem, including more frequent and aggressive internal inspection, offer little promise and cost money.

11   The final link between drugs and crime is the tautological connection: producing, selling, buying, and consuming drugs is a crime in and of itself that occurs billions of times each year nationwide. Last year alone, about 30 million Americans violated a drug law, and about 750,000 were arrested, mostly for mere possession, not dealing. In New York City almost half the felony indictments were on drug charges, and in Washington, D.C., the figure was more than half. Close to 40 percent of inmates in federal prisons are there on drug-dealing charges, and that population is expected to more than double within 15 years.

12   Clearly, if drugs were legalized, this drug-crime connection—which annually accounts for around $10 billion in criminal justice costs—would be severed. (Selling drugs to children would, of course, continue to be prosecuted.) And the benefits would run deeper than that. We would no longer be labeling as criminals the tens of millions of people who use drugs illicitly, subjecting them to the risk of arrest, and inviting them to associate with drug dealers (who may be criminals in more senses of the word).

The attendant cynicism toward the law in general would diminish, along with the sense of hostility and suspicion that otherwise law-abiding citizens feel toward police. . . .

Thinking It Through

1. Nadelmann states the main idea of his argument in paragraph 2: "But the historical link between the two [drugs and crime] is more a product of drug laws than of drugs." This main idea is based on understanding cause and effect; do drug laws *cause* the crimes? Try to answer this question for yourself as you look at each of the four "connections" discussed. Then be prepared to discuss with your class or in small groups of class members whether drug laws are a cause or an effect of crimes involving drugs.

2. In discussing the second connection between drugs and crime in paragraph 5, Nadelmann concludes that "even if the drugs were taxed heavily to discourage consumption, prices probably would be much lower than they are today." Is this a sound argument? Would it be possible for drug prices to be low enough to support drug habits without users turning to robbery, burglary, prostitution, and numbers-running? Form your own opinion, and be ready to discuss your ideas in class.

3. Reread paragraphs 7 and 8 and then state in your own words Nadelmann's reasons for believing that legalizing drugs would reduce criminal behavior, especially among children, in the ghettos. Do you find these reasons logical and convincing? Why or why not?

4. What, in your opinion, causes police and other law enforcement officials to accept bribes and participate in other illegal drug-related activities? Would legalization of drugs prevent this corruption of law enforcement?

5. Why does Nadelmann believe that legalizing drugs would increase Americans' respect for the law? Review and restate the reasons given in paragraphs 11 and 12.

Thinking and Writing

1. Review the article and list the four chief connections that, according to Nadelmann, link drugs and crime. Try to rewrite these four ideas in your own words. Now write a paragraph of 75 to 100 words in which you summarize the main idea of the article, including the four points you have just identified.

2. Begin your prewriting for an essay on the legalization of drugs by listing all the points you can think of to support the position that

drugs *should* be legalized. (Make sure you include any points you agree with from Nadelmann's essay.) Then list the problems that legalization of drugs would cause or the reason that drugs *should not* be legalized. It would be helpful for you to discuss this issue with your classmates and make notes as good ideas are shared. Make sure you have written down several points on each side of the argument before you complete your prewriting.

Now write an essay in which you discuss the pros and cons surrounding the issue of the legalization of drugs. As you write down a point for or against the position, make sure you develop and clarify the point with explanations, examples, or illustrations—whatever is needed to make the point clear to the reader.

You will need to decide how to arrange the positive and negative points you want to make. Will it be best to discuss all the positive points first or all the negative points first? Should you alternate positive and negative? Experiment with a scratch outline of key words to decide which arrangement will be most effective for your paper.

If possible, share a draft of your essay with a small group of students from your class or with a group of friends before you complete the draft you turn in to your instructor. Ask the group if you have presented the positive and negative positions clearly and fairly. A person reading your paper should finish it with a clear understanding of the issues.

Television

Television—a medium. So called because it is neither rare nor well-done.
—Ernie Kovacs

Exposing Media Myths: TV Doesn't Affect You as Much as You Think

JOANMARIE KALTER

First Thoughts

This article contradicts several widely believed myths or misconceptions about television news. Notice how Joanmarie Kalter organizes her essay: she states a "myth," states the "truth," and then gives support for her viewpoint. This is an effective way to structure a refutation or counterargument to something that has already been written or stated.

In the final paragraphs Kalter expands her argument to consider the advantages of tossing out the myths and thinking of TV news differently. Notice how this gives her earlier argument added importance.

Word List

VIRTUAL TRUISM (paragraph 1):   a statement almost wholly accepted as true

PREMISE (paragraph 2):   one of a series of statements leading to a logical conclusion

CANARD (paragraph 3):   a false report

QUERIED (paragraph 3):   asked

SUCCINCTLY (paragraph 7):   briefly

INDISPUTABLE (paragraph 7):   not arguable

BREVITY (paragraph 8):   briefness

BELATEDLY (paragraph 10):   later than might be expected

RAPT (paragraph 13):   deeply engaged or absorbed; entranced

GLITZED (paragraph 21):   overwhelmed or distracted by impressive, flashy techniques

1   Once upon a time, there was a new invention—television. It became so popular, so quickly, that more American homes now have a TV set (98 per cent) than an indoor toilet (97 per cent). Around this new invention, then, an industry rapidly grew, and

around this industry, a whole mythology. It has become a virtual truism, often heard and often repeated, that TV—and TV news, in particular—has an unparalleled influence on our lives.

2   Over the past 20 years, however, communications scholars have been quietly examining such truisms and have discovered, sometimes to their surprise, that many are not so true at all. *TV Guide* asked more than a dozen leading researchers for their findings and found an eye-opening collection of mythbusters. Indeed, they suggest that an entire body of political strategy and debate has been built upon false premises. . . .

3   **Myth No. 1:** Two-thirds of the American people receive most of their news from TV. This little canard is at the heart of our story. It can be traced to the now-famous Roper polls, in which Americans are queried: "I'd like to ask you where you usually get most of your news about what's going on in the world today. . . ." In 1959, when the poll was first conducted, 51 per cent answered "television," with a steady increase ever since. The latest results show that 66 per cent say they get most of their news from TV; only about a third credit newspapers.

4   Trouble is, that innocent poll question is downright impossible to answer. Just consider: it asks you to sort through the issues in your mind, pinpoint what and where you learned about each, tag it, and come up with a final score. Not too many of us can do it, especially since we get our news from a variety of sources. Even pollster Burns Roper concedes, "Memories do get fuzzy."

5   Scholars have found, however, that when they ask a less general, more specific question—Did you read a newspaper yesterday? Did you watch a TV news show yesterday?—the results are quite different. Dr. John Robinson, professor of sociology at the University of Maryland, found that on a typical day 67 per cent read a newspaper, while 52 per cent see a local or national TV newscast. Dr. Robert Stevenson, professor of journalism at the University of North Carolina, analyzed detailed diaries of TV use, and further found that only 18 per cent watch network news on an average day, and only 13 per cent pay full attention to it. Says Robinson, "TV is part of our overall mix, but in no way is it our number one source of news."

6   Yet it's a myth with disturbing consequences. Indeed, it is so widespread, says Dr. Mark Levy, associate professor of journalism at the University of Maryland, that it shapes—or misshapes—our political process. In the words of Michael Deaver, White House deputy chief of staff during President Reagan's first term, "The majority of the people get their news from television, so . . . we construct events and craft photos that are designed for

30 seconds to a minute so that it can fit into that 'bite' on the evening news." And thus the myth, says Levy, "distorts the very dialogue of democracy, which cannot be responsibly conducted in 30-second bites."

7   **Myth No. 2:** TV news sets the public agenda. It was first said succinctly in 1963, and has long been accepted: while the mass media may not tell us what to think, they definitely tell us what to think about. And on some issues, the impact of TV is indisputable: the Ethiopian famine, the Challenger explosion. Yet for the more routine story, new research has challenged that myth, suggesting TV's influence may be surprisingly more limited.

8   For one thing, TV news most often reacts to newspapers in framing issues of public concern. Dr. David Weaver, professor of journalism at Indiana University, found that newspapers led TV through the 1976 campaign. Given the brevity of broad-casts, of course, that's understandable. "TV has no page 36," explains Dr. Maxwell McCombs, professor of communications at the University of Texas. "So TV journalists have to wait until an issue has already achieved substantial public interest." TV, then, does not so much set the public agenda as spotlight it.

9   Even among those issues spotlighted, viewers do make independent judgments. It seems the old "hypodermic" notions no longer hold, says Dr. Doris Graber, political science professor at the University of Illinois. "We're not sponges for this stuff, and while TV may provide the raw material, people do select."

10   Indeed, even TV entertainment is less influential than once was thought. According to Robinson, studies found no difference in racial attitudes among those who saw *Roots* and those who didn't. Ditto "The Day After" on nuclear war, and *Amerika* on the Soviets. As for news, Graber notes that the public took a long time to share the media's concern about Watergate, and even now are lagging the media on Iran-Contragate. And finally, there are many issues on which the press must belatedly catch up with the public. Which brings us to . . .

11   **Myth No. 3:** TV news changed public opinion about the war in Vietnam. Contrary to this most common of beliefs, research shows just the opposite. Lawrence Lichty, professor of radio/television/film at Northwestern University, analyzed network war coverage and found that it did not become relatively critical until 1967. By then, however, a majority of Americans already thought U.S. involvement in Vietnam was a mistake. And they thought so not because of TV coverage, but because of the number of young Americans dying.

12   Yet this fable about the "living-room war" is so accepted it has become "fact": that gory TV pictures of bloody battles under-

mined public support for the war; that, in a 1968 TV-news special, Walter Cronkite mistakenly presented the Tet offensive as a defeat for the U.S.; and that, because President Johnson so believed in the power of TV, he concluded then that his war effort was lost.

13   In fact, Lichty found few "gory" pictures. "TV presented a distant view," he says, with less than five per cent of TV's war reports showing heavy combat. Nor, as we now know, was a rapt audience watching at home in their living rooms. As for Cronkite's report on the Tet offensive, the CBS anchor said on the evening news, "First and simplest, the Vietcong suffered a military defeat." And, in his now-famous TV special, Cronkite concluded, "we are mired in a stalemate," and should "negotiate." By that time, Lichty says, "public opinion had been on a downward trend for a year and a half. A majority of Americans agreed." And so Johnson's concern, it seems, was not that Cronkite would influence public opinion, but rather that he reflected it.

14   Indeed, Prof. John Mueller of the University of Rochester has compared the curve of public opinion on the war in Vietnam, covered by TV, with that of the war in Korea, hardly covered. He found the two curves strikingly similar: in both cases, public support dropped as the number of American deaths rose.

15   Disturbingly, the misconception about TV's influence in Vietnam has had broad consequences, for it has framed an important debate ever since. Can a democratic society, with a free flow of dramatic TV footage, retain the public will to fight a war? Many argue no. And this has been the rationale more recently for censoring the Western press in the Falklands and Grenada. Yet it is, says Lichty, a policy based on a myth.

16   **Myth No. 4:** TV today is the most effective medium in communicating news. Most of us think of TV fare as simple, direct, easy to understand—with the combination of words and pictures making it all the more powerful. But recent research shows that TV news, as distinct from entertainment, is often very confusing. In study after study, Robinson and Levy have found that viewers understand only about a third of network news stories.

17   Why is TV news so tough to understand? Dr. Dan Drew, professor of journalism at Indiana University, suggests that the verbal and visual often conflict. Unlike TV entertainment, in which the two are composed together, TV-news footage is gathered first, and the story it illustrates often diverges. We may see fighting across the Green Line in Beirut—for a story about peace talks. We may see "file footage" of Anglican envoy Terry Waite walking down the street—for a story on his disappearance. As viewers try to make sense of the visual, they lose the gist of the

verbal. "The myth," says Levy, "is that since we are a visual medium, we must always have pictures. . . . But that's a disaster, a recipe for poor communication."

18   Journalists also are much more familiar with the world of public affairs, says Levy, and rely on its technical jargon: from "leading economic indicators" to "the Druse militia." Their stories, say researchers, are overillustrated, with most pictures on the screen for less than 20 seconds. They assume, mistakenly, that viewers pay complete attention, and so they often do not repeat the main theme. Yet while understanding TV news takes concentration, watching TV is full of distractions. In one study, researchers mounted cameras on top of sets and recorded the amount of time viewers also read, talked, walked in and out of the room. They concluded that viewers actually watch only 55 per cent of what's on.

19   The audience does recall the extraordinary, such as a man on the moon, and better comprehends human-interest stories. But since most news is not covered night after night, tomorrow's broadcast tends to wash away today's. "People don't remember much from TV news," says Graber. "It's like the ocean washing over traces that have been very faintly formed."

20   Today's TV news is carefully watched by politicians, who keep a sharp eye on how they're covered. But while it may provide theater for a handful, this research increasingly shows it's lost on the American public. And sadly, then, hard-working TV journalists may be missing an opportunity to inform.

21   Yet TV remains a medium with great potential. And studies show that it does extend the awareness of the poor and ill-educated, who cannot afford additional sources. What's more, research suggests that the clarity of TV news can be improved—without compromising journalistic standards. "We have been glitzed by the glamour of TV, all these gee-whiz gimmicks," says Robinson. "And we have lost sight of one of the oldest and most durable findings of communications research. . . . The most important element is the writer, who sits at a typewriter and tries to tell the story in a simple and organized way. That's the crucial link."

22   Research also shows that viewers want a broadcast they can understand. The success of "60 Minutes" proves there's an audience still hungry for sophisticated factual information. "When someone does this for news, they'll grab the ratings," says Levy. "Nobody loses!" Ironically, no corporation would launch an ad campaign without extensive testing on how best to reach its audience. But many broadcast journalists, working under intense pressure, remain unaware of the problems. "There's a lot we have to learn about how people comprehend," says William

Rubens, NBC research vice-president. "But no, it hasn't been the thrust of our research." According to Robinson and Levy, this requires the attention of those in charge, a collective corporate will. With the networks under a financial squeeze, their news audiences having recently declined some 15 per cent, "This may be the time for them to rethink their broadcasts," says Levy.

23   And if they do, they may just live . . . happily ever after.

Thinking It Through

1. What exactly is a myth? If you are not sure of the various definitions of the word, check your dictionary. Why does Kalter use the word as she does in her article?

2. In discussing myths 1 and 2, and to some extent myth 4, Kalter adds information between the statement of the myth and her statement of the truth. What kind of information is it, and why does she introduce it?

3. Why does Kalter consider the results of the Roper polls that she discusses in paragraphs 3 and 4 unreliable?

4. When Kalter mentions her sources of information in paragraphs 5, 6, 8, 9, and elsewhere, how does she help to establish them as authorities?

5. In paragraph 17 the author asks: "Why is TV news so tough to understand?" What answers does she give?

6. In paragraph 21 Kalter says that "TV remains a medium with great potential." Why does it have such potential? What changes are necessary before this potential can be realized?

Thinking and Writing

1. If you have an opportunity, watch the report of an important event on network news and read the report of that same event in a large daily newspaper. When you see the report on TV, note what seem to be the most important facts. Briefly describe your reaction to the news story. Do the same when you read the newspaper account. Then write a brief (two- or three-paragraph) paper describing the differences in the two types of reporting and your responses to them. Mention whether or not the two presentations have any effect on your understanding of the event.

2. A number of TV critics claim that watching soap operas and popular crime shows affects the attitudes and behavior of viewers. If you and others you know watch such shows, do you think this claim is accurate, or is it another myth? Write a paper supporting one side or the other of this question. You will strengthen your case by mentioning specific programs and the response you and others have to them.

~~~~~~

Hooked Parents

MARIE WINN

First Thoughts   "Hooked Parents" is from a chapter in Marie Winn's popular book, *The Plugged-In Drug*. A clue to the main ideas developed in this essay come in paragraph 3: "Two factors combine to 'hook' parents on using television: its unique ability to pacify children and its ready availability."

   Look for the two factors named here and find where each is discussed in the essay. Evidence to show television's "unique ability to pacify children" includes a contrast between children's behavior when watching and not watching TV. Evidence to show the effect of TV's "ready availability" is made up of a series of real-life examples. The essay ends with comments about some of the problems of parents' decreasing involvement with children.

Word List   READY (paragraph 3):   convenient

HYPOTHESIS (paragraph 4):   an idea that has not yet been proved

RESORT TO (paragraph 8):   turn to for help

ASPECT (paragraph 13):   appearance

SUBTLE (paragraph 13):   difficult to notice

PERSISTENTLY (paragraph 27):   determinedly

IMPETUS (paragraph 27):   motivation

~~~~~~~~~~~~~~~~~~~~~   1   A mother of three children admits:

2   "I'm afraid not to have a television set even though I know the kids would probably be a lot better off without it. What would I do when I needed it? I'd just go to pieces. I can't imagine managing without it. I'm hooked on using it."

3   Two factors combine to "hook" parents on using television: its unique ability to pacify children and its ready availability.

4   It may seem obvious that when children watch television they are less troublesome to their supervisors than when they engage in normal play. Nevertheless a research study was devised and carried out to establish the truth of just such a hypothesis.

5   The study set out to answer these questions: Are children quieter while viewing television than while playing? What kinds of activities are engaged in during television viewing relative to the kinds of activities occurring during ordinary play time? Is there

less need for parental control and supervision during television viewing than during play?

6   A team of trained observers visited a selected number of young children in their homes and compared their behavior while watching television with their conduct while playing with another child. The following acts were noted and scored when they appeared, either while the child watched television or while he played: talking, laughing, crying, sitting, walking, running, self-stimulation (rubbing the body, playing with hair, sucking a finger, etc.), aggression toward another person, destructive play, leaving the room. Controlling behavior on the part of the mother was also noted when it occurred.

7   The results of the study revealed that notably different behaviors occurred in the course of each condition—viewing and playing. Television viewing proved to be associated with more sitting, less walking, less talking, fewer attempts to leave the room, less aggression toward others, and, most important, less need for maternal interference.

8   The simple presence of the set is an important factor in parents' growing dependence on television. It is there at all times, in every home (sometimes in every room). When the parent is faced with annoying behavior on the part of a child, the temptation to resort to television is strong, far stronger than if it were not so handy, easy to use, and swiftly effective.

9   A New York City mother of two young children reports:

10   "My husband is definitely more concerned about the children's television watching than I am. He thinks it prevents them from thinking. Well, maybe he's right, but I think being with children all day gives you a different attitude than if you only see them evenings. If you've had a hectic day and they want to go to their room and watch TV and leave you alone, well, you're not going to say, 'Don't do that. It's not intellectually stimulating.' You'll say, 'Fine. I want some peace.' I think that's something you don't understand unless you spend all day with the kids. My husband would say, 'You shouldn't give in like that. We've set up the rules about TV and they should stick to them.' But men who are not with children all day don't understand. Sometimes when you're exhausted, it's a lot easier to give in." . . .

11   Interviews with mothers reveal a pattern of growing dependence upon television as a child-rearing tool. This occurs even when the mother does not start off using television to suit her own purposes but introduces it for the child's sake alone:

12   "When I first started turning on the television for the children," relates a Denver mother of two preschool girls, "it wasn't out of need, but because I thought it was a good thing to offer.

I'd turn on the television set and say, 'It's time for "Sesame Street,"' even if it meant interrupting the girls in the middle of play. They didn't need to be coaxed to watch television. They enjoyed watching, and I often watched with them.

13   "But after a time television took on a different aspect in our household. The change was subtle, but looking back now, it's clear that a real change did take place. I suppose it was because I discovered how dependable an amusement television was, more dependable than any other. After a time whenever things came up, tiny domestic emergencies—when I had to talk to somebody on the phone, or when somebody dropped in, or when Marty called that he was bringing somebody home for dinner—that sort of thing—then I would turn to television for help.

14   "Suddenly I realized that I was no longer using television as an experience to offer the children, but as something with value for me. But by now it was hard to change my operating procedure. Now I no longer had to remind the children that it was time for their program, or interrupt them in their play. They really wanted to watch and were quite unwilling to find amusements when I wasn't able to play with them myself." . . .

15   While some mothers first set their children before the television primarily for the child's benefit, the majority of parents begin using television in an open quest for relief. They look forward to those hours of peace so eagerly that sometimes they actually push the child into watching. . . .

16   As parents depend more and more on television until they find they cannot manage without it, television slowly infiltrates family life. One day they make the disturbing discovery that they have lost control over their child's television viewing.

17   Helen S., a part-time musician and mother, began using television as a handy child sedative while she prepared dinner. She describes the evolution of a serious television problem:

18   "There was a time when Kitty and John were both little, about two and three, when they watched nothing but 'Mr. Rogers.' Our whole dinner schedule was geared to that program, and I'd have dinner ready for them exactly at five-thirty when 'Rogers' was over. That was a nice useful time to have them salted away watching TV. I was the one who turned on the set at that time, and I didn't turn it on any other time. But that program was very convenient.

19   "Then there was a time when they watched 'Sesame Street' and 'Mr. Rogers.' That didn't seem too much television to me. But pretty soon a time came when 'Mr. Rogers' became too tame for John. When he was four he discovered 'Batman.' So now there was 'Sesame Street' and 'Batman.' And sometimes 'Under-

dog,' which both of them liked a lot. And then they developed a great fondness for 'The Flintstones.' I don't know where they got interested in all those other programs, maybe from baby-sitters, who always let them watch TV.

20 "Now I began to feel a bit uneasy about television. You see, I had been in such complete control at first. But then, slowly, all these other programs infiltrated, and they seemed to want to watch so many things! So I decided to limit the time they spent watching instead of worrying too much about what programs they watched, since they seemed to like some programs so much.

21 "But what began to bother me was that John often refused to go out and ride his bike in the afternoon because he preferred to stay at home and watch TV. Well, I fought that tooth and nail! I'd explode and have a tantrum and say, 'We're not going to watch any television if it has that sort of a hold on you!' I'd make a scene about it and declare that we were going to have some new rules about television! But those never lasted very long. Also, I talked to the school psychologist about the television problem and she told me not to worry, that if John wanted to watch two or three hours of television, it was probably the best thing for him to do. Well, that went against all my instincts, but it was the easiest thing to do, to just let him watch.

22 "When they were six and seven they discovered the Saturday morning cartoons. They adored them and would watch them all morning. I can't deny that this was great for us, because we'd be able to lie in bed nice and late while they watched their programs.

23 "Then last year they discovered 'Jeannie.' [Groan]. The combined message of 'Jeannie' and 'The Flintstones' is so sexist that it makes me furious. But the school psychologist assured me that TV is just TV and that kids know it isn't real.

24 "Last year our pattern was a terrible one. 'Jeannie' was on from five-thirty to six-thirty, but our dinnertime was six o'clock. I'd tell the kids that if they insisted on watching 'Jeannie,' they'd have to turn it off when dinner was ready. They'd say, 'Yeah, sure, we'll turn it off.' Then I'd come and warn them that dinner would be ready in five minutes. Then I'd come in and tell them to turn it off at the next commercial. Of course, they didn't turn it off. I'd always have to come in and turn it off and they'd be very angry about this. They'd say, 'I hate you,' and come into dinner shoving and kicking each other, angry and pouty, very, very angry. So dinnertime would be very unpleasant for all of us.

25 "They'd stay grumpy for the whole meal. It was the worst time of the day, really! And this went on all year. Every once in a while I'd get fed up and make threats like 'We won't watch TV

anymore if this is what happens when you watch!' I don't think I ever made good on those fancy threats."

26   At this point in the narrative the mother stopped and said to the interviewer in a changed voice, "This is really a terrible saga, isn't it?"

27   What emerges from talks with parents about their children's television watching is a picture of parents' steady loss of control as they gradually withdraw from an active role in their children's upbringing. And as the parents grow less powerful, they discover themselves less and less capable of coping with their strong but undisciplined, grumpy, threatening children. Common sense suggests that without television, parents would have been unable to survive life under such circumstances; they would have been forced to socialize their children more persistently, forced to work a little harder at making them speak more agreeably or behave more considerately. But television, as the mothers' testimonies indicate, abolishes the need to establish those sorts of disciplines. There is no longer the impetus to ensure the sort of behavior that would allow a mother to cook dinner or talk on the telephone or assert herself as a parent in any way without being eaten alive, in a manner of speaking, by her children. . . .

Thinking It Through

1. Describe the process by which, according to Winn, children and parents usually get "hooked" on television.

2. After reading Winn's essay, do you believe that children or parents are more to blame for kids' excessive TV watching? Explain your reasons for thinking so.

3. Do children gain anything from watching television? If you believe so, explain what benefits you think are possible.

4. For the most part, Winn allows mothers to tell their own stories about their children's TV habits. Is this device effective or not? Why do you think so?

5. Would you describe Helen S. (see paragraphs 17 and following) as an unusually weak parent? Give several reasons for your answer.

Thinking and Writing

1. Write an essay of several paragraphs in which you describe and evaluate your own television viewing habits. Begin by explaining when you started to watch and what you watched. Continue your description until the present. Be as specific as you can, naming particular shows you watched and estimating the approximate number of

hours. Did your parents or others encourage or discourage your TV viewing? Did you go through stages of liking particular programs or kinds of programs? Use specific details in your description.

Then explain what you believe the effects of your TV watching have been. Were they positive, negative, mixed, or neutral? Would you be different now if you had not watched TV at all? Be fair and open-minded in making your evaluation.

2. In a recently published book, *The Difficult Child*, the psychiatrist and child specialist Stanley Turecki takes a position on television viewing opposite to Winn's. He writes: "The 'electronic baby-sitter' can be a valuable tool in the management of a difficult child. . . . Sometimes it may be the only thing that pacifies a child who would otherwise be running wild. It may be the only way a mother can buy a few free moments for herself."

If you agree with Turecki rather than Marie Winn, write a short essay supporting the points he makes. Use examples from your experience with children in your family or children you have kept or observed closely.

The Chuck Show

GARRISON KEILLOR

First Thoughts   In this satirical essay the well-known humorist Garrison Keillor takes a look at TV talk shows. Keillor's satire raises questions about the taste (and perhaps the intellect) of some of America's TV talk-show hosts and viewers.

Word List   OBESE (paragraph 2):   seriously overweight

CHRONICALLY (paragraph 8):   over a long period of time

ABDICATED (paragraph 8):   gave up

ILK (paragraph 8):   kind or sort

MUTANT (paragraph 24):   an altered species

MONDAY

1   Donahue: Top Men Who Can't Stand It and Quit
Oprah Winfrey: A Former Lover of Mine (In Person, Along with His Wife and Three Kids)
Geraldo: The Fattest People You Ever Laid Eyes On
Darin: Cross-Dressing at the Washington *Post*
Sally Jessy Raphael: Kids from Nice Homes Who Eat Dirt
Morton Downey, Jr.:   Please Don't Watch This Show if You Weep at the Sight of Cruelty!
Chuck: Parents from District 18 Discuss Bus Transportation

2   This was the week after Flag Day, traditionally a slow time for morning talk shows. Donahue did ambitious young Wall Street executives who suddenly cut loose and become primitive herdsmen roaming the Adirondacks and living on roots and berries and milking elk, and Oprah talked with George (who was as slim and rich and good-looking as when they couldn't keep their hands off each other and whose dumpy little wife, Sally, was very sweet about the whole thing, though was pretty obvious that her man still had eyes for Oprah), and Geraldo did grossly obese men who must be moved by crane, three of whom were hoisted on tiptoe and danced around to the "Waltz of the Sugarplum Fairy," from "The Nutcracker," and Darin decided that even though six times as many guys at the Washington *Post* are wearing bras and panty hose as in

1969 it does not seem to affect their reporting so far, and Sally
Jessy showed kids from *extremely* nice homes who were devour-
ing dirt *by the shovelful*, and Morton Downey ran around the
studio with a pickaxe and did one hundred and fifty thousand
dollars' worth of property damage.

3   Meanwhile, on "The Chuck Show of Television" (the Peterson Cable Network, Minneapolis) you saw four parents discussing the fact that the school had cancelled the late bus,
which made it necessary for them to drive all the way into
Tarryville every afternoon and pick up the kids after field-
hockey practice and choir rehearsal. "It would've been nice if
the process had allowed for some input from the parents," one
parent said.

4   *"You guys are dumber than dirt! Gosh, you're a bunch of dummies!*
Whose dumb, dumb, dumb, dumb, dumb idea was this, anyway?" said
Chuck's producer, Al, when he saw how bad Chuck got
creamed in the overnight ratings. "A zero point six! *That's as*
low as you can go and still be talking English! We're talking tiny!" In
fact, Chuck got beat out even by Miklo Pstachek's talk show,
which is in Latvian. Mik had a woman guest who picked up
and threw three spinet pianos and then lowered her head and
busted through an oak door and ran down the alley with her
clothes off. Mik got a one point two. By the time Al saw the
overnights and sat the Chuck staff down for a meeting, however, it was Tuesday already.

TUESDAY

5   Donahue: Top Men You Like a Lot Until You Talk To Their
       Wives and Suddenly The Subject of Sex Comes Up
    Oprah Winfrey: George Alone (by Audience Request) to
       Discuss "Sensuality and the Talk-Show Gal"
    Geraldo: Big Huge Blubbery Guys in Their Poofy Dresses
       (Ones We Didn't Dare Show Yesterday, Afraid You'd be
       Offended)
    Darin: How About *Time* and *Newsweek*? Is Transvestism As
       Big a Problem There as an Awful Lot of People Are Saying
       Now?
    Sally Jessy Raphael: They Eat Dirt and Touch Themselves in
       Bad Places
    Morton Downey, Jr.:   He Will Rage and Foam and Screech
       and Pound—He Will Rip His Clothes to Shreds and Shake
       the Bars of His Cage Until They Are So Loose You Are
       Sure He Will Jump Out in the Audience and Whomp You
    Chuck: What's New These Days In Vocational Counselling in
       and Around Tarryville?

6   *"Who is killing this show by booking guests who are dumber than stumps?"* inquired Al when the whole Chuck crew assembled in his office on Tuesday afternoon—Mike and Melody and Fielding and Trevor and Shazzaba and Bob, all drinking coffee out of plastic cups, and each with a clipboard and a stopwatch. *"Fess up and tell me which of you dumbbells is stiffing this show by hauling in dead meat on trucks and dumping it on Chuck."* But in fact it had been the Chucker himself who booked those two shows, and here in the paper swamp on Al's desk was a Chuck memo saying they ought to do a show on recycling. Chuck's wife, Marge, is a lifelong recycler, a fanatic who carries a garbage bag everywhere, even to other people's garden parties, and collects cans and bottles, and one of Chuck's big interests at Peterson Cable has been recycling: he's the one who got management to put a recycling bin next to the soda machine.

7   "One problem is that here in Minneapolis it's hard to find that many cross-dressers—at least, any who care to come on TV and talk about it," said Fielding. "We have a few fatties, but nothing like what you see in New York or L.A. I was in New York once and I saw a man as wide as the whole sidewalk. He was driving himself along on a forklift and singing in a sweet, high-pitched voice and lifting up his T-shirt to show his belly button."

8   *"No more of these Dumb Dora guests or I'll throw you all out the window. We got to have some sad weird people—some people who make you go, Whoa-a-a-a—or else I'm going to start kicking some fanny around here,"* said Al. Ironically, he was an ideal guest himself—forty-seven, unable to read or write, terrified of cats, addicted to sugar, chronically depressed because of a rare disease called Phelps—but as the producer he needed to be in the control room, not sitting on the white couch sobbing over the bum hand that life had dealt him, though he could have cried plenty about his dad, who abdicated the parental role and married Al's beautiful Aunt Nora and became his uncle, a kindly but distant figure who sat on the porch chuckling and spitting but never giving the boy a smidgen of discipline. But was that the reason Al was lesbian? And did it matter? Loneliness was Al's big bugaboo. He felt like the only male lesbian in the whole world. There were no books about his ilk, not even a small brochure. The problem was apparently so unspeakably vile that nobody dared breathe a word about it. Was that why he always yelled—to cover up his unique sexuality? *"What's the matter with you people!"* he said. *"How come you can't think? You want this show to go down the toilet?"*

9   "I don't think it's just guests. The star has been looking a little peaked since the show started to cool off," said Bob. "We need him looking fresh and eager again, like when we had the barking spiders on the show."

10   True. That *had* been good. Six months after Chuck went into syndication, he had four Girl Scouts on the show, and one of them, a spider hobbyist, owned three rare barking spiders, and it was fascinating to see the tiny hairy insects and hear their unmistakable woofing and arfing. It got Chuck in papers from coast to coast, and the next day thirty-six million Americans tuned in, but his guests that day were four old farts from the Legion club who sat and grumped about high property taxes, and the Chuck show was dead in the water again. *"Animals,"* said Al. *"Go out there and bring back live animals!"*

WEDNESDAY

11   Donahue: $500,000-a-Year Guys Who Come Home From Work and Lie Weeping in Dark Basements

Oprah Winfrey: George and Me and What We Said Yesterday After the Show—When We Thought the Cameras Were Off!

Geraldo: Will Guys This Fat Bounce if We Drop Them? Will They Roll? What Do They Look Like Hanging Upside Down?

Darin: What About the TV Anchors? Do One or Two of Them Wear High Heels During News?

Sally Jessy Raphael: Parents Who Sit and Watch Kids Stuff Fistfuls of Dirt in Their Mouths

Morton Downey, Jr.:   He Escapes from His Trainer! He Leaps Into the Crowd of Innocent Bystanders! He Has a Small Child in His Hands and is About to Crush Its Head Like a Beer Can!

Chuck: Rabbits Copulating in Cages

12   The rabbits belonged to Melody's brother Donald, three males and three females in heat. The males mounted the females and pumped furiously for six seconds like furry pistons and then fainted and toppled over and lay on their backs twitching, with their legs sticking up in the air, and then awoke and jumped up and remounted.

13   The PCN crew did some fantastic camerawork—slow-mo and stop-action and split-frame—and the minute Chuck went off the air all three major networks were calling and begging for footage. All three evening newscasts ran a story on it, and that night Al took the Chuck staff out for prime rib at Sammy's. He was so happy and got so drunk that he almost

stood up and said, "I'm illiterate, sugar-dependent, cat-ophobic, Phelps-infected, and lesbian, and every day I feel sadder than you'll ever know, but I still love you so much I could hug you to pieces!" Chuck wasn't there—he and Marge had Amnesty on Wednesday nights—but he sent a cake that said "Congratulations to a Great Bunch of Persons!"

14   *"The dumbest thing we could do would be to sit on our laurels at this point,"* Al said. *"We've got our work cut out for us now. The hardest thing is to stay on top!"*

THURSDAY

15   Donahue: What Does It Take to Open These Men Up?
Oprah Winfrey: George—I Can't Stop Thinking About Him. It's Driven Me Off My Diet. I Sit in My $10 Million Chicago Apartment Eating Nachos and Chili Dogs and Fried Potatoes, Getting Big As a Barn
Geraldo: Much Fatter People Than the Ones We Showed Before. Those Were Just the Tip of the Iceberg. These Fatsos Make Them Look Teeny-Weeny
Darin: I Must Confess That I Myself Am Wearing a Pink Lacy Slip Under My Suit—Would You Like to See It?
Sally Jessy Raphael: Mothers Whose Kids Eat Dirt: Should They Be Shot? Or Helped?
Morton Downey, Jr.:   The Child Weeps Copiously, the Parents Scream in Terror, But It's Too Late—In Another Second, Mort Will Rip It to Shreds
Chuck: Hypnotizing Chickens

16   Bob's brother learned about hypnotizing chickens when he was in 4-H. You hold the chicken gently and stroke its beak until the bird's eyes cross and it goes limp in your hands. Then you can stand it up on the ground (the chicken locks its knees when it's hypnotized; nobody knows why) and it'll stand, mo-tionless, its white feathers riffling in the breeze, the eyes fo-cussed on the tip of the beak, until suddenly it falls over on its side. Or you can prop it against a stake.

17   The PCN crew shot some footage of hypnotized chickens on location at several egg ranches in the area, including the controversial segment in which a chicken under hypnosis is beheaded with an axe and tears around in circles for a full fif-teen seconds, blood pouring from its neck. Some stations cut that segment from the Chuck show, and then all three net-works did stories that showed the execution segment, and switchboards were jammed and Thursday night the radio call-in shows were full of it and Friday morning there were big newspaper stories and the overnight ratings showed Chuck with the highest numbers ever recorded by a daytime talk

host. Phenomenal. Al burst into Chuck's office laughing and screaming, waving the survey, and what did Chuck say? He glanced at the numbers and said, "This is great. You know why? Because it gives us a platform to say some things about urban planning. I'm troubled by these Republican lobbyists and their three-hundred-thousand-dollars kickbacks on federal housing contracts, but in a larger sense I'm concerned about the whole urban picture nowadays. It's terribly serious."

18   Al felt sick. He thought to himself, *You dumb Chuck, we beat our brains out for you and all you can think about is your dumb agenda.*

19   Al went to his office and got a sawed-off shotgun out of his desk drawer and came back to Chuck's office and stood in the doorway with the muzzle pointed at his own head and told Chuck the truth. *"I cannot read or sign my own name, I am dying of Phelps, I drink three six-packs of Coke every day, my cat terrifies me at night, and all I think about is having unnatural sex with women. If you don't quit being so dumb and ruining this show, I am going to blow my head off."*

FRIDAY

20   Donahue: An Open Plea to My Wife: I Wield Vast Influence and Earn Zillions yet You and I Never Talk Anymore and So You Have No Idea of the Depth of My Obsessive Fantasies. Love Me! Or I Will Don Female Apparel in Front of Millions!

Oprah Winfrey: Thinking About George I Put on 118 lbs. in Four Days—but Did I *Really* Eat All Those Potatoes? Or Am I Carrying Elvis's Baby?

Geraldo: Obese Psychologists Discuss Inhumane Practices on Talk Shows: Is Chuck Kidnapping Cats and Torturing Them and Mutilating Their Bodies in Secret Satanic-Cult Rites? (Extremely Vivid Photographs. No Children, *Please*)

Darin: Four Topics I Refuse to Discuss on This Show, Including Bestiality, Phone Calls from the Dead, Rumors About Nuns, and My Recent Operation

Sally Jessy Raphael: You Were Right, Viewers, I Was Wrong! Millions of You Told Me, "Don't Knock It if You Haven't Tried It!"—So Today I Will! A Whole Big Bucket!

Morton Downey, Jr.:   Look! A Dog Rushes In! He Barks, "Mort! Mort!" And Big Tears Run Down the Arch-Fiend's Cheeks and He Returns the Child Unharmed to Its Parents! It Is His Boyhood Dog, Chipper, Who Ran Away and Now Has Come Back! The Child Is Saved and the Monster Redeemed by the Love of a Pet!

Chuck: My Producer and My Best Friend, Al

21   Al knew it was a major mistake the minute the "On Air" light flashed, but what could he do? Too late. He told everything in five minutes, and it was nothing. Male lesbianism—*big deal*. Adult illiteracy. Sugar addiction. Cat Fear. Depression. Phelps. It was just a bunch of words. Noise. He wished so badly that he'd listened to the staff—the great stuff they'd gone out and found. The world's smallest horse! A cow with two heads and two separate udders with a total of ten teats! A pig with a wooden leg who rides a Harley and swims and attacks on command!

22   Chuck finished the week on top, and there were a hundred and eighteen press requests for personal interviews with him, but still there was quite a big of soul-searching around Chuck Productions that afternoon. Chuck was gone—he and Marge were spending the weekend at a conference on Central America—and so was Al. His dad saw the show and called up, and they went out for dinner and drinks. Mike ran the meeting, and basically what he said was, "c'mon, guys. Lesbianism isn't what got us here. We gotta get back to the basics." It was reported that Geraldo was planning a whole week on capital punishment and Donahue would do the Black Plague and Oprah the Inquisition.

23   "Don't worry about them," said Mike. "We're going to play our game and do what we do best. Otherwise you'll be fired and hurled naked into a vat of acid."

24   By five o-clock Friday, every slot on the Chuck show was filled for the next two weeks with snakes, lizards and horned toads, live rats, giant cock-roaches, rabid dogs, alligators, weird neon fish with balloon eyes, mutant pets from isolated towns near Army testing sites, dogs that looked *exactly* like different celebrities, and a four-hundred-foot-long white whale, named Ruby, which was captured from the North Atlantic and which has swallowed several men (maybe six or seven) thought perhaps to be still alive inside. Doctors listening with powerful infrared stethoscopes hear what sounds like English from within. The gigantic creature will be carefully anesthetized and opened up on Monday morning at ten-thirty.

Thinking It Through

1. What is Keillor's main technique for humor when he describes the subjects for the nationally broadcast talk shows?

2. What sorts of people often appear on daytime TV talk shows? Do any of them fit the description given by Al, the producer: "sad weird people—some people who make you go, Whoa-a-a"?

3. Keillor deliberately deals in stereotypes. In fact, Chuck himself is a stereotype. Describe him.

4. Would a serious discussion of the quality of talk shows be as effective as this humorous essay?

Thinking and Writing

Many sociologists and professional people in communications believe that television is largely a reflection of those who watch it—that when we look at the TV screen, we see ourselves. Think about this idea as well as about the kinds of topics discussed on talk and advice shows and other popular television programs. Your instructor may want you to discuss this topic in class or in small groups.

When you have given this issue some thought, write an essay in which you agree or disagree with this statement: "We are what we watch." Give specific examples from modern television programming to support your point of view.

The Meaning of TV

WILLIAM HENRY III

First Thoughts

William Henry's article is part of a special feature that *Life* printed in 1989 to celebrate the first fifty years of television. Henry looks over TV's brief history and notes how far the medium has advanced and how much it has become a part of our lives. As you read about the TV viewers and the effects that TV can have on them, consider your own viewing habits.

Word List

AUTEURS (paragraph 1):   individual authors or originators

POTENT (paragraph 1):   powerful

CONGENIAL (paragraph 2):   friendly, easy to get along with

ASSERT (paragraph 3):   declare

INERT (paragraph 3):   inactive

AVID (paragraph 4):   eager

INNOCUOUS (paragraph 5):   innocent

CATHARSIS (paragraph 5):   purging, release (of emotions)

SUSCEPTIBLE (paragraph 5):   open (to influence)

ENTICINGLY (paragraph 6):   temptingly

LIBERTINE (paragraph 6):   morally loose

REVERED (paragraph 6):   honored

CONFERRED (paragraph 6):   given, awarded

1   We tend to talk about television as though it has always been there, as though it provides the same experience for everyone, as though it were a single, living organism. In conversation almost everyone speaks of "television" doing this or that, intending this or that. A moment's thought is enough to recall that "television" is made up of a score and more broadcast and cable networks, some 1,300 local stations and countless production companies. The medium is collaborative; there are few if any *auteurs*. Yet TV is so potent a presence that it seems to have a mind, and personality, of its own.

2   If TV has changed over time, we take it mostly as a reflection of how we who view it have changed, and in a sense that is right. While TV may not sense our moods and respond to them like a friend or family member, the people who administer, advertise on and program television all devote themselves to research that tracks each zig and zag of national mood. Their goal is to keep television exactly in step with mainstream taste, so that in most homes it will resemble a family member or a congenial neighbor. If television really were a personality, it would qualify as almost everyone's closest friend.

3   The average American watches TV about four hours a day; the average household has the set on for seven hours in all. Even people who say they "don't watch much television" turn out to be forgetting to count news, or sports, or Mister Rogers with the toddlers, or old movies, or vintage reruns, or something or other that they somehow consider to be not mere TV. Just why do people in all walks of life feel such guilt about watching TV, or assert such superiority in pretending that they do not? Because, despite their affection for TV, they think watching it is too passive, an inert substitute for exercise or reading or conversation—or study.

4   The reality is that TV can provide plenty of learning, and not merely on Sunrise Semester. For every schoolchild whose reading problems might be blamed on an excess of TV, there is probably another who learned the alphabet from Sesame Street and began see-and-say reading with the on-screen words of commercials. High school students may have trouble spotting South America on a map, but through TV they have grasped some basic truths about the planet. Wherever they live, they were shaken last summer by images of beaches closed to bathers because the sands were strewn with toxic hospital waste. Among television's diehard critics, the print journalists, it is an open secret that the most important source of news flow during any election night or political crisis is the television set, around which editors and reporters cluster to stay abreast and to test their news judgment. And the same scholars and opinion-makers who profess to view television with disdain are nearly always avid to appear on it— fully expecting that their friends will see them. Most of the nation's elite seem to live by at least the latter half of Gore Vidal's reported dictum: "There are two things in life one must never refuse. One is sex, and the other is television."

5   Perhaps TV's deepest power is not the change it works on sports or commerce or any other branch of reality, but the way its innocuous-looking entertainment reaches deep into the national mind. TV has the ability to generate, or regenerate, national mythology. The great characters of television embody

human truths as profound as the great characters in Moliere or Ibsen, and for vastly bigger audiences. The viewership for even one modestly successful airing of a prime-time series would fill every theater on Broadway, eight performances a week, for a couple of years. These characters linger in memory because they epitomize what the nation feels about itself. They teach behavior and values. They enter the language. Say the name Falstaff, and some minority of the population will know that you mean a vainglorious coward; say Ralph Kramden, and everyone will know what you mean. The Mary Richards character created by Mary Tyler Moore summed up their own lives for a whole generation of thirtysomething single women who could have any careers they wanted, but often at the expense of satisfaction at home. This is not new with television. The great civilizing effect of all literature is that it takes people's vision beyond the immediate, the clan and the tribe. It enables them to make the philosophical leap that Jean-Paul Sartre described as "seeing the other as another self." Television simply does this more effectively, more touchingly, than any kind of art that went before. Unlike the stage and movies, the episodic TV series does not end in catharsis. The characters come back week after week, evolving at the slow pace of ordinary life, exposing themselves more fully than most relatives or friends. Other literature provides occasional experiences. Television becomes an ongoing part of life and for some susceptible people is only barely distinguishable from real life itself.

6   It is hard to imagine a world without television, harder still to imagine what the world of the last half century would have been without those first flickering images from NBC and all that followed. We might have fewer terrorists, because there would be no worldwide pulpit for their propaganda. We might have a less violent society, because the typical child would not have been exposed to tens of thousands of actual and simulated violent crimes on news and entertainment by the time he or she reached adulthood. We might have a society in which people still felt respect for established institutions and their leaders, instead of one in which TV-bred skepticism had lowered the approval rating for Congress, business executives and even judges to between 20 and 40 percent. We might have a healthier society, one in which children played outside instead of watching the box hour after hour, one in which meals cooked from scratch at home had not been outdistanced by snacks and fast food loaded with sugar, salt and fat, all enticingly advertised. We might have a more restrained, less libertine world, one in which virginity and marriage were still revered while premarital pregnancy and divorce were still treated

with distaste rather than sympathy. All of these effects have been attributed, sometimes convincingly, to TV. But we might also have a less alert world, one in which citizens were not so widely informed about the economy, about medical matters, about foreign military adventures that run the risk of war. We might have a less concerned world, one in which starvation in Ethiopia could never inspire Live Aid, one in which the homeless of Manhattan or Chicago might remain unseen by the rest of the nation. We might have a lonelier, more isolated world in which the old lived without much entertainment, without much company, without the sense of involvement in life that can be conferred even by watching Donahue.

7   Only one thing can be said for certain. Whatever world we would have, it would be different in many and unimaginable ways from this one. Like fire and the wheel and the alphabet, television has changed the world that humans live in. And more, perhaps than any invention or discovery before it, television has changed the definition of what it means to be human.

Thinking It Through

1. Do you believe that TV reflects or influences changes in lifestyle? Or does it sometimes do both? Explain your answer.

2. In paragraph 4 Henry says that "TV can provide plenty of learning." Do you believe that TV has educational value? Why or why not?

3. Let us test Henry's statement in paragraph 5 about TV characters and literary characters. Are you familiar with Falstaff? How about Ralph Kramden and Mary Richards?

4. The writer says that TV characters teach behavior and values. Does this contradict his statement in paragraph 2 that TV mainly reflects? If he is correct, can you think of characters from whom we can learn positive behavior and values? How about negative ones?

5. Analyze paragraph 6. How is it organized? Does this paragraph present a successful persuasive argument? Why or why not?

6. If you read Joanmarie Kalter's "Exposing Media Myths," summarize the points on which Kalter and Henry agree and disagree.

Thinking and Writing

1. Choose a TV show that offers a view of one group in modern American society. (Note that there are TV shows about kids, divorced persons, single parents, widows or widowers, blacks, two-income working couples, the mentally handicapped, and so forth.) Briefly

describe the characters and a few of the situations in which they are presented. Then show why you believe that the show gives a realistic or an unrealistic picture of this part of society.

2. If you are familiar with two TV shows about one of the groups mentioned in topic 1, compare the two. First indicate whether the shows are comic, serious, or perhaps both. Indicate how the characters and situations are similar or different. Conclude by showing how they compare in presenting a realistic or unrealistic view.

   The planning stage for a paper like this is very important. Be sure to begin by making full lists of similarities and differences. Then divide your material into categories (facts about characters, facts about situations, and so forth). Decide whether you want to tell everything about show 1 and then show 2 or whether you want to move back and forth from one to the other.

3. "I like _____ (name of TV show) _____ because _____."
   Using this sentence or one similar to it as your topic sentence, write a general-to-particular paragraph explaining why you enjoy a certain TV show. (Paragraph order is described in Chapter 7.)

The Natural Environment

The environment is everything that isn't me.
—Albert Einstein

A Fable for Tomorrow

RACHEL CARSON

First Thoughts

"A Fable for Tomorrow" is the first chapter of Rachel Carson's popular and highly influential book, *Silent Spring*. Written in the early 1960s, Carson's book documents the enormous damage caused by the uncontrolled use of pesticides. This is a pioneering work in the early environmental movement in the United States.

Word List

VIBURNUM (paragraph 2):   a type of flowering shrub

MALADIES (paragraph 3):   illnesses

STRICKEN (paragraph 3):   afflicted, made seriously ill

MORIBUND (paragraph 4):   dying

SPECTER (paragraph 9):   ghost, phantom

1   There was once a town in the heart of America where all life seemed to live in harmony with its surroundings. The town lay in the midst of a checkerboard of prosperous farms, with fields of grain and hillsides of orchards where, in spring, white clouds of bloom drifted above the green fields. In autumn, oak and maple and birch set up a blaze of color that flamed and flickered across a backdrop of pines. Then foxes barked in the hills and deer silently crossed the fields, half hidden in the mists of the fall mornings.

2   Along the roads, laurel, viburnum and alder, great ferns and wildflowers delighted the traveler's eye through much of the year. Even in winter the roadsides were places of beauty, where countless birds came to feed on the berries and on the seed heads of the dried weeds rising above the snow. The countryside was, in fact, famous for the abundance and variety of its bird life, and when the flood of migrants was pouring through in spring and fall people traveled from great distances to observe them. Others came to fish the streams, which flowed clear and cold out of the hills and contained shady pools where trout lay. So it had been from the days many years ago when the first settlers raised their houses, sank their wells, and built their barns.

3   Then a strange blight crept over the area and everything began to change. Some evil spell had settled on the community:

mysterious maladies swept the flocks of chickens; the cattle and sheep sickened and died. Everywhere was a shadow of death. The farmers spoke of much illness among their families. In the town the doctors had become more and more puzzled by new kinds of sickness appearing among their patients. There had been several sudden and unexplained deaths, not only among adults but even among children, who would be stricken suddenly while at play and die within a few hours.

4   There was a strange stillness. The birds, for example—where had they gone? Many people spoke of them, puzzled and disturbed. The feeding stations in the backyards were deserted. The few birds seen anywhere were moribund; they trembled violently and could not fly. It was a spring without voices. On the mornings that had once throbbed with the dawn chorus of robins, catbirds, doves, jays, wrens, and scores of other bird voices there was now no sound; only silence lay over the fields and woods and marsh.

5   On the farms the hens brooded, but no chicks hatched. The farmers complained that they were unable to raise any pigs—the litters were small and the young survived only a few days. The apple trees were coming into bloom but no bees droned among the blossoms, so there was no pollination and there would be no fruit.

6   The roadsides, once so attractive, were now lined with browned and withered vegetation as though swept by fire. These, too, were silent, deserted by all living things. Even the streams were now lifeless. Anglers no longer visited them, for all the fish had died.

7   In the gutters under the eaves and between the shingles of the roofs, a white granular powder still showed a few patches; some weeks before it had fallen like snow upon the roofs and the lawns, the fields and streams.

8   No witchcraft, no enemy action had silenced the rebirth of new life in this stricken world. The people had done it themselves.

9   This town does not actually exist, but it might easily have a thousand counterparts in America or elsewhere in the world. I know of no community that has experienced all the misfortunes I describe. Yet every one of these disasters has actually happened somewhere, and many real communities have already suffered a substantial number of them. A grim specter has crept upon us almost unnoticed, and this imagined tragedy may easily become a stark reality we all shall know.

10   What has already silenced the voices of spring in countless towns in America?

**Thinking It
Through**

1. Why does Carson call this short chapter "A Fable for Tomorrow"?

2. This description has the atmosphere of a mystery story. How does the writer get this effect?

3. Why does Carson choose spring as the season for this description of sickness and death?

**Thinking and
Writing**

1. Most people have seen (either first hand or in pictures) the results of environmental pollution. In a few paragraphs describe a scene that shows the effects of pollution. You may choose a rural or urban setting, for both are affected. Your scene may be actual or imaginary, but the details must be realistic. If you wish, you may look through current magazines and newspapers for pictures and descriptions of areas blighted by pollution. Be sure, however, that your description is written in your own words.

2. If you have some knowledge of or interest in the current debate over pesticides, write a paper giving your views of this issue. Here are some questions you could consider: Should all chemical pesticides be banned? What would be the result? Can insects be adequately controlled by organic compounds, natural enemies, or genetic alteration? In a time when great numbers of people are starving and the food supply in many areas is limited, is there some reasonable compromise between the usefulness and the danger of pesticides? If your instructor wishes, you may check the library for recent information and statistics.

Will Earth Survive Man?

UN CHRONICLE

First Thoughts The United Nations Environmental Programme (UNEP) has been studying changes in the Earth's environment for over twenty years. This recent (1988) article in the *UN Chronicle* reports many of UNEP's findings and makes some disturbing predictions about the future.

Word List IRREPLACEABLE (paragraph 2): incapable of being replaced

ARCHIPELAGO (paragraph 7): group of islands

INUNDATE (paragraph 9): flood

MAGNITUDE (paragraph 11): size (suggesting largeness)

DEPLETED (paragraph 12): exhausted

RECOURSE (paragraph 22): resort

HECTARES (paragraph 26): one hectare = approximately 2.5 acres

EXTRACTION (paragraph 27): removal

1   A brutal life or death struggle is taking place each day everywhere on this planet.

2   At times, it is invisible, as when a plant species, with its set of irreplaceable genes, disappears forever from an Amazon forest. Other times, it is painfully visible: a man chokes to death in a Mexico City subway, killed by a pollution-triggered asthma attack; the face of a New York woman is disfigured by skin cancer, one of 200,000 such cases predicted to occur over the next decades by the thinning of the protective ozone layer around the Earth.

3   . . . One million species may be extinct by the year 2000; a cure for AIDS or cancer or heart attacks may be lost forever with their genes.

4   Dirty water kills 25,000 people every day in developing countries. Air pollution makes people sick in the developed world. Lakes and forests are destroyed. In developing countries, the poor continue to damage an already frail environment in order

to survive. Third world cities burst at the seams, their populations fleeing exhausted countrysides. Tropical forests, the Earth's greatest genetic reservoir, are being cut for fuel, agriculture or highways.

5   Much of the destruction is irreversible.

IT'S GETTING HOT

6   In September 2078 the General Assembly meets in emergency session to discuss a crisis in the Maldives. The ambassadors arrive by boat and make their way to the new Assembly Hall, on the 10th floor of the United Nations building in New York. Not one boat is propelled by a motor, since delegates want to set an example for the rest of the world. Manhattan island, now entirely under water, is called the city of a thousand bridges. All traffic is on foot or by water.

7   During a dramatic all-night session, delegates are told that two of the dikes built a generation ago to contain the sea around the main islands of the Maldivian archipelago in the Indian Ocean have collapsed, and all life within three miles has been wiped out. The President of the Maldives asks that the entire population of his nation be immediately relocated to the mainland of the African continent. The Assembly agrees and the largest evacuation operation of the 21st century starts two days later. A few hours after the last Maldivian is ferried out of his homeland, the sea swallows those picturesque coral reef islands.

8   The above scenario of the future may not be far-fetched. Oceans inevitably expand as they are heated. The global "warming" already under way could therefore push sea levels everywhere to more than six feet. One third of the world's population that lives within 60 kilometres of coastlines would be threatened.

9   A rise of less than two feet in sea level might inundate 27 percent of Bangladesh, displacing 25 million people. Egypt could lose 20 percent of its productive land, the United States, between 50 and 80 percent of its coastal wetlands. A 6-foot rise could wipe out the 1,190-island Maldivian archipelago.

10   If the Arctic and the Antarctic glaciers were to melt, sea levels would rise nearly 300 feet, flooding many major world cities and all ports.

11   Average global temperatures may rise by 4.5 degrees centigrade by the year 2030. To understand the magnitude of this occurrence, one only must realize that the planet's climate has not varied by more than 2 degrees centigrade over the past 10,000 years and that during the last Ice Age global temperatures averaged some 5 degrees colder than now.

12   A six-foot sea level rise, dramatic as that might be, would be among the milder consequences of a global warming. Agriculture would be hardest hit. Wheat production would have to move north, where depleted soils could result in crop reduction. The production of rice—crucial to the diets of 60 percent of the world's population—would suffer in a drier world. Dust bowls, dying forests, unbearably hot cities, more frequent storms, forest fires and outbreaks of pestilence and disease would also occur.

WHY IS THE EARTH WARMING UP?

13   Carbon dioxide—mainly released by the burning of coal, oil and other fossil fuels—and other industrial gases are trapping heat in the atmosphere and warming the Earth as if it were a greenhouse.

14   Since the Industrial Revolution, carbon dioxide levels in the atmosphere have increased by some 25 percent. They are expected to increase another 30 percent over the next 50 years.

15   Other greenhouse gases are nitrous oxide (laughing gas), methane, ozone and the ozone-depleting chlorofluorocarbons. Their collective presence in the atmosphere will double the carbon dioxide effect.

16   At the end of March 1988, American, British and Soviet scientific data showed that the decade of the 1980s has been the warmest in over a century. The warmest year on record was 1987, according to the Climatic Research Unit at the University of East Anglia in the United Kingdom.

17   Some scientists attribute this to the "greenhouse effect." Others prefer to wait and see if the pattern persists into the next decade before deciding. Tom Wigley, head of the British research unit, told *The New York Times* that if "the next 10 years are as warm or warmer, it would be very hard to deny the greenhouse effect," adding "it is very hard to deny now."

18   Little has been done to tackle this problem which is, in many ways, a more serious issue than ozone loss.

19   For the United Nations Environment Programme (UNEP), which pioneered studies on the subject in the early 1970s, its reality is no longer at issue: the only questions remaining are when the effects will occur and to what degree. With ozone loss widely acknowledged as a major threat in need of urgent solution, the "greenhouse effect" is moving to the top of UNEP's agenda.

20   UNEP's first goal is to advance scientific research to obtain specific data on consequences for regions and countries. Existing data now are mostly global and general. With specific data in hand, UNEP can then ask Governments to either control the

greenhouse effect or be ready for the consequences and adopt contingency measures, such as planning evacuation from flooded cities.

21   There is only one practical way to control the greenhouse problem: to slash energy production. It is unlikely that countries will be willing to do this. For industrialized nations, it would mean a radical shift to energy conservation or alternative energy sources. In developing countries, while technologically easier to accomplish, that shift might not be possible for political and economic reasons.

22   Adapting to a changing climate might be the only recourse.

THE WAY OF THE DINOSAUR

23   It took 8 million years for the dinosaurs to disappear. Today extinction of species can be quick—and is often man-made.

24   Every year between 10,000 and 35,000 species become extinct when their forest habitat is destroyed. Tropical forests are the planet's genetic storehouses—home to half the world's species. These are quiet deaths: most species on Earth are insignificant, even invisible to the eye—micro-organisms, insects, protozoa, worms.

25   Forests also regulate the climate, protect the soil against erosion and help control floods. They are the only source of fuel for about 2 billion people—40 percent of the world's population. Fodder for domestic animals and cash crops crucial to the survival of poor rural families also come from the forests.

26   There are 250 million landless people in the world. Pushed into the forests, they destroy an estimated 5 million hectares a year. After two or three years the land becomes barren. The settlers move on again, deeper and deeper into wooded areas. They become the greatest threat to the rain forests.

27   An authoritative three-year study by the United Nations Environment Programme (UNEP) and the Food and Agriculture Organization of the United Nations (FAO) published in 1981 states that extraction of fuel-wood and charcoal, along with logging, are not the major causes of tropical deforestation. Clearing for agriculture, particularly shifting agriculture, was found to be the main culprit.

*HOW FAST ARE FORESTS
DISAPPEARING?*

28   Every minute, 21.5 hectares of tropical forest are destroyed.

29   Unless something is done quickly, closed forests will totally disappear within 25 years in four Latin American, three African

and two Asian countries. Thirteen other countries will lose them within 50 years.

30   Since the 1960s, a quarter of the Central American rain forest has been felled to give way to cattle pastures. Much of the meat is exported to North America, to be used by the fast-food industry.

31   "Every time we eat a hamburger, half a ton of rain forest may be destroyed," says Dr. George Schaller, Science Director of Wildlife Conservation International, an environment group based in the United States.

32   Developed countries have more forests now than a century ago, and severely deforested areas have been successfully replanted. But acid rain and pollution are killing trees fast in many European and other industrialized countries.

WHAT CAN BE DONE?

33   UNEP has lobbied successfully to introduce environmental concerns into the 1985 International Tropical Timber Agreement. With the United Nations Educational, Scientific and Cultural Organization (UNESCO), it is helping to establish and support protected areas; with FAO it is involved in protecting genetic resources. It is also working with FAO, the United Nations Development Programme, the World Bank and the World Resources Institute on a new plan calling for $8 billion to be spent on tropical forests over the next five years.

34   So far, attempts to convince some nations to conserve their forests have failed. The focus is now shifting to a more realistic goal: convincing them to manage their forests wisely.

35   Last year, Conservation International, a United States-based environment group, bought a piece of the debt of Bolivia at a discount. In exchange that country agreed not to touch 3.7 million hectares of its natural forests. That kind of pragmatic approach might prove to be the wave of the future.

Thinking It Through

1. The first five paragraphs provide an overview of the information that follows. Is this an effective technique? Would the article catch the reader's attention more quickly if it started with paragraph 6?

2. Do you think that the "scenario of the future" (paragraphs 6 and 7) add to or take away from the factual evidence presented elsewhere? Explain.

3. This article suggests that if the world does not change its ways, "adapting to a changing climate might be the only recourse." What kind of adaptations might we have to make?

4. What do you think the writers might see as the *best* solution to these environmental problems? What do they see as the *most practical* solution?

Thinking and Writing

1. Reread paragraphs 13–15. In one paragraph summarize the process by which scientists believe the greenhouse effect causes the Earth to grow warmer.

2. If the Earth's temperature should rise 4.5 degrees centigrade (slightly more than 8 degrees Fahrenheit), what effect would that increase have on the place where you now live? In two or three paragraphs describe how your surroundings might look in the year 2030 after such a global warming.

What Is the Truth About Global Warming?

ROBERT JAMES BIDINOTTO

First Thoughts In this essay Robert Bidinotto examines one of the most familiar debates in modern science, one side of which is presented in "Will Earth Survive Man?" Bidinotto does not agree with many of the conclusions stated in that article. Here, he presents the evidence for the other side clearly and fairly, using well-established persuasive techniques.

Word List

SPECULATED (paragraph 2): theorized

INUNDATE (paragraph 2): flood

DRACONIAN (paragraph 3): extremely harsh

POTENT (paragraph 11): strong

IMPLICATED (paragraph 11): involved (used negatively)

FLUCTUATES (paragraph 13): changes, rises and falls

DEPLETION (paragraph 16): exhaustion

PARADOXICALLY (paragraph 25): seeming to be contradictory, but not actually so

JIBE (paragraph 25): agree

ATTRIBUTE (paragraph 26): credit, assign

DILEMMA (paragraph 31): difficulty, problem

INCONCLUSIVE (paragraph 33): indefinite, not final

ADVOCACY (paragraph 33): support, promotion

PRUDENT (paragraph 35): wise

1 In the summer of 1988, one of the century's worst heat waves gripped the East Coast and had Midwest farmers wondering if the Dust Bowl had returned. On June 23, at a Senate hearing on global climate change, James Hansen, a respected atmospheric

scientist and director of NASA's Goddard Institute for Space Studies, gave alarming testimony. "The earth is warmer in 1988 than at any time in the history of instrumental measurements," he said. "The greenhouse effect is changing our climate now."

2 Hansen's remarks touched off a firestorm of publicity. A major news magazine speculated that the Great Plains would be depopulated. On NBC's "Today" show, biologist Paul Ehrlich warned that melting polar ice could raise sea levels and inundate coastal cities, swamping much of Florida, Washington, D.C., and the Los Angeles basin. And in his recent book, *Global Warming*, Stephen Schneider of the National Center for Atmospheric Research imagined New York overcome by a killer heat wave, a baseball double-header in Chicago called because of a thick black haze created by huge forest fires in Canada, and Long Island devastated by a hurricane—all spawned by the "greenhouse effect."

3 In Paris last July, the leaders of seven industrial democracies, including President Bush and British Prime Minister Margaret Thatcher, called for common efforts to limit emissions of carbon dioxide and other "greenhouse gases." To accomplish this, many environmentalists have proposed draconian regulations—and huge new taxes—that could significantly affect the way we live. Warns Environmental Protection Agency head William Reilly: "To slow down the global heating process, the scale of economic and societal intervention will be enormous."

4 The stakes are high: the public could be asked to decide between environmental catastrophe and enormous costs. But do we really have to make this choice? Many scientists believe the danger is real, but others are much less certain. What is the evidence? Here is what we know:

5 **What is the greenhouse effect?** When sunlight warms the earth, certain gases in the lower atmosphere, acting like the glass in a greenhouse, trap some of the heat as it radiates back into space. These greenhouse gases, primarily water vapor and including carbon dioxide, methane and man-made chloro-fluorocarbons, warm our planet, making life possible.

6 If they were more abundant, greenhouse gases might trap too much heat. Venus, for example, has 60,000 times more carbon dioxide in its atmosphere than Earth, and its temperature averages above 800 degrees Fahrenheit. But if greenhouse gases were less plentiful or entirely absent, temperatures on Earth would average below freezing.

7 Because concentrations of greenhouse gases have been steadily rising, many scientists are concerned about global warming. Researchers at the Goddard Institute and at the University of

East Anglia in England foresee a doubling of greenhouse gas concentrations during the next century, which might raise average global temperatures as much as nine degrees Fahrenheit.

8   **What is causing the buildup?** Nature accounts for most of the greenhouse gases in the atmosphere. For example, carbon dioxide (CO_2), the most plentiful trace gas, is released by volcanoes, oceans, decaying plants and even by our breathing. But much of the buildup is man-made.

9   CO_2 is given off when we burn wood or such fossil fuels as coal and oil. In fact, the amount in the atmosphere has grown more than 25 percent since the Industrial Revolution began around 200 years ago—over 11 percent since 1958 alone.

10   Methane, the next most abundant greenhouse gas, is released when organic matter decomposes in swamps, rice paddies, livestock yards—even in the guts of termites and cud-chewing animals. The amount is growing about one percent per year, partly because of increased cattle raising and use of natural gas.

11   Chlorofluorocarbons (CFCs), a third culprit, escape from refrigerators, air conditioners, plastic foam, solvents and spray cans. The amount in the atmosphere is tiny compared with CO_2, but CFCs are thousands of times more potent in absorbing heat and have also been implicated in the "ozone hole."

12   **What does the ozone hole have to do with the greenhouse effect?** For all practical purposes, nothing. Ozone, a naturally occurring form of oxygen, is of concern for another reason. In the upper atmosphere it helps shield us from ultraviolet sunlight, which can cause skin cancer. In 1985, scientists confirmed a temporary thinning in the ozone layer over Antarctica, leading to a new concern: if ozone thinning spreads to populated areas, it could cause an increase in the disease.

13   The ozone hole appears only from September to November, and only over the Antarctic region, and then it repairs itself when atmospheric conditions change a few weeks later. It also fluctuates: in 1988, there was little ozone thinning.

14   Ozone is constantly created and destroyed by nature. Volcanoes, for example, can release immense quantities of chlorine, some of which may get into the stratosphere and destroy ozone molecules.

15   But the most popular theory to explain the appearance of the ozone hole is that man-made chlorofluorocarbons release chlorine atoms in the upper atmosphere.

16   Despite thinning of upper atmospheric ozone over Antarctica, no increase in surface ultraviolet radiation outside of that area is expected. John E. Frederick, an atmospheric scientist who chaired a United Nations Environment Program panel on trends

in atmospheric ozone, has dismissed fears of a skin-cancer epidemic as science fiction. "You would experience a much greater increase in biologically damaging ultraviolet radiation if you moved from New York City to Atlanta than you would with the ozone depletion that we estimate will occur over the next 30 years," he says.

17 **Will destruction of forests worsen the greenhouse effect?** When trees and plants grow, they remove CO_2 from the air. When they are burned or decay, they release stored CO_2 back into the atmosphere. In nations such as Brazil, thousands of square miles of tropical rain forests are being cleared and burned, leading many to be concerned about further CO_2 buildup.

18 Worldwide, millions of acres are planted with seedling trees each year, however; and new studies reveal that there has been no reliable data about the impact of forest destruction on global warming. Research by Daniel Botkin and Lloyd Simpson at the University of California at Santa Barbara and by Sandra Brown at the University of Illinois at Urbana shows that the carbon content of forests had been vastly overestimated, suggesting that deforestation is not as great a source of CO_2 as was once thought.

19 **Can we be certain that global warming will occur?** Virtually all scientists agree that if greenhouse gases increase and all other factors remain the same, the earth will warm up. But "the crucial issue," explains Prof. S. Fred Singer, an atmospheric scientist at the Washington Institute for Values in Public Policy, "is to what extent other factors remain the same." Climatic forces interact in poorly understood ways, and some may counteract warming.

20 At any given time, for example, clouds cover 60 percent of the planet, trapping heat radiating from its surface, but also reflecting sunlight back into space. So, if the oceans heat up and produce more clouds through evaporation, the increased cover might act as a natural thermostat and keep the planet from heating up. After factoring more detailed cloud simulations into its computer models, the British Meteorological Office recently showed that current global-warming projections could be cut in half.

21 Oceans have a major effect upon climate, but scientists have only begun to understand how. Investigators at the National Center for Atmospheric Research attributed the North American drought in the summer of 1988 primarily to temperature changes in the tropical Pacific involving a current called El Niño—not to the greenhouse effect. And when ocean currents were included in recent computerized climate simulations, the

Antarctic Ocean didn't warm—diminishing the likelihood that part of its ice sheet will break up and add to coastal flooding.

22   How heat travels through the atmosphere and back into space is another big question mark for the global-warming theory. So is the sunspot cycle, as well as the effect of atmospheric pollution and volcanic particles that can reflect sunlight back into space. Such factors throw predictions about global warming into doubt.

23   **So what is the bottom line? Has the earth begun to heat up?** Two widely reported statistics seem to present a powerful case for global warming. Some temperature records show about one degree Fahrenheit of warming over the past century, a period that has also seen a noticeable increase in greenhouse gases. And the six warmest years globally since record keeping began 100 years ago have all been in the 1980s.

24   As for the past decade, the increased warmth in three of its hottest years—1983, 1987 and 1988—is almost certainly associated with El Niño events in the Pacific.

25   Paradoxically, the historical records of temperature change do not jibe with the greenhouse theory. Between 1880 and 1940, temperatures appeared to rise. Yet between 1940 and 1965, a period of much heavier fossil-fuel use and deforestation, temperatures dropped, which seems inconsistent with the greenhouse effect. And a comprehensive study of past global ocean records by researchers from Britain and M.I.T. revealed no significant rising temperature trends between 1856 and 1986. Concludes Richard Lindzen of M.I.T.'s department of Earth, Atmospheric and Planetary Sciences, "The data as we have it does not support a warming."

26   Taking everything into account, few climatologists are willing to attribute any seeming warming to the greenhouse effect. Last May, 61 scientists participating in a greenhouse workshop in Amherst, Mass., declared that "such an attribution cannot now be made with any degree of confidence."

27   **Is there any other evidence of global warming?** Atmospheric researchers use complex computer programs called General Circulation Models (GCMs) to plot climate change. But a computer is no more reliable than its input, and poorly understood oceanic, atmospheric and continental processes are only crudely represented even in the best GCMs.

28   Computer calculations do not even accurately predict the past: they fail to match historical greenhouse-gas concentrations to expected temperatures. Because of these uncertainties, Stephen Schneider says in *Global Warming*, it is "an even bet that the GCMs have overestimated future warming by a factor of two."

29   In time, the computer models will undoubtedly improve. For now, the lack of evidence and reliable tools leaves proponents of global warming with little but theory.

30   **Should we do anything to offset the possible warming up of the globe?** Fossil fuels now provide 90 percent of the world's energy. Some environmentalists have advocated huge tax increases to discourage use of coal and other fossil fuels. Some have suggested a gasoline tax. There are also proposals that the government subsidize solar, windmill and geothermal power; that some foreign debts be swapped for protecting forests; and that worldwide population growth be slowed.

31   The buildup of greenhouse gases is cause for scientific study, but not for panic. Yet the facts sometimes get lost in the hysteria. Stephen Schneider confesses to an ethical dilemma. He admits the many uncertainties about global warming. Nevertheless, to gain public support through media coverage, he explains that sometimes scientists "have to offer up scary scenarios, make simplified, dramatic statements, and make little mention of any doubts we might have." Each scientist, he says, must decide the "right balance" between "being effective and being honest. I hope that means being both."

32   The temptation to bend fears for political ends is also ever present. "We've got to ride the global-warming issue," Sen. Timothy Wirth (D., Colo.) explained to a reporter. "Even if the theory is wrong, we will be doing the right thing in terms of economic and environmental policy."

33   But many scientists are troubled when inconclusive evidence is used for political advocacy. "The greenhouse warming has become a 'happening,'" says Richard Lindzen. To call for action, he adds, "has become a litmus test of morality."

34   We still know far too little to be stampeded into rash, expensive proposals. Before we take such steps, says Patrick J. Michaels, an associate professor of environmental sciences at the University of Virginia, "the science should be much less murky than it is now."

35   Further research and climatic monitoring are certainly warranted. If the "greenhouse signal" then emerges from the data, we can decide on the most prudent course of action.

Thinking It Through

1. What climatic conditions first led scientists to advance the theory of the greenhouse effect? Bidinotto and the writers of "Will Earth Survive Man?" look at the same climatic evidence, but they draw differ-

ent inferences from it. What are their inferences? (You can review inferences in Chapter 2.)

2. The writer structures his essay by asking questions and then answering them. Why does he do this? Is it effective?

3. What is the writer's final view of the issue of global warming? Do you think that his evidence supports his view? Explain.

4. Disagreeing with a number of the views expressed in "Will Earth Survive Man?" Bidinotto says that the evidence is not strong enough to cause nations to stop cutting tropical rain forests, to cut back on the use of fossil fuels, or to attempt to slow population growth in an attempt to halt global warming. Are there any other reasons for taking these actions? Explain.

Thinking and Writing

More and more frequently, there are conflicts—both small and large—between environmental and economic groups. A major hospital agrees to redesign a parking garage in order to spare a 300-year-old tree, but construction costs (and no doubt patient fees) go up. We stop strip-mining in some areas, but the miners are then unemployed. We may save ancient forests (and the northern spotted owl), but many loggers will lose their jobs.

Using your own knowledge or information gathered from reading newspapers and current magazines, write an essay in which you describe a recent conflict between those seeking to protect the environment and others following economic interests. You may either remain neutral or argue a particular point of view, but try to present a balanced view of the conflict.

~~~~~~

Let's Start Saving the Planet

BELVA PLAIN

First Thoughts In January 1990 Belva Plain wrote this New Year's wish for the world. Though she mentions the usual concerns of environmentalists, her approach to these problems is very personal.

Word List

RAMPANT (paragraph 1):   widespread

ARABLE (paragraph 4):   tillable, capable of being cultivated

CARCINOGENIC (paragraph 4):   cancer-causing

PANDERING TO (paragraph 8):   catering to (used negatively)

ARMAMENTS (paragraph 12):   weapons

ASSUREDLY (paragraph 14):   certainly

1   Like many Americans, as 1990 dawns, I hope this is the start of the decade when we will begin making improvements here at home. Better education. No more drugs. Stronger families with fewer divorces. No more homeless on the streets. A cleanup of the stupid, corrupting material with which television clutters the airwaves. A crackdown on the rampant crime that puts triple locks on our doors. Let's begin.

2   And I have larger concerns: My dearest hopes are for the small planet on which we live. With all proper respect for the gigantic intelligence that conceived the possibility of man's upward leap into space, for the technical skill of the hands that build the machinery and the courage of the individuals who make the leap toward Mars, I must still remind myself that for the present and the foreseeable future, this planet is our only home.

3   And we are destroying it! We Americans, along with the rest of the world, are destroying it.

4   All of us read the statistics: So many acres of arable land turned into desert when forests are leveled; so many tons of carbon dioxide released in to the air to produce the stifling greenhouse effect; so many tons of garbage dumped into the ocean that kill the fish and the dolphins and their nourishment. We go

254

to the beaches and watch the tides float filth back onto the shore. We cough in bitter smog. We worry about carcinogenic foods. We crawl bumper-to-bumper on the highways. We mourn— some of us do, at any rate—the pitiable suffering of the noble elephant shot dead and left to rot so that somebody can make money out of ivory ornaments for our necks and wrists. We wonder—some of us do, and some of us don't because we know—why there are so few songbirds in the trees on summer mornings. And more. And more.

5   We see all this, read about it and contribute to organizations that are trying to do something about it. Some of us even vote for people who promise to work on behalf of this lovely, mistreated earth. And all of this effort is good, but still it's not enough.

6   So my hope for the new year is that we will do more before it is too late.

7   Let our lumber companies stop stripping our great western forests to export lumber for Japanese houses, for how can we ask Brazil to preserve its forests when we don't cherish our own?

8   Let our manufacturers make a real and honest effort to perfect an electric car, a silent, clean and nonpolluting vehicle. Let us have no more delays, no more excuses, no more pandering to the oil companies or wreckage of our irreplaceable wilderness to make way for oil drills.

9   Let our builders stop filling the countryside with flimsy tract houses—that fall apart before the mortgage is paid off—strung along some of the ugliest highways in the entire world. Let the countryside remain green while, instead, we tear down slums and fashion the cities richly into the "alabaster cities" of "America the Beautiful," cities where people live or to which they come to enjoy parks and theater, music and museums.

10   When I was young, if you spoke about things in this way, you were laughed at. Whether you were one or not, they called you a "little old lady in tennis shoes." You were comical because "progress" was all, industry was all, profits were all, and bigger was better. But people don't laugh anymore now that so many dreary prophecies have come true. People are considering the fact that smaller is often better. Smaller cars. Smaller cities. Using less. Recycling. Saving instead of wasting. Remodeling old buildings. Preserving the historic neighborhoods.

11   I hope, too, for smaller population growth as the 1990s begin. "Be fruitful and multiply," the Bible says. But we are finally multiplying ourselves out of house and home! Most of our babies live to reach adulthood; no longer do we need to bear large numbers of children in order that a few may survive. How wonderful that

is! Yet there are still too many parts of the world where large numbers are born, and where they die, too, because there is no food for them. I hope that we can begin a truly serious effort toward population control everywhere so that no human being will be hungry or homeless and there will be pleasant space for all. We must remember that the earth is finite.

12　　Then, if everyone can be decently housed and fed, I believe that the chance for peace will be improved one-hundredfold. I hope so much that armaments can be decreased and money used to better purpose, like ridding mankind of mental illness and of cancer.

13　　Are all of these things too much to hope for, too many New Year's wishes? I don't think so. It's a long list, but not one item on it is impossible to achieve, if we simply put our minds to it. I want to see our country, this wonderful, free nation where, so it seems, half the world's people would like to live if they could, take the lead by example and persuasion in the saving of the planet.

14　　Then one day when the first men speed off toward Mars, as assuredly they will, from dark space they will look back at a blue-green Earth as bright and warm and fertile as it was on the day it was created. Happy New Year.

Thinking It Through

1. If you have read all the selections in this unit, summarize the major environmental problems that all the writers discuss.

2. Though Plain mentions statistics, she doesn't quote any. What kind of evidence does she use to persuade her readers? (To review types of evidence, see Chapter 6.) Do you think her technique works well? Why or why not? How do you feel she could have strengthened her persuasive appeal?

3. What suggestions does the writer offer for dealing with environmental problems? Does she propose specific ways of putting these suggestions into effect?

Thinking and Writing

Though Plain is writing specifically about the environment, her technique can be adapted to other subjects. This is basically an "I wish . . ." essay.

Write an essay expressing your own wishes for the environment or any other issue of wide concern. Though essays of this kind are personal and informal, they do take careful planning and organization. Otherwise, they ramble.

The Human Environment

Mankind owes to the child the best it has to give.
—UN Declaration on the Rights of the Child

Distancing the Homeless

JONATHAN KOZOL

First Thoughts   Jonathan Kozol writes often about education and social issues. The selection here condenses part of his long-term study of the homeless. His complete findings are published in his award-winning book, *Rachel and Her Children: Homeless Families in America* (1989).

Word List   AFFORDED (paragraph 1):   given

CHRONICALLY (paragraph 4):   over a long time

DEINSTITUTIONALIZED (paragraph 4):   released from an institution

SUPPOSITION (paragraph 4):   theory, idea

VAGRANT (paragraph 5):   homeless wanderer

DEPRIVATION (paragraph 6):   lack

DEBILITATED (paragraph 6):   weakened

SPORADIC (paragraph 9):   infrequent, irregular

COMMUNAL (paragraph 9):   shared by a group

PRENATAL (paragraph 13):   before birth

CONTEMPLATED (paragraph 14):   thought about, considered

~~~~~~~~~~~~~~~~   1   Last summer, some twenty-eight thousand homeless people were afforded shelter by the city of New York. Of this number, twelve thousand were children and six thousand were parents living together in families. The average child was six years old, the average parent twenty-seven. A typical homeless family included a mother with two or three children, but in about one-fifth of these families two parents were present. Roughly ten thousand single persons, then, made up the remainder of the population of the city's shelters.

2   These proportions vary somewhat from one area of the nation to another. In all areas, however, families are the fastest-growing sector of the homeless population, and in the Northeast they are by far the largest sector already. In Massachusetts, three-fourths

of the homeless now are families with children; in certain parts of Massachusetts—Attleboro and Northhampton, for example— the proportion reaches ninety percent. Two-thirds of the homeless children studied recently in Boston were less than five years old.

3   Of an estimated two to three million homeless people nationwide, about 500,000 are dependent children, according to Robert Hayes, counsel to the National Coalition for the Homeless. Including their parents, at least 750,000 homeless people in America are family members.

4   What is to be made, then, of the supposition that the homeless are primarily the former residents of mental hospitals, persons who were carelessly released during the 1970s? Many of them are, to be sure. Among the older men and women in the streets and shelters, as many as one-third (some believe as many as one-half) may be chronically disturbed, and a number of these people were deinstitutionalized during the 1970s. But in a city like New York, where nearly half the homeless are small children with an average age of six, to operate on the basis of such a supposition makes no sense. Their parents, with an average age of twenty-seven, are not likely to have been hospitalized in the 1970s, either.

5   Nor is it easy to assume, as was once the case, that single men—those who come closer to fitting the stereotype of the homeless vagrant, the drifting alcoholic of an earlier age—are the former residents of mental hospitals. The age of homeless men has dropped in recent years; many of them are only twenty-one to twenty-eight years old. Fifty percent of homeless men in New York City shelters in 1984 were there for the first time. Most had previously had homes and jobs. Many had never before needed public aid. . . .

6   A young man who had lost his job, then his family, then his home, all in the summer of 1986, spoke with me for several hours in Grand Central Station on the weekend following Thanksgiving. "A year ago," he said, "I never thought that somebody like me would end up in a shelter. Nothing you've ever undergone prepares you. You walk into the place [a shelter on the Bowery]—the smell of sweat and urine hits you like a wall. Unwashed bodies and the look of absolute despair on many, many faces there would make you think you were in Dante's Hell. . . . What you fear is that you will be here forever. You do not know if it is ever going to end. You think to yourself: It is a dream and I will awake. Sometimes I think: It's an experiment. They are watching you to find out how much you can take. . . . I was a pretty stable man. Now I tremble when I meet somebody in the ordinary world. I'm trembling right now. . . . For me, the loss of

work and loss of wife had left me rocking. Then the welfare regulations hit me. I began to feel that I would be reduced to trash. . . . Half the people that I know are suffering from chest infections and sleep deprivation. The lack of sleep leaves you debilitated, shaky. You exaggerate your fears. If a psychiatrist came along he'd say that I was crazy. But I was an ordinary man. There was nothing wrong with me. I lost my kids. I lost my home. Now would you say that I was crazy if I told you I was feeling sad?"

7   "If the plight of homeless adults is the shame of America," writes Fred Hechinger in the *New York Times*, "the lives of homeless children are the nation's crime."

8   In November 1984, a fact already known to advocates for the homeless was given brief attention by the press. Homeless families, the *New York Times* reported, "mostly mothers and young children, have been sleeping on chairs, counters and floors of the city's emergency welfare offices." Reacting to such reports, the mayor declared: "This woman is sitting on a chair or on a floor. It is not because we didn't offer her a bed. We provide a shelter for every single person who knocks on our door." On the same day, however, the city reported that in the previous eleven weeks it had been unable to give shelter to 153 families, and in the subsequent year, 1985, the city later reported that about two thousand children slept in welfare offices because of lack of shelter space.

9   Some eight hundred homeless infants in New York City, reported the National Coalition for the Homeless, "routinely go without sufficient food, cribs, health care and diapers." The lives of these children "are put at risk," while "high-risk pregnant women" are repeatedly forced to sleep in unsafe "barracks shelters" or welfare offices called Emergency Assistance Units (EAUs). "Coalition monitors, making sporadic random checks, found eight women in their ninth month of pregnancy sleeping in EAUs. . . . Two women denied shelter began having labor contractions at the EAU." In one instance, the Legal Aid Society was forced to go to court after a woman lost her child by miscarriage while lying on the floor of a communal bathroom in a shelter which the courts had already declared unfit to house pregnant women.

10   The coalition also reported numerous cases in which homeless mothers were obliged to choose between purchasing food or diapers for their infants. Federal guidelines issued in 1986 deepened the nutrition crisis faced by mothers in the welfare shelters by counting the high rent paid to the owners of these buildings as a part of family income, rendering their residents ineligible for food stamps. Families I interviewed who had received as

much as $150 in food stamps monthly in June 1986 were cut back to $33 before Christmas.

11 "Now you're hearing all kinds of horror stories," said President Reagan, "about the people that are going to be thrown out in the snow to hunger and [to] die of cold and so forth. . . . We haven't cut a single budget." But in the four years leading up to 1985, according to the *New Republic*, Aid to Families with Dependent Children had been cut by $4.8 billion, child nutrition programs by $5.2 billion, food stamps by $6.8 billion. The federal government's authority to help low-income families with housing assistance was cut from $30 billion to $11 billion in Reagan's first term. In his fiscal 1986 budget, the president proposed to cut that by an additional ninety-five percent.

12 "If even one American child is forced to go to bed hungry at night," the president said on another occasion, "that is a national tragedy. We are too generous a people to allow this." But in the years since the president spoke these words, thousands of poor children in New York alone have gone to bed too sick to sleep and far too weak to rise the next morning to attend a public school. Thousands more have been unable to attend school at all because their homeless status compels them to move repeatedly from one temporary shelter to another. Even in the affluent suburbs outside New York City, hundreds of homeless children are obliged to ride as far as sixty miles twice a day in order to obtain an education in the public schools to which they were originally assigned before their families were displaced. Many of these children get to school too late to eat their breakfast; others are denied lunch at school because of federal cuts in feeding programs.

13 Many homeless children die—and others suffer brain damage—as a direct consequence of federal cutbacks in prenatal programs, maternal nutrition, and other feeding programs. The parents of one such child shared with me the story of the year in which their child was delivered, lived, and died. The child, weighing just over four pounds at birth, grew deaf and blind soon after, and for these reasons had to stay in the hospital for several months. When he was released on Christmas Eve of 1984, his mother and father had no home. He lived with his parents in the shelters, subways, streets, and welfare offices of New York City for four winter months, and was readmitted to the hospital in time to die in May 1985.

14 When we met and spoke the following year, the father told me that his wife had contemplated and even attempted suicide after the child's death, while he had entertained the thought of blowing up the welfare offices of New York City. I would tell him that to do so would be illegal and unwise. I would never tell him it was crazy.

15   "No one will be turned away," says the mayor of New York City, as hundreds of young mothers with their infants are turned from the doors of shelters season after season. That may sound to some like denial of reality. "Now you're hearing all these stories," says the President of the United States as he denies that anyone is cold or hungry or unhoused. On another occasion he says that the unsheltered "are homeless, you might say, by choice." That sounds every bit as self-deceiving. . . .

Thinking It Through

1. Locate examples of several types of evidence used in this essay. (Types of evidence are discussed in Chapter 6.) Is one more effective than the others?

2. How does Kozol counter the claim (often used by the federal government) that most of the homeless are former inmates of mental institutions?

3. Reread the remarks of the young man who lost his job, family, and home (paragraph 6). What does his language tell you about him? What do examples like this suggest about the stereotypes of the homeless that are given by former President Reagan and former Mayor Koch?

4. In persuasive writing we often quote authorities. Kozol quotes government officials in paragraphs 11, 12, and 15. How does he use these quotations?

5. In March 1990 a government commission released a study that included these findings: (1) the infant death rate has risen, reversing a fifty-year decline; (2) the number of babies with low birth weights is up, increasing the risk of deafness, blindness, and mental retardation in these infants; (3) the number of pregnant women who receive no medical care has increased more than 50 percent in ten years. Based on these data and on information that Kozol gives, what inferences might we draw? (Inferences are discussed in Chapter 2.)

Thinking and Writing

1. Look over Kozol's essay again, noting the major points that you underlined and marked in the margin. Summarize these major points in a short paragraph.

2. Look again at question 1 in "Thinking It Through." Alone or in small groups, consider Kozol's evidence carefully. Then write a brief essay in which you explain what type of evidence seems most effective to you and why. (This is one way of evaluating evidence, a necessary step in analyzing any piece of persuasive writing.)

Reporter Gives Birth on Assignment

YEVGENIA ALBATS

First Thoughts   Yevgenia Albats is a reporter and analyst for *Moscow News* (often called simply *MN*), a weekly newspaper published by the Soviet Union. In this selection from *MN*, Albats reprints and reflects on entries from a diary she kept during her days in a Moscow maternity hospital. Though Albats is writing specifically of conditions in Soviet hospitals, her concerns are shared in various parts of the world. Addressing her newborn daughter in a diary entry, the author speaks for many parents, especially mothers, when she writes: ". . . it is for you and for the sake of what you are going to experience one day (I hope you won't have to experience much of what I have experienced) that I'm writing this report. It is for your sake that I'm writing this, my girl. . . ."

Word List   PEREMPTORILY (paragraph 1):   in a domineering way

MAGNITUDE (paragraph 1):   great size

EXPELLED (paragraph 5):   pushed out

PREFERENTIAL (paragraph 8):   special, uncommon

COMPENSATE (paragraph 9):   make up for

DIATHESIS (paragraph 14):   tendency to contract a disease

NAPPIES (paragraph 16):   cloth diapers

AESTHETIC TASTE (paragraph 19):   knowledge of or sense of beauty

ALLOCATIONS (paragraph 27):   portions, amounts (as of funds)

1   **SECOND DAY**. From my diary: "He came into our ward where four women who had given birth the previous evening were resting, and, without saying hello, told us in a tired, mechanical voice what we could and could not have. We are allowed to have two towels, a toothbrush and paste, some soap, eau-de-cologne for our hands, and nothing more. The white-capped doctor Oleg Nikolayevich poked each of us in the belly, asked peremptorily if we had any complaints, and went out. He didn't have time to say 'Congratulations!' or any such phrase. In fact none of the medical personnel had said anything like that to me yesterday or today. The four of us—pale, tired and dead-beat, hardly realizing

the magnitude of yesterday's event—kept silent. I recollected the day before, the first day."

2   The delivery room had eight beds covered in orange oil-cloth with bits of laundered stained linen thrown over. Midwife Lydia Gavrilovna had strong manly hands and gentle words to soothe us, but she came off her duty too soon. Then I kept pleading with the pretty young nurse, "Olechka, don't go away, don't leave me alone, please. . . ." There was a nurse's assistant too, who bumped into the room from time to time to yell at me: "Stop screaming!"

3   I put all my lung power into those screams. Not for pain, although the pain of childbirth is considerable. I'm no specialist and cannot judge how well-justified, from the medical point of view, is the thesis "a child must be born through suffering." Childbirth is hard work, but why should it be suffering? In my view the above thesis is born of our poverty. An old obstetrician explained that pain relief by anesthetics, hypnosis or electric sleep is expensive and requires permanent attendance, for which there aren't enough nurses. So I kept yelling—not so much through pain as to follow some wise women's advice. They said it seemed easier that way, and there was also hope that someone might attend to you. . . .

4   Our women will certainly cope. They can unload freight cars and lay down asphalt. But I'm worried about the babies.

5   According to the statistics, four out of five babies are born with abnormalities. The well-known pediatrician Nina Znamenskaya said, "something terrible is happening before our very eyes: the percentage of 'squeezed out' babies has grown sharply," which means that children do not pass through the birth passages naturally, but are forcefully expelled from the womb. No wonder the number of children with brain damage is climbing.

6   A very young woman, a teenager by the look of her, was in labour in the bed next to mine. In my presence the doctor told her that her physique threatened grave complications to herself and the baby. Yet she was not overindulged with medical attention. Later I learned that the delivery was very hard, and the doctors did not guarantee her child would be normal.

7   My case was trivial, thank God, and I had the benefit of publicity after my previous report was published in *MN*. But here is a dialogue in the delivery room when the time came for my baby daughter to be born: "Will you please call the doctor and the pediatrician?" A few minutes later she returned saying, "None of them are there."

8   If this is preferential treatment, what about run-of-the-mill cases? If this is the situation in one of Moscow's best maternity

hospitals, famous for its obstetricians, what can be said about other clinics?

9   One more detail to finish off the picture. What does a woman who has just given birth need for perfect happiness? A glass of hot sweet tea to compensate for the heavy loss of blood, and a bite. "It's long past supper time," the assistant said. Did she mean I ought to have hurried up with my business?

10   **THIRD DAY**. From my diary: "The doctor's morning round. Lena complains: 'I have a belly ache.' 'It's unimportant,' says the doctor. Galya complains: 'My stitches ache.' 'It's unimportant. . . .' We all laughed when he left."

11   You ought not to have your child in the summer, because half of the clinics are closed down for repairs, and in the remaining ones beds fill up corridors and nurses are run off their feet.

12   You ought not to have your baby on Friday, because the pediatrician who is to examine your child and tell you if it is all right—the information most important for every mother—will not turn up until Monday.

13   You ought not to have your baby at a clinic where everything is unimportant.

14   Today we were given our babies to feed for the first time. My God, I was afraid to handle the creature, let alone feed her. How should I hold her? How should I arrange myself on the sagging mattress? What should I do if she falls asleep while suckling? And why was she given to me only today? It's common knowledge that the best way to prevent diathesis is to put the baby to breast on the very first day.

15   I look at the small warm bundle swaddled to the neck in the wrap stamped with the full name of the maternity hospital with the inscription, "Ministry of Health," and am unable to understand that it is my daughter, part of myself only a couple of days earlier.

16   **FOURTH DAY**. From my diary: "The woman who has just delivered becomes positively stupid. She starts asking silly questions and gets terribly upset by the answers. I asked the nurse who brings our babies to feed, placed like pieces of firewood on the trolley, how many babies each of them had to look after. 'Thirty-two,' she answered. 'But this is incredible! How do you manage to wash and change nappies for each of them six times a day, before every suckling?'

17   'But we only change nappies three times a day. We are short of nappies, you see. And we've got no baby's vests at all . . . .'"

18   Let me quote the *Parents' Book About Children*: "From the fourth day on, the baby urinates 21 to 25 times a day."

19   I'm so happy our babies don't see things straight for the time being! Otherwise, their aesthetic taste would have been spoiled

once they set their eyes on their mummies. The things we wear! Hideous faded dressing gowns with pockets, lapels and belts torn off, men's yellow plastic slippers and nighties often torn from top to waist—all of these must look disgusting from the outside. But for those inside it's just everyday life you get used to. Getting an extra towel is a stroke of luck. An extra square of linen (called nappy here) is a sign of good fortune, and obtaining a clean nightie by begging from the linen mistress is an achievement that can make your day! . . .

20   Six times a day my baby daughter is brought to my filthy bed where I was dumped three days earlier after delivery, smeared in blood. She runs the risk of being infected with all sorts of streptococcal, staphylococcic and Gram-negative infections. Incidentally, before we are allowed to touch our babies, we must cleanse our hands with alcohol, the doctors say.

21   **FIFTH DAY**. From my diary: "The doctor monitoring our ward is called Vyacheslav Borisovich. A civilized and well-informed young man, he asked me: 'Have you got any questions or requests?' 'I have a request, please. Will you please prescribe me a shower?'

22   "'But you know there's no shower room in our department.' . . ."

23   Well, all this is going on in a country capable of landing an unmanned spacecraft returning from the orbit! The country that occupies 50th place in the world—immediately after Barbados —for infant mortality. A strangely high rating. Our infants must have enormous survival potential.

24   Do you feel ashamed? I feel disgusted! . . .

25   Add to that the approach of AIDS whose virus lives in the blood and is especially dangerous where there is direct contact with infected blood. Well, in a maternity clinic you face direct contact round the clock. Don't you think that this makes newly-born babies the greatest risk group to date? We are infecting our future. The future of the nation is in peril.

26   I cannot write about it any longer. I shudder at the thought of what might happen to my daughter. I'm terrified. . . .

27   My whys are endless. They tormented me at the maternity clinic, and then keep tormenting me now that I'm writing this report. We are fond of going to extremes in that we either see all the negative aspects of our health service as "separate shortcomings" or as global problems like the budget deficit, inadequate allocations for medical science, and lack of modern equipment. I can see all that, but to my mind, our greatest, in fact, global shortcoming is the lack of personal responsibility and personal commitment: "Who will do that if I don't?" As well as the lack of personal answerability for the existing order of things.

28   If the doctor says about a patient's complaint, "It's unimportant," no computer tomographs are going to save you. . . .

29   **SIXTH DAY**. No entry in my diary. There's a cluster of cars in the clinic's courtyard. Many will go home today. We shall be discharged, too. Daddy is waiting downstairs with flowers. As I watch the nurse change my girl into the things brought from home (the first baby's vest in her life!) I feel terrified at the thought that a few hours from now I'll have to change her myself. I notice intertrigo on my daughter's behind but say nothing. "Never mind intertrigo! The important thing is she's got no birth trauma." I don't yet know anything about the trouble lying in wait inside my daughter's system already. She has caught staphylococcic infection at the clinic. But, for the time being, we are happy.

30   A month later I wrote this in my diary: One should give birth to a child if only to realize how fearful life can be when you know you might lose your child any minute.

Thinking It Through

1. This article does not look or sound like the typical expository or persuasive essays in this text, but it does have a thesis. How would you state it?

2. The article follows the arrangement of the diary entries: second day, third day, and so forth; however, there is more than simple chronological order here. How does the writer's view of her surroundings and her understanding of the conditions of the hospital change as time goes on?

3. Though this article is strongly personal and obviously based on firsthand experience, the writer skillfully introduces information based on research and a reporter's knowledge of conditions in health care facilities. Point out some of this information.

4. After reading Albats's account, who or what do you think is mainly to blame for conditions in the maternity hospitals?

Thinking and Writing

Choose a subject about which you feel strongly and with which you have had some personal experience. Some possible examples: gun control; use of seat belts; drunk driving; controlling the spread of communicable diseases; drug testing; discrimination on the basis of age, race, or gender; equal access for the handicapped; and so on.

Write a personal narrative that tells your own story but that, at the same time, makes a persuasive point. If you wish, you may work in outside material—statistics, facts, even quotations—that you already have or can get at a library.

If you wish to review narrative writing, see Chapter 4.

Brave New World

ALDOUS HUXLEY

First Thoughts It was nearly sixty years ago that the British writer Aldous Huxley published his startling vision of what the world could become. The world in 632 A.F. (after Ford) is one in which traditional values and moral or ethical standards are turned upside down. As we see in this selection from the first chapter of Huxley's novel, the key to maintaining this new society is genetic control and early conditioning. Chapter 1 opens in the Central London Hatchery and Conditioning Centre. Some new students (taking notes, of course) are being taken on a tour by the Director of Hatcheries and Conditioning (the D.H.C.) and an assistant, Mr. Foster.

Word List ZEALOUS (paragraph 1):   earnest

OVA (paragraph 1):   eggs

GAMETES (paragraph 1):   sperm cells

EXCISED (paragraph 2):   cut out; surgically removed

POROUS RECEPTACLE (paragraph 2):   absorbent container

IMMERSED (paragraph 2):   submerged or bathed

PROLIFERATE (paragraph 4):   reproduce

BURGEONED (paragraph 7):   budded

PRODIGIOUS (paragraph 7):   huge

VIVIPAROUS (paragraph 7):   developed in a mother and live-born

PERITONEUM (paragraph 15):   lining of the abdominal cavity

MORULA (paragraph 16):   cell mass in the early embryonic stage

PREDESTINE (paragraph 17):   determine beforehand

DECANT (paragraph 17):   unbottle

SPANNER (paragraph 19):   wrench (British usage)

SURROGATE (paragraph 19):   substitute

CASTE (paragraph 24):   class

SENTENTIOUSLY (paragraph 29):   speaking in a moralizing way

(*A note on vocabulary:* Huxley uses a number of technical terms—a few of which he makes up—in order to set the high-tech tone of this chapter. Readers, like the students on tour, are supposed to be impressed and even slightly puzzled. You need not be concerned if some of these words are unfamiliar.)

1   "I shall begin at the beginning," said the D.H.C. and the more zealous students recorded his intention in their notebooks: *Begin at the beginning.* "These," he waved his hand, "are the incubators." And opening an insulated door he showed them racks upon racks of numbered test-tubes. "The week's supply of ova. Kept," he explained, "at blood heat; whereas the male gametes," and here he opened another door, "they have to be kept at thirty-five instead of thirty-seven. Full blood heat sterilizes."

2   Still leaning against the incubators he gave them, while the pencils scurried illegibly across the pages, a brief description of the modern fertilizing process; spoke first, of course, of its surgical introduction—"the operation undergone voluntarily for the good of Society, not to mention the fact that it carries a bonus amounting to six months' salary"; continued with some account of the technique for preserving the excised ovary alive and actively developing; passed on to a consideration of optimum temperature, salinity, viscosity; referred to the liquor in which the detached and ripened eggs were kept; and, leading his charges to the work tables, actually showed them how this liquor was drawn off from the test-tubes; how it was let out drop by drop onto the specially warmed slides of the microscopes; how the eggs which it contained were inspected for abnormalities, counted and transferred to a porous receptacle; how (and he now took them to watch the operation) this receptacle was immersed in a warm bouillon containing free-swimming spermatozoa—at a minimum concentration of one hundred thousand per cubic centimetre, he insisted; and how, after ten minutes, the container was lifted out of the liquor and its contents re-examined; how, if any of the eggs remained unfertilized, it was again immersed, and, if necessary, yet again; how the fertilized ova went back to the incubators; where the Alphas and Betas remained until definitely bottled; while the Gammas, Deltas and Epsilons were brought out again, after only thirty-six hours, to undergo Bokanovsky's Process.

3   "Bokanovsky's Process," repeated the Director, and the students underlined the words in their little notebooks.

4   One egg, one embryo, one adult—normality. But a bokanovskified egg will bud, will proliferate, will divide. From eight to ninety-six buds, and every bud will grow into a perfectly formed embryo, and every embryo into a full-sized adult. Making ninety-six human beings grow where only one grew before. Progress.

5   "Essentially," the D.H.C. concluded, "bokanovskification consists of a series of arrests of development. We check the normal growth and, paradoxically enough, the egg responds by budding."

6   *Responds by budding.* The pencils were busy.

7   He pointed. On a very slowly moving band a rack-full of test-tubes was entering a large metal box, another rack-full was emerging. Machinery faintly purred. It took eight minutes for the tubes to go through, he told them. Eight minutes of hard X-rays being about as much as an egg can stand. A few died; of the rest, the least susceptible divided into two; most put out four buds; some eight; all were returned to the incubators, where the buds began to develop; then, after two days, were suddenly chilled, chilled and checked. Two, four, eight, the buds in their turn budded; and having budded were dosed almost to death with alcohol; consequently burgeoned again and having budded—bud out of bud out of bud—were thereafter—further arrest being generally fatal—left to develop in peace. By which time the original egg was in a fair way to becoming anything from eight to ninety-six embryos—a prodigious improvement, you will agree, on nature. Identical twins—but not in piddling twos and threes as in the old viviparous days, when an egg would sometimes accidentally divide; actually by dozens, by scores at a time.

8   "Scores," the Director repeated and flung out his arms, as though he were distributing largesse. "Scores."

9   But one of the students was fool enough to ask where the advantage lay.

10   "My good boy!" The Director wheeled sharply round on him. "Can't you see? Can't you see?" He raised a hand; his expression was solemn. "Bokanovsky's Process is one of the major instruments of social stability!"

11   *Major instruments of social stability.*

12   Standard men and women; in uniform batches. The whole of a small factory staffed with the products of a single bokanovskified egg.

13   "Ninety-six identical twins working ninety-six identical machines!" The voice was almost tremulous with enthusiasm. "You really know where you are. For the first time in history." He quoted the planetary motto. "Community, Identity, Stability." Grand words. "If we could bokanovskify indefinitely the whole problem would be solved."

14   Solved by standard Gammas, unvarying Deltas, uniform Epsilons. Millions of identical twins. The principle of mass production at last applied to biology. . . .

15   In the Bottling Room all was harmonious bustle and ordered activity. Flaps of fresh sow's peritoneum ready cut to the proper size came shooting up in little lifts from the Organ Store in the sub-basement. Whizz and then, click! the lift-hatches flew open; the bottle-liner had only to reach out a hand, take the flap, insert, smooth-down, and before the lined bottle had had time to travel out of reach along the endless band, whizz, click! another flap of peritoneum had shot up from the depths, ready to be slipped into yet another bottle, the next of that slow interminable procession on the band.

16   Next to the Liners stood the Matriculators. The procession advanced; one by one the eggs were transferred from their test-tubes to the larger containers; deftly the peritoneal lining was slit, the morula dropped into place, the saline solution poured in . . . and already the bottle had passed, and it was the turn of the labellers. Heredity, date of fertilization, membership of Bokanovsky Group—details were transferred from test-tube to bottle. No longer anonymous, but named, identified, the procession marched slowly on; on through an opening in the wall, slowly on into the Social Predestination Room. . . .

"We also predestine and condition [said Mr. Foster]. We decant our babies as socialized human beings, as Alphas or Epsilons, as future sewage workers or future . . ." He was going to say "future World controllers," but correcting himself, said "future Directors of Hatcheries," instead.

18   The D.H.C. acknowledged the compliment with a smile.

19   They were passing Metre 320 on Rack 11. A young Beta-Minus mechanic was busy with screw-driver and spanner on the blood-surrogate pump of a passing bottle. The hum of the electric motor deepened by fractions of a tone as he turned the nuts. Down, down . . . A final twist, a glance at the revolution counter, and he was done. He moved two paces down the line and began the same process on the next pump.

20   "Reducing the number of revolutions per minute," Mr. Foster explained. "The surrogate goes round slower; therefore passes through the lung at longer intervals; therefore gives the embryo less oxygen. Nothing like oxygen-shortage for keeping an embryo below par." Again he rubbed his hands.

21   "But why do you want to keep the embryo below par?" asked an ingenuous student.

22   "Ass!" said the Director, breaking a long silence. "Hasn't it occurred to you that an Epsilon embryo must have an Epsilon environment as well as an Epsilon heredity?"

23   It evidently hadn't occurred to him. He was covered with confusion.

24   "The lower the caste," said Mr. Foster, "the shorter the oxygen." The first organ affected was the brain. After that the skeleton. At seventy per cent of normal oxygen you got dwarfs. At less than seventy eyeless monsters.

25   "Who are no use at all," concluded Mr. Foster. . . .

26   Their wanderings through the crimson twilight had brought them to the neighborhood of Metre 170 on Rack 9. From this point onwards Rack 9 was enclosed and the bottles performed the remainder of their journey in a kind of tunnel, interrupted here and there by openings two or three metres wide.

27   "Heat conditioning," said Mr. Foster.

28   Hot tunnels alternated with cool tunnels. Coolness was wedded to discomfort in the form of hard X-rays. By the time they were decanted the embryos had a horror of cold. They were predestined to emigrate to the tropics, to be miners and acetate silk spinners and steel workers. Later on their minds would be made to endorse the judgment of their bodies. "We condition them to thrive on heat," concluded Mr. Foster. "Our colleagues upstairs will teach them to love it."

29   "And that," put in the Director sententiously, "that is the secret of happiness and virtue—liking what you've *got* to do. All conditioning aims at that: making people like their unescapable social destiny." . . .

30   On Rack 10 rows of next generation's chemical workers were being trained in the toleration of lead, caustic soda, tar, chlorine. The first of a batch of two hundred and fifty embryonic rocket-plane engineers was just passing the eleven hundred metre mark on Rack 3. A special mechanism kept their containers in constant rotation. "To improve their sense of balance," Mr. Foster explained. "Doing repairs on the outside of a rocket in mid-air is a ticklish job. We slacken off the circulation when they're right way up, so that they're half starved, and double the flow of surrogate when they're upside down. They learn to associate topsy-turvydom with well-being; in fact, they're only truly happy when they're standing on their heads.

31   "And now," Mr. Foster went on, "I'd like to show you some very interesting conditioning for Alpha Plus Intellectuals. We have a big batch of them on Rack 5. First Gallery level," he called to two boys who had started to go down to the ground floor.

32   "They're round about Metre 900," he explained. "You can't really do any useful intellectual conditioning till the foetuses have lost their tails. Follow me."

33   But the Director had looked at his watch. "Ten to three," he said. "No time for the intellectual embryos, I'm afraid. We must

go up to the Nurseries before the children have finished their afternoon sleep."

34   Mr. Foster was disappointed. "At least one glance at the Decanting Room," he pleaded.

35   "Very well then." The Director smiled indulgently. "Just one glance."

∿∿∿∿∿∿∿∿∿∿∿

Thinking It Through

1. The process by which human eggs are fertilized and developed at the Hatchery is discussed in great technical detail. What effect does this have on the reader?

2. The terms *Alphas*, *Betas*, *Gammas*, *Deltas*, and *Epsilons* are not specifically explained. What do you assume they refer to?

3. How do the processes of hatching and conditioning work together to produce the population needed for this brave new world?

4. The motto of the World State is "Community, Identity, Stability." What do these familiar words really mean in the year 632 A.F.?

Thinking and Writing

Though we have not reached the stage Huxley describes, we can (as the next essay shows) to some extent medically alter the beginning of life. And by medically shortening or prolonging life, we can also alter the end. Today, private citizens, doctors, hospital staff, Supreme Court Justices, and others are struggling with scientific and ethical questions that previous generations hardly considered. In your view, what changes in the beginning or the end of human life do we have the right to make? What changes do we not have the right to make?

Write an essay in which you address this issue. You may choose to focus on either birth or death. (You may want to read the next essay, "Made to Order Babies," before you write.) If your instructor wishes, you may spend some group time discussing or brainstorming this topic.

```
^^^^^^^^^^^^^^^^^^^^^^^^^^^^^^^^^^^^^^^^^^^^^^^^^^^^^^^^^^^^^^
```

Made to Order Babies

GEOFFREY COWLEY

First Thoughts   In the early 1930s Huxley imagined a world in which human development could be controlled even before conception. In the late 1980s, as Geoffrey Cowley reports, that world is here. Huxley's vision was frightening and sometimes disgusting. The modern reality, as we read of it here, has great potential for both good and bad.

Word List   DEMENTED (paragraph 1):   insane

PROSPECTIVE (paragraph 2):   likely to become

ANALOGOUS (paragraph 6):   comparable

PRENATAL (paragraph 6):   before birth

MUTATIONS (paragraph 7):   changes, deviations

ADAMANT (paragraph 8):   determined

DORMANT (paragraph 8):   inactive

DILEMMAS (paragraph 10):   problems, difficulties

IMPETUS (paragraph 10):   motivation

ETHICIST (paragraph 13):   one who studies ethics or the ethical choices that people make

PRECEDENT (paragraph 14):   example, model for future action

BIZARRE (paragraph 15):   strange, very unusual

STIGMATIZED (paragraph 16):   characterized as undesirable or in some way disgraceful

EUGENICS (paragraph 17):   the belief in or study of improving a species through genetic control

RIFE (paragraph 18):   plentiful, thick or crowded

```
^^^^^^^^^^^^^^^^^^
```
1   For centuries, Jewish communities lived Job-like with the knowledge that many of their babies would thrive during infancy, grow demented and blind as toddlers and die by the age of 5. Joseph Ekstein, a Hasidic rabbi in Brooklyn, lost four children to Tay-Sachs disease over three decades, and his experience was not unusual. Some families were just unlucky.

2   Today, the curse of Tay-Sachs is being lifted—not through better treatments (the hereditary disease is as deadly as ever) but through a new cultural institution called Chevra Dor Yeshorim, the "Association of an Upright Generation." Thanks largely to Rabbi Ekstein's efforts, Orthodox teenagers throughout the world now line up at screening centers to have their blood tested for evidence of the Tay-Sachs gene. Before getting engaged, prospective mates simply call Chevra Dor Yeshorim and read off the code numbers assigned to their tests results.

3   If the records show that neither person carries the gene, or that just one does, the match is judged sound. But if both happen to be carriers (meaning any child they conceive will have a one-in-four chance of suffering the fatal disease), marriage is virtually out of the question. Even if two carriers wanted to wed, few rabbis would abet them. "It's a rule of thumb that engagements won't occur until compatibility is established," says Rabbi Jacob Horowitz, codirector of the Brooklyn-based program. "Each day, we could stop many marriages worldwide."

4   Marriage isn't the only institution being reshaped by modern genetics; a host of new diagnostic tests could soon change every aspect of creating a family. Physicians can now identify some 250 genetic defects, not only in the blood of a potential parent but in the tissue of a developing fetus. The result is that, for the first time in history, people are deciding, rather than wondering, what kind of children they will bear.

5   Choosing to avoid a horrible disease may be easy, at least in principle, but that's just one of many options 21st century parents could face. Already, conditions far less grave than Tay-Sachs have been linked to specific genes, and the science is still exploding. Researchers are now at work on a massive $3 billion project to decipher the entire human genetic code. By the turn of the century, knowledge gained through this Human Genome Initiative could enable doctors to screen fetuses—even test-tube embryos—for traits that have nothing to do with disease. "Indeed," says Dr. Paul Berg, director of the Beckman Center for Molecular and Genetic Medicine at Stanford, "we should be able to locate which [gene] combinations affect kinky hair, olive skin and pointy teeth."

6   How will such knowledge be handled? How should it be handled? Are we headed for an age in which having a child is morally analogous to buying a car? There is already evidence that couples are using prenatal tests to identify and abort fetuses on the basis of sex, and there is no reason to assume the trend will stop there. "We should be worried about the future and where this might take us," says George Annas, a professor of health law

at Boston University's School of Medicine. "The whole definition of normal could well be changed. The issue becomes not the ability of the child to be happy but rather our ability to be happy with the child."

7   So far, at least, the emphasis has been on combating serious hereditary disorders. Everyone carries four to six genes that are harmless when inherited from one parent but can be deadly when inherited from both. Luckily, most of these mutations are rare enough that carriers are unlikely to cross paths. But some have become common within particular populations. Five percent of all whites carry the gene for cystic fibrosis, for example, and one in 2,000 is born with the disease. Seven percent of all blacks harbor the mutation for sickle-cell anemia, and one in 500 is afflicted. Asian and Mediterranean people are particularly prone to the deadly blood disease thalassemia, just as Jews are to Tay-Sachs.

8   When accommodating the disability means watching a toddler die of Tay-Sachs or thalassemia, few couples hesitate to abort, and only the most adamant pro-lifer would blame them. But few of the defects for which fetuses can be screened are so devastating. Consider Huntington's disease, the hereditary brain disorder that killed the folk singer Woody Guthrie. Huntington's relentlessly destroys its victim's mind, and anyone who inherits the gene eventually gets the disease. Yet Huntington's rarely strikes anyone under 40, and it can remain dormant into a person's 70s. What does a parent do with the knowledge that a fetus has the gene? Is some life better than none?

9   Most carriers think not. . . .

10   As more abnormalities are linked to genes, the dilemmas can only get stickier. Despite all the uncertainties, a positive test for Down or Huntington's leaves no doubt that the condition will set in. But not every disease-related gene guarantees ill health. Those associated with conditions like alcoholism, Alzheimer's disease and manic-depressive illness signal only a susceptibility. Preventing such conditions would thus require aborting kids who might never have suffered. And because one gene can have more than one effect, the effort could have unintended consequences. There is considerable evidence linking manic-depressive illness to artistic genius, notes Dr. Melvin Konner, an anthropologist and nonpracticing physician at Emory University. "Doing away with the gene would destroy the impetus for much human creativity."

11   The future possibilities are even more troubling when you consider that mere imperfections could be screened for as easily as serious diseases. Stuttering, obesity and reading disorders are

all traceable to genetic markers, notes Dr. Kathleen Nolan of The Hastings Center, a biomedical think tank in suburban New York. And many aspects of appearance and personality are under fairly simple genetic control. Are we headed for a time when straight teeth, a flat stomach and a sense of humor are standards for admission into some families? It's not inconceivable. "I see people in my clinic occasionally who have a sort of new-car mentality," says Dr. Francis Collins, a University of Michigan geneticist who recently helped identify the gene for cystic fibrosis. "It's got to be perfect, and if it isn't you take it back to the lot and get a new one."

12   At the moment, gender is the only nonmedical condition for which prenatal tests are widely available. There are no firm figures on how often people abort to get their way, but physicians say many patients use the tests for that purpose. The requests have traditionally come from Asians and East Indians expressing a cultural preference for males. But others are now asking, too. "I've found a high incidence of sex selection coming from doctors' families in the last two years," says Dr. Lawrence D. Platt, a geneticist at the University of Southern California—"much higher than ethnic requests. Once there is public awareness about the technology, other people will use the procedure as well."

13   Those people will find their physicians increasingly willing to help. A 1973 survey of American geneticists found that only 1 percent considered it morally acceptable to help parents identify and abort fetuses of the undesired sex. Last year University of Virginia ethicist John C. Fletcher and Dr. Mark I. Evans, a geneticist at Wayne State University, conducted a similar poll and found that nearly 20 percent approved. Meanwhile, 62 percent of the geneticists questioned in a 1985 survey said they would screen fetuses for a couple who had four healthy daughters and wanted a son.

14   Right or wrong, the new gender option has set an important precedent. If parents will screen babies for one nonmedical condition, there is no reason to assume they won't screen them for others. Indeed, preliminary results from a recent survey of 200 New England couples showed that while only 1 percent would abort on the basis of sex, 11 percent would abort to save a child from obesity. As Dr. Robin Dawn Clark, head of clinical genetics at Loma Linda Medical Center observes, the temptation will be to select for "other features that are honored by society."

15   The trend toward even greater control could lead to bizarre, scifi scenarios. But it seems unlikely that prenatal swimsuit competitions will sweep the globe anytime soon: most of the globe

has yet to reap the benefits of 19th-century medicine. Even in America, many prospective parents are still struggling to obtain basic health insurance. If the masses could suddenly afford cosmetic screening tests, the trauma of abortion would remain a powerful deterrent. And while [geneticist] John Buster's dream of extracting week-old embryos for a quick gene check could ease the trauma, it seems a safe bet many women would still opt to leave their embryos alone.

16   The more immediate danger is that the power to predict children's medical futures will diminish society's tolerance for serious defects. Parents have already sued physicians for "wrongful life" after giving birth to disabled children, claiming it was the doctor's responsibility to detect the defect in the womb. The fear of such suits could prompt physicians to run every available test, however remote the possibility of spotting a medical problem. Conversely, parents who are content to forgo all the genetic fortune-telling could find themselves stigmatized for their backward ways. When four-cell embryos can be screened for hereditary diseases, failing to ensure a child's future health could become the same sort of offense that declining heroic measures for a sick child is today.

17   In light of all the dangers, some critics find the very practice of prenatal testing morally questionable. "Even at the beginning of the journey the eugenics question looms large," says Jeremy Rifkin, a Washington activist famous for his opposition to genetic tinkering. "Screening is eugenics." Perhaps, but its primary effect so far has been to bring fewer seriously diseased children into the world. In Britain's Northeast Thames region, the number of Indian and Cypriot children born with thalassemia fell by 78 percent after prenatal tests became available in the 1970s. Likewise, carrier and prenatal screening have virtually eliminated Tay-Sachs from the United States and Canada.

18   Failing to think, as a society, about the appropriate uses of the new tests would be a grave mistake. They're rife with potential for abuse, and the coming advances in genetic science will make them more so. But they promise some control over diseases that have caused immense suffering and expense. Society need only remember that there are no perfect embryos but many ways to be a successful human being.

Thinking It Through

1. Skimming Cowley's article again, summarize the positive and negative possibilities resulting from early genetic testing.

2. Dr. Robin Clark believes (and fears) that it may become possible to screen embryos for "features that are honored by society." If this

should happen, what traits would the perfect child possess in modern American society?

3. Why does Cowley believe that "the power to predict children's medical futures [could] diminish society's tolerance for serious defects" (paragraph 16)?

4. How is modern genetic science similar to and different from the reproductive science described in Huxley's *Brave New World*?

Thinking and Writing

Even if early testing of a human embryo can reveal the sex, physical and mental characteristics, and possible life-threatening defects, some parents-to-be say they do not want to know. Would you?

Write a paper in which you explain why you would or would not want to know before its birth what your child would be like and what kind of development it might have. A subject like this requires a good bit of thought. As you consider it, write down the positive and negative features of having such knowledge before birth. Weigh them carefully as you make a decision.

Notice that the topic simply asks whether you would want to *know*. It does not ask whether you would take any action based on such knowledge. Whether or not you wish to consider this angle in your paper is up to you.

A Future Denied:
Children Who Work

UN CHRONICLE

First Thoughts

In 1959 the United Nations issued the Declaration on the Rights of the Child. Part of that statement appears on the first page of this chapter: "Mankind owes to the child the best it has to give." Thirty years later the UN was working on a revision of this declaration, as well as new plans for putting beliefs into practice. In the following article the writer looks at some countries where children are still not getting the best mankind has to offer and measures the progress that world society has made toward achieving that goal.

Word List

PAUPER (paragraph 1):   poor, impoverished

EXPLOITED (paragraph 1):   made unfair use of, abused

ARCHAIC (paragraph 1):   old, out of date

RAVAGES (paragraph 2):   damage, destruction

RAMPANT (paragraph 4):   widespread, out of control

FLOUT (paragraph 5):   defy, openly ignore

CLANDESTINELY (paragraph 6):   secretly

PRAGMATIC (paragraph 7):   practical

SPECTRE (paragraph 8):   phantom, ghost (something that haunts)

DETRIMENTAL (paragraph 8):   damaging

SOLE (paragraph 11):   unit of money worth much less than one cent

AGRARIAN (paragraph 14):   agricultural

~~~~~~~~~~~~~~~~~   1   In 19th century Europe, pauper children were sometimes apprenticed to factory owners, who mercilessly exploited them. In recent years, children have panned gold in sweltering, malaria-ridden jungles of South America, faced sharks and suffered ruptured eardrums when engaged in deep-sea fishing in tropical ocean waters, and risked physical deformity in archaic leather

tanning workshops in the Middle East. They are among the more than 100 million working children around the world.

2 Ravages such as those inflicted by the industrial revolution on European and North American children about a century ago are now being felt by third world children amidst slum-filled megacities, abandoned countrysides, swelling populations and near-bankrupt economies struggling to meet next month's external debt interest payment.

NO OTHER CHOICE

3 In those countries, poor parents are sending their children to work because they have no other choice. Sometimes there are no schools or they are too expensive or their quality is so low and the drop-out rate so high that parents perceive them as irrelevant.

4 While child labour seems to have been more or less abolished in large, modern enterprises in most developing countries, it is still rampant in the huge "informal sector," a vast unorganized array of small enterprises.

5 But even where child labour is legally banned, employers openly flout the law, knowing that it won't be enforced: a handful of overworked labour inspectors cannot possibly cope with the thousands of illegal enterprises operating in the back alleys of a sprawling third world metropolis.

6 Legislation backfires when it ignores the realities of hunger and need and when it is not properly enforced. Banning child labour has often only meant forcing children to work clandestinely. It has also made child labour regulation and assistance to working children politically impossible for many Governments since public opinion may see that as a betrayal of the abolitionist ideal.

7 But attitudes are changing and public policy is becoming more pragmatic in countries such as Colombia, Brazil, Peru, India, and the Philippines. Today, the reality that millions of children work in the developing world is being acknowledged. While abolition remains the goal, greater protection for working children is recognized as an immediate need.

8 Another new development is that not all child labour is now automatically seen as evil. It is not work as such that is damaging to children, but the conditions under which most children work. Idleness—with the triple spectre of drug abuse, gang violence, and social alienation—can be as detrimental to children as exploitative work.

AMONG THE LOWEST PAID

9   Children work too long and are among the lowest paid. They are often forced to do tasks for which they are entirely unprepared, physically and mentally.

10   Children are more prone than adults to suffer occupational injuries and have far more serious health problems than adults exposed to the same working environment.

11   Everywhere, girls are far more exploited than boys. While boy gold panners work eight hours a day for about 15 to 17,000 Peruvian soles a day and can take Sundays off, girls cooking for them work 15 hours a day all week long, for an average 8,500 soles a day.

12   Very often exploitation goes well beyond low wages, subhuman working conditions and long hours. In one Asian nation's deep-sea fishing operation, now banned, food on board, transportation, medicines and even equipment maintenance costs were deducted from the young workers' meager salaries.

UNIONS IGNORE CHILDREN

13   Children have no protection when they work in industries, mining, household services or on the street. Labour unions largely ignore them and generally children do not organize themselves and fight for their rights. They are also less likely than adults to change jobs. Therefore, employers have tremendous power over them—a quasi parental power.

14   In agrarian societies, working children are at least protected by parents. But rural work can also be hazardous. Children are being mauled by farm machinery, not only in third world countries where that technology is new, but in the American mid-West, where near-bankrupt farmers are counting more and more on their children's after-school work. . . .

A GRASS-ROOTS APPROACH

15   Most innovative programmes to help working children are run by private voluntary groups throughout the world, the ILO reports.

16   In Brazil, where millions of children live and work on the streets, the Government supports a vast network of community-based groups that is starting to successfully deal with the problem.

17   India is concentrating on wiping out the most hazardous types of child labour and regulating all others. A target is to provide all children under 14 with free and compulsory education by 1995.

18   In Manila, Philippines, voluntary groups have set up mobile schools in tents near places where children work. Meals and health services are also provided.

19   Working children are proving in Peru that they are not only capable of organizing themselves but that they can also play a leadership role in their communities. Manthoc, a social action movement launched in 1976 in southern Lima by a group of teenagers, is run by children themselves, with help from Catholic Youth volunteers.

20   Local chapters have successfully mobilized their communities to clean up hazardous garbage, fumigate malaria-carrying mosquitoes, and raise funds to help working children in case of illness.

21   Working conditions of some 350 children who arrange flowers in Bogota's cemeteries have dramatically improved since "Villa Javier," a project of the Colombian Institute for Family Welfare, helped them get organized in 1986.

22   Although extremely effective, most of these voluntary programmes lack sufficient funds and a national scope. Direct governmental involvement "remains far too limited," a new ILO study says.

Thinking It Through

1. According to the author, what are the major reasons that child labor is so widespread in developing countries?

2. What is one positive outcome of child labor in these countries? Do you agree with this view? Why or why not?

3. In paragraph 14 there is one example of the dangers to children working in the United States. Do you know of other American businesses or industries besides agriculture in which children and early teens are employed? Do you know of other possible dangers to child workers?

Thinking and Writing

As a child or a teenager, did you hold a job? If so, tell about your experience as a child or teen worker. What kind of work did you do? What reward (if any) did you receive for doing it? Was your work voluntary or required? How did you feel about your job? As you have done before, list as many details as you can remember, cluster them into groups or categories, and decide how you will organize the major points of the essay. If your instructor wishes, you can exchange and comment on early drafts in small groups before you write the draft you will submit for evaluation.

Credits and Acknowledgments

Pages on which material appears are indicated in **boldface** in parentheses at the end of each acknowledgment.

Chapter 2

Ray Bradley, three photos. (**19, 20**)

Celia E. Picazo, "Donna's Li'l Brother," student essay. Reprinted with permission. (**22–23**)

Chapter 4

Ernest Hemingway, "The Short, Happy Life of Francis Macomber," *The Short Stories of Ernest Hemingway*. Copyright 1936 by Ernest Hemingway; renewal copyright © 1964 by Mary Hemingway. Reprinted with permission of Charles Scribner's Sons, an imprint of Macmillan Publishing Company. (**48**)

Maxine Hong Kingston, *China Men*. Copyright © 1977, 1978, 1979, 1980 by Maxine Hong Kingston. Reprinted with permission of Alfred A. Knopf, Inc. (**49, 57–58**)

Ernest Hemingway, "Hills Like White Elephants," *Men Without Women*. Copyright 1927 by Charles Scribner's Sons; renewal copyright 1965 by Ernest Hemingway. Reprinted with permission of Charles Scribner's Sons, an imprint of Macmillan Publishing Company. (**50**)

Donald Hall, "Winter," *Seasons at Eagle Pond*. Copyright © 1987 by Donald Hall. Reprinted by permission of Houghton Mifflin Co. (**53–54, 55–56**)

Joan Didion, "Letter from Los Angeles," *The New Yorker*, September 4, 1989. Copyright © 1989 by Joan Didion. Reprinted by permission of the Wallace Literary Agency. (**54, 56**)

Chapter 5

John Bonnett Wexo, *Elephants*. Copyright 1980, 1986 by Wildlife Education, Ltd. Reprinted by permission. (**66**)

285

Index